The Aesthetics of
Everyday Life

The Aesthetics of
Everyday Life

Edited by

Andrew Light and
Jonathan M. Smith

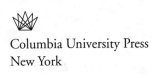

Columbia University Press
New York

Columbia University Press
Publishers Since 1893
New York   Chichester, West Sussex

Library of Congress Cataloging-in-Publication Data

The aesthetics of everyday life / edited by Andrew Light and Jonathan M. Smith.
    p. cm.
    Includes bibliographical references and index.
    ISBN 0–231–13502–5 (cloth : alk. paper)—ISBN 0–231–13503–3 (pbk : alk. paper)
    1. Environment (Aesthetics)   I. Light, Andrew, 1966–   II. Smith, Jonathan M.

  BH301.E58A37 2004
  111'.85—dc22

2004056133

Columbia University Press books are printed on
permanent and durable acid-free paper.

Printed in the United States of America
c 10 9 8 7 6 5 4 3 2 1
p 10 9 8 7 6 5 4 3 2 1

Contents

Acknowledgments   vii

Jonathan M. Smith
Introduction   ix

I. Theorizing the Aesthetics of the Everyday

Tom Leddy
1. The Nature of Everyday Aesthetics   3

Arnold Berleant
2. Ideas for a Social Aesthetic   23

Arto Haapala
3. On the Aesthetics of the Everyday: Familiarity,
Strangeness, and the Meaning of Place   39

Michael A. Principe
4. Danto and Baruchello: From Art to the
Aesthetics of the Everyday   56

II. Appreciating the Everyday Environment

Pauline von Bonsdorff
5. Building and the Naturally Unplanned   73

Allen Carlson
6. What Is the Correct Curriculum for Landscape?   92

Andrew Light

7. Wim Wenders's Everyday Aesthetics   109

III. Finding the Everyday Aesthetic

Wolfgang Welsch

8. Sport Viewed Aesthetically, and Even as Art?   135

Yuriko Saito

9. The Aesthetics of Weather   156

Emily Brady

10. Sniffing and Savoring: The Aesthetics of Smells and Tastes   177

Glenn Kuehn

11. How Can Food Be Art?   194

About the Authors   213

Index   217

Acknowledgments

Chapter 6, "What Is the Correct Curriculum for Landscape?" reprinted by permission of the University of Illinois Press from *Journal of Aesthetic Education* 35 (2000).

Chapter 7 adapted from "Wim Wenders and the Everyday Aesthetics of Technology and Space." Reprinted by permission of the University of Wisconsin Press from *Journal of Aesthetics and Art Criticism* 55.2 (Spring 1997): 215–229.

Introduction

Jonathan M. Smith

OUR SUBJECT MATTER is everyday aesthetics, both as an extension beyond the traditional domain of the philosophical study of aesthetics, usually confined to more conventionally understood works of art, and as a step into a new arena of aesthetic inquiry—the broader world itself. This introduction summarizes the contents of the papers that follow, aiming to guide the reader on the common themes arising in the chapters and explaining the reasoning behind the organization of the volume.

The chapters in the first section of this book make general arguments for application of aesthetic criticism to objects and events that have been, until recently, exempt from this sort of scrutiny. In chapter one Tom Leddy offers an outline of the field of everyday aesthetics. This chapter admirably provides an overview of this topic in relation to traditional work in aesthetic theory and thus stands in for such a discussion that could have been provided in this introduction. Looking at colloquial usage of aesthetic terms, Leddy proposes that everyday aesthetics be taken to include inquiries into all aesthetic experiences that fall outside of existing domains of aesthetic theory, such as aesthetics of art, aesthetics of nature, and aesthetics of mathematics. Everyday aesthetics is not, in other words, limited to study of the aesthetic experience of humble objects and quotidian acts, although such are often of interest to everyday aesthetics. It is concerned with all of the undeniably aesthetic experiences that do arise when one contemplates objects or performs acts that are not traditionally categorized as aesthetic objects or acts, be they rare or frequent, fugitive or profound. What sets the everyday aesthetic experience apart is the fact that it seems to be prompted by something that should not be able to cause such an experience, at least according to conventional aesthetic theory. Leddy maintains that this is because the aesthetic properties of everyday aesthetic experience inhere in the fusion of sense and imagination that is the experience itself, and not in the object of the aesthetic experience. The question for everyday aesthetics therefore becomes not what are the formal properties of this object that make it beautiful, but rather what is the relation between subject and object that makes this particular experience of that object beautiful. There are, Leddy concedes, difficulties with this approach. Many subjects do, after all, find beauty in maudlin kitsch, and it is not entirely clear how, say, Hummel figurines should be treated in Leddy's everyday aesthetics. There is also a danger that this theory of the aesthetics of everyday life might seem to lend intellectual support to the commercial aestheticization of everyday life that one finds in advertisements. Finally, it is unclear what should be done with the promiscuous aesthetic experiences of individuals who, due to a temporarily or permanently ecstatic state of mind, find beauty everywhere.

Like Leddy, Arnold Berleant believes that aesthetic properties are present in places other than those covered by traditional aesthetic theory. In chapter two he argues that aesthetic properties can be discerned in human relations when these are ethical and just. Berleant grounds his argument in a model of the aesthetic situation that details the many conditions that must be met for an aesthetic experience to occur. These include: the belief that aesthetic experience is possible in any particular situation, a lively sensory awareness (with all of the senses) of all that is present in that situation, the discipline to keep this sensory awareness from fading into a stereotype of that situation, and the ability to enter into unreserved communion with that situation. Berleant insists that traditional art objects cannot be aesthetically appreciated if these conditions are not met; he then postulates that things other than traditional art objects can be aesthetically appreciated when these conditions are met. Indeed it appears that we are prepared to recognize and appreciate beauty in social forms and relationships, as is evident in theater, film, television, etiquette, and ritual. When we speak of a beautiful marriage, or family, or friendship, we are not, of course, praising the pulchritude of the parties involved in these unions, but rather some quality in the union itself. This quality, Berleant suggests, is love, and he goes on to detail the many parallels between love and beauty. Expanding this notion of the beauty of loving relations to the scale of the political unit, he describes an aesthetic community that is anarchistic, socialistic, and in some ways reminiscent of nineteenth-century utopian movements.

Berleant's everyday aesthetics requires one to preserve one's sense of wonder, to look upon a familiar thing with the same wide eyes one had when one looked upon that thing for the first time. In chapter three Arto Haapala pursues an existentialist argument to the opposite conclusion. He insists that the preoccupation of aesthetic theory with aesthetics of art, and more particularly modern art, has led to a widespread but erroneous assumption that the experience of art, especially modern art, is the only form of aesthetic experience. Thus strangeness, surprise, shock, and wonder, which are integral to the experience of modern art, are supposed by many to be indispensable ingredients in all aesthetic experiences. Haapala does not deprecate this aesthetics of strangeness, but argues that it is limited. Most individuals live most of their lives surrounded by familiar things, persons, and activities, whose beauty is to be found not by treating them as if they were endlessly novel, but by delighting in their easy familiarity. Like Heidegger's hammer, everyday things have a beauty that is present only when the things themselves are little noticed. The hammer is a simple tool adapted to a simple task; places, according to Haapala, are complex tools adapted to the complex task of living an individual life. The carpenter delights in his hammer because it allows him to be a carpenter; he scrutinizes the object only when it fails, and thereby interrupts his being. Likewise, one delights in the places that allow one to be one's self, to act out one's existential structure; one is surprised by, and grows sensible of, these places only when they fail and thereby disrupt one's way of being-in-the-world.

Each of the preceding essays in some way challenges the notion that artworks properly inhabit a world apart from everyday things, and more particularly everyday and useful things. Michael Principe approaches this problem squarely in chapter four. Drawing from published works by the critic Arthur Danto and the painter Gianfranco Baruchello, he discusses the state of affairs when artwork is very much part of the everyday world (performance art) and the everyday world is very much part of artwork (ready-mades). Unlike Danto, who sees this promiscuous mingling of art and the everyday as the end of art history and the beginning of aimless pluralism, Principe sees in it an opportunity for art, its independent history having ended, to find direction and purpose in the concerns of political struggles and history. Inspired by Baruchello's claim that his farm is art because it is a stimulating and nurturing context for creativity, Principe suggests that serving as the occasion for further aesthetic statements is itself an aesthetic quality. Aimless pluralism may ensue when we lift the barrier that has for centuries separated artworks from everyday things, but this can be averted if we at the same time lift the barrier that has for centuries separated artworks from the world of everyday struggles and projects.

The second section of this book contains essays on the aesthetics of everyday environments. These environments are shaped by the intentions of designers and the actions of builders, but as Pauline von Bonsdorff argues in chapter five, their beauty often depends on shaping forces that designers and builders do not, by choice or necessity, control. Juxtapositions with adjacent buildings, the nature of the site, marks of wear and weathering, all play a part in lending character to a building, and it is the grace with which a building accepts these mundane exactions on its individual being that in large part determines its aesthetic value. A building cannot do other than actively shape an environment, but a good building also abides that environment; a good builder regards nature as not simply a plastic medium for the expression of his artistic intentions, but also as a creative agent in its own right. Because a good building does not appear to repudiate its surroundings or controvert time (made evident in wear and weathering), it conveys to those who know it a tacit knowledge that abiding *and* active shaping can be reconciled into a highly satisfactory way of being in the world. What we experience as the beauty of everyday environments is, in fact, according to Bonsdorff, tacit knowledge of this reciprocal way of being in the world.

In chapter six Allen Carlson argues that aesthetic appreciation of landscape requires much more than tacit knowledge, and in fact depends on articulate knowledge drawn from a range of academic and cultural discourses. The forms of landscape on which all aesthetic enjoyment depends are selected and made clearly visible by the viewer's understanding of the meaning, significance, or content of the scene. Much of this content is furnished by the common knowledge of objects that one learns with language, so that one sees as significant forms those things that one has nouns to name. This content is enriched by scientific knowledge that categorizes these forms and explains the creative processes by which they have been shaped, so that knowledge of convection, say, enhances the beauty of a cumulus cloud, just as knowledge of the Renaissance enhances the beauty of a painting by Giotto. Because a landscape, unlike a painting, is always a work in progress, appreciation of its formal characteristics is also enhanced by knowledge of past and present human land use. Thus articulate knowledge of the history that produced a landscape is, for Carlson, necessary to appreciation of that landscape, just as articulate knowledge of the history that produced a work of art is necessary to appreciation of that work of art. This articulate knowledge of the processes that have produced a landscape is properly augmented by articulate knowledge of the accretions of cultural meaning that incorrigibly color any given viewer's reception of that landscape. Thus appreciation of landscape is enriched by knowledge of myths and legends, the use of landscapes as symbols that connote ideas, and of the consequent representation of these landscapes in art, because this grants the viewer a degree of self consciousness of the ways in which he himself, as a member of a particular culture, shapes the scene before his eyes.

Many of the authors collected here explain everyday aesthetics as an experience of pleasure and meaning that results when a special relationship exists, or is established, between a subject and an object, or between several subjects brought together and coordinated by an object. This theme is made explicit in chapter seven, in which Andrew Light attempts to reconcile elements from the competing philosophies of technology of Andrew Feenberg and Albert Borgmann through a close reading of Wim Wenders's film, *Alice in the Cities* (1973). Light poses two central questions. How can one account for the fact that one experiences some spaces as satisfying and thick, and others as alienating and thin? Are thin spaces necessarily alienating, or can they be, so to speak, thickened by regarding them in a new light? He draws on Borgmann to answer the first question. Thick spaces, like Borgmann's "focal things," cause those who inhabit them to assume roles, enter into relationships, and cultivate relevant skills, demands that serve to give these inhabitants a sense of meaning and identity. Thin spaces, like Borgmann's "devices," demand little from their inhabitants (except, often enough, cash payment), and consequently lend no significant shape to their lives. The second question, prompted by Feenburg, is whether this spectral and amorphous existence is an inescapable consequence of thin spaces or can be subverted. Light answers this question with a close reading of Wenders's film that shows how apparently thin spaces aesthetically thicken once they become a setting for roles, relationships, and meaningful projects.

The third section of this book contains essays that describe and interpret particular everyday events, experiences, and objects that have aesthetic qualities. In chapter eight Wolfgang Welsch questions why sport, with its generally acknowledged grace and beauty, is not considered an art and subjected to aesthetic criticism. He argues that the prejudice is based on outdated definitions of art and understandings of sport. As other authors in this volume have argued, the concept of aesthetic quality can be abstracted from artworks, and that something very similar can be found to subsist, if perhaps less potently, in objects that are not conventional works of art. Artists themselves have in many cases taken the lead in questioning art as a valid category of reality, and have busied themselves blurring boundaries between high art and popular art, between the various high arts, and between art and life. Given these relaxed criteria, there is, Welsch contends, no reason not to consider the possibility that sport is art. Indeed the athlete is increasingly understood in terms appropriate to an artist: he does not, as was formerly thought, discipline his body so much as allow it to express the perfection of its own nature. Having stated why we may wish to view sport as art, Welsch works to eliminate the more obvious objections to such a view. Although sport, unlike art, contains an explicit purpose of winning, it is also driven, as art is driven, by a desire to be a perfect instance of the type of performance that it is. Although sport, unlike (modern) art, does not strive to break the rules, it does strive, as (traditional) art strove, to realize new possibilities within rules. Although sport does not have clear meaning, in the sense of referents outside the sport event itself, it nevertheless expresses in highly stylized ways basic human traits such as pluck, desire, exaltation, or loss of nerve. Sport is, therefore, but one of the many forms of demotic entertainment that satisfy the aesthetic needs of ordinary people; it cannot replace difficult art, but neither should we allow it (or its counterparts) to be entirely overshadowed by difficult art when we set to describing the aesthetics of today's world.

In chapter nine Yuriko Saito makes a similar argument for aesthetic appreciation of weather. Like Welsch, she does this with a series of responses to possible objections against consideration of weather as an aesthetic object. One cannot, for instance, separate weather from the context of nature in general in the same way that Western culture has, traditionally, separated aesthetic objects from the context of objects in general. Nor can one discipline the manner in which people view weather in the same way that Western culture has, traditionally, disciplined the manner in which people view art. Saito counters such objections by noting that, in the West, the work of art was separated from ordinary objects (in museums, for instance), and viewed according to definite conventions, largely to protect its meaning from distortion by extraneous associations and ignorant interpretations. Since weather, viewed aesthetically, has no such purport, such precautions are unnecessary. A second objection to weather as an aesthetic object is that it has practical consequences, and cannot therefore be viewed with the impersonal disinterestedness that many aestheticians believe is necessary to appreciate the "sensuous surface" of an aesthetic object. Against this Saito contends that feelings aroused by weather become part of the experienced aesthetic object, and therefore may, when sufficiently mild, be viewed with disinterest even by the person feeling them. Illustrating her point with Japanese poetry, Saito notes that aesthetically satisfying weather is often sufficiently inconvenient to arouse feelings, but seldom so threatening as to prohibit disinterested enjoyment. The last objection to weather as an aesthetic object is that it is evanescent, unlike great art, which is thought to endure. Yet most will agree that many of the keenest beauties of weather are fleeting, as in the moment when rain gives way to sunshine or the cold shadow of an ominous thunderhead creeps across the land. Such beauties of weather are, in fact, strangely absent from those monotonous spans of stable temperatures and sunshine that we call, by convention, beautiful weather. Drawing again from Japanese poetry, Saito suggests that this may be because transient beauty reconciles us, in some degree, to our own mortal transience, while unpredicted beauty assures us that goodness can at least sometimes spring from natural processes that are wild and beyond human control.

Emily Brady argues for formal aesthetic appreciation of tastes and smells in chapter ten, and, as in the two previous chapters, does so by answering objections that might be raised against attempts at such appreciation. Traditional Western aesthetics, has, for instance, deprecated smelling and tasting as low pleasures of the body, animal pleasures without appeal for the incorporeal mind. Brady deflects this objection with an appeal to materialist philosophies of mind, which deny that there is a difference between mind and brain and thereby demote the mind and its allegedly lofty pleasures to the same level as the body and its enjoyments. In addition to their stigmatization as low pleasures, smell and taste are deemed by many unsuited to aesthetic appreciation because their close connection to appetites makes them impossible to appreciate in a disinterested manner. And even if it is allowed that some tastes and smells are savored simply for the pleasure they afford, it may be objected that they lack the complex structure necessary for a sensation to be more than what Kant described as agreeable. Against these objections Brady raises the examples of connoisseurship in costly drink, cigars, and perfume, a well-developed form of aesthetic appreciation that also disproves the allegation that tastes and smells are not susceptible to critical standards or terminology. These commodified tastes do not exhaust the range of tastes and fragrances that can be subjected to aesthetic criticism and analysis; they do make it clear that such analysis and criticism is possible. Indeed Brady encourages us to develop this sort of gustatory, and more especially this sort of olfactory, discrimination in our dealings with the tastes and smells of the everyday world.

In chapter eleven Glen Kuehn enlarges on Elizabeth Telfer's 1996 argument that food is a minor art, making more robust claims on the strength of ideas drawn from John Dewey. Dewey famously argued that because art is a distillation of experience it must, like experience, transform its subject in such a way that he or she grows capable of additional, more fully integrated experience. With this description of the aesthetic experience in hand, Kuehn is able to dismiss the scruples that prevented Telfer from affirming that some food might, in certain circumstances, be considered the equal of any of the arts. He insists that certain experiences of eating do transform the eater's understanding, not only of the possibilities inherent in that particular food, or of food and eating in general, but also of the possibilities inherent in life itself. Kuehn concludes that the best argument against consideration of food as high art is that food has not traditionally been considered as high art, but that this reliance on tradition is incongruent with the prevailing belief that all such categories are fluid social constructions.

Kuehn's analysis of food brings the collection full circle to the theme of experience first raised by Leddy in chapter one. Indeed, viewed as a set, these chapters disclose a degree of unanimity remarkable for a field as young and undeveloped as everyday aesthetics. Perhaps the clearest and most consistent of these is that the everyday aesthetic experience arises when a certain, often evanescent, relationship exists, either between a subject and an everyday object, or between subjects brought into a happy configuration by their mutual relation to an object. This should, of course, come as no surprise, since the relational basis of the everyday aesthetic experience would seem to account for the facts that nothing in the everyday world is invariably beautiful, even to those who wish that some things were, and that nothing in the everyday world (or at least very little) can be supposed devoid of the power to excite an aesthetic response in the proper circumstances. As if in some great dance, we move among the twirling things of the everyday world, enjoying but for a moment the beauty in their already half-averted faces.

The Aesthetics of
Everyday Life

Part I

Theorizing the Aesthetics of the Everyday

CHAPTER 1

The Nature of Everyday Aesthetics

Tom Leddy

WHAT IS EVERYDAY AESTHETICS? It would be a mistake to take the term *everyday* too literally. A musician who practices and plays every day can justly say that her everyday aesthetic experience is mainly connected with music. A naturalist could similarly say that his everyday aesthetic experience is of nature. Yet when we talk about everyday aesthetic experience, we are thinking of aesthetic issues that are *not* connected closely with the fine arts or with the natural environment, or with other areas that form well-established aesthetic domains, for example, the aesthetics of mathematics, science, or religion. We are thinking instead of the home, the daily commute, the workplace, the shopping center, and places of amusement.

The issues that generally come up have to do with personal appearance, ordinary housing design, interior decoration, workplace aesthetics, sexual experience, appliance design, cooking, gardening, hobbies, play, appreciation of children's art projects, and other similar matters.[1] Of course the boundaries are not clearly drawn. Everyday aesthetics is a loose category. For example, the aesthetics of weather seems to fall equally within everyday aesthetics and the aesthetics of nature. Children's art projects fall somewhere between everyday aesthetics and the aesthetics of art. I hope to show in this chapter what the boundaries might be, and give some idea of the scope of inquiry.

Discussion of everyday aesthetics allows us to talk about things that do not generally come up in traditional aesthetics. It opens a whole new domain of inquiry. Yet, this domain is closely related to more traditional fields of aesthetics. For example, terms are often shared between it and the aesthetics of art. Also, much art is based on, or inspired by, everyday aesthetic experience. Vermeer, for example, draws our attention to the aesthetic pleasures of bourgeois Dutch house interiors. We see art, at least in part, in terms of everyday aesthetics, and we see everyday aesthetics, at least partially, in terms of art. Nor should we forget that we see both, at least in part, in terms of the aesthetics of nature.

Of special importance is the relationship between everyday aesthetics and environmental aesthetics. There is considerable overlap. Environmental aesthetics points the way to appreciation of everyday aesthetics by focusing on the entire lived experience, for example, of a walk in the woods. One could certainly approach everyday aesthetics in the holistic manner of environmental aesthetics. My own daily walk to work is an example of a fairly complex experiential whole that may be analyzed along the lines of environmental aesthetics. I may appreciate the nature of the day (sunny and fresh), the seasonal variations of the plant life (spring has arrived!), the flowery smells of plant-clippings (brought out by a recent rain), the cultural richness of our ethnically diverse community (notice that statue of the Virgin!), architectural niceties of ordinary buildings (the California bungalow that looks a bit like a Frank Lloyd Wright), the physical pleasure of my own bodily movement, the quick vision of a white crane in Coyote creek as I walk over the bridge (a fragment of nature appreciation), and the fashion statements of students as I enter the campus. All of the senses are involved.

But notice that the aesthetic delights of my walk may also be relatively isolated and less holistic. I am an amateur photographer, and I often look at scenes of everyday life as potential shots through an imagined frame. For this, and other reasons, I would not make everyday aesthetics just a branch of environmental aesthetics. It will be helpful to turn to a recent work in environmental aesthetics by Arnold Berleant to explore this point.[2] Berleant recognizes that environmental aesthetics was originally focused on the natural environment, but wishes to expand it to include the aesthetics of everyday life. Thus, he informs us that environmental aesthetics will deal with "how we engage with the prosaic landscapes of home, work, local travel, and recreation" (16). He notes that "we engage the landscape aesthetically as we drive to work or school, go shopping, walk the dog, or picnic in a park" (20). Although Berleant's contribution is valuable, I believe that taking the aesthetics of the natural environment as paradigmatic places unnecessary limitations on everyday aesthetics. First, contemporary photography, assemblage, and 3D work have taught us to appreciate many landscapes that would be repulsive to most nature lovers (for example, German sculptor Olaf Metzel's "Outdoors," 1992, which creates a work of art out of camping tents and netting, and his "112–104," 1991, which uses debris from a destroyed basketball court; and Swiss artists Peter Fischli and David Weiss's wonderful film, *The Way Things Go*, 1985–87, both featured in *Art in America*, June 1997). Some of my own strongest aesthetic experiences have come from viewing the display of junkyards and storage yards along the train route from San Jose to San Francisco. Berleant implies that such things as telephone poles, power lines, commercial strips, trailer parks, suburban malls, and parking lots necessarily "embody negative aesthetic values" (20). Yet, these are often the subjects of contemporary painting and photography, which provide mediation for our experiencing them in aesthetically positive terms.

Second, an exclusive focus on landscape would draw our attention away from appreciation of relatively isolated objects. Consider a key scene in the 2001 Academy-Award-nominated movie, *American Beauty.* The boy-next-door is a drug-pusher and a voyeur, and yet he shows his new girlfriend a video he made of a plastic bag shuffling back and forth against a building wall in a gentle swirl of local wind—an image of extraordinary beauty. From a traditional environmentalist perspective, this video simply records the existence of a plastic bag not properly recycled. From a landscape environment perspective, it shows lack of concern for the total environment: there is no landscape present, and only one of the senses is engaged. Yet, this video-within-a-movie makes us aware of possibilities of powerful aesthetic experience that are not particularly environmental or landscape-oriented.

Third, Berleant's attack on traditional aesthetics goes too far when he says that "the conscious body does not observe the world contemplatively but participates actively in the experiential process" (12). Why should we accept this strict dichotomy? Why cannot we enjoy both? Berleant discourages the detached visual contemplation exemplified by the above-mentioned video, and would disallow my own contemplative appreciation of urban scenes from a train window. Although engagement of all of the senses can contribute to a powerful aesthetic experience, this should not preclude the possibility, and value, of aesthetic experience that focuses on one sense, and is relatively disengaged.

Allen Carlson, another major figure in environmental aesthetics, insists that experiencing nature as a static two-dimensional object unduly limits our appreciation of it, and that we must appreciate natural objects in terms of correct scientific knowledge. Carlson rejects appreciation of nature in pictorial terms, which he believes is to misunderstand it. Whether this is the right approach to appreciating nature I cannot say, but it would seem somewhat bizarre to approach the aesthetics of everyday life in terms of this primacy of scientific cognition, for example, the home in terms of the science of house management, or the aesthetics of sex in terms of sexology. Moreover, we do not *need* the cognitive approach to help us appreciate the "scenically challenged" (to borrow a term from Yuriko Saito) aspects of everyday life in the way we might need it to help us appreciate something scenically challenged in nature—such as a dead elk filled with crawling maggots.[3] We already have the above-mentioned mediation of contemporary visual arts. (I do not intend to exclude the other fine art traditions here. The contemporary aural arts may do something similar with respect to the noises of everyday life. The contemporary novel often engages us descriptively and imaginatively with the same material represented in contemporary visual art.)

Kantian Attempt to Define Everyday Aesthetics

It might be thought that everyday aesthetics could be correlated with Kant's notion of "the agreeable." Kant says, "That is agreeable which the senses find pleasing in the sensation."[4] He distinguishes two kinds of aesthetic experience: the agreeable and the beautiful. Unlike beauty, the agreeable does not merely please, but gratifies. Thus, whereas beauty is disinterested, the agreeable is not. When we judge an object as agreeable we are expressing an interest in it. This is shown by the fact that it provokes a desire for similar objects. Although the agreeable may be experienced by irrational animals, Kant believes beauty is only available to man.

Kant argues that the agreeable is relative to inclination. Hence, the hungry man will find something agreeable that others may not. Taste, in the sense of "discrimination," does not enter into the agreeable. The judgment of the agreeable rests, rather, on private feeling. As opposed to the beautiful, when we talk of the agreeable there is no disputing about tastes.

Kant seems to think there are specific kinds of things that are objects of the agreeable, for example, canary wine, violet color, and the smell of a rose. He speaks of "the taste of the tongue, the palate, and the throat," and also of that which is agreeable to the eye and the ear. When he discusses violet color, he notes that it may be soft and lovely to one, and dull and faded to another. He also refers to the tones of wind and string instruments as examples of the agreeable. However, he insists that *pure* tones are objects of beauty.

Can the concept of the agreeable be used to define everyday aesthetics? Much of this domain could be included in the agreeable as Kant defines it; for example, all of the pleasures of the senses when they are unmediated by reflection. There are, however, various problems with a strictly Kantian definition of everyday aesthetics.

(1) Recent aestheticians have rightly questioned the idea that aesthetic appreciation can be completely disinterested, and that aesthetic objects can be completely formal. This has undercut Kant's distinction between the agreeable and the beautiful. For example, Kant's view of disinterestedness implies that we do not want to hear more of some beautiful music after we have had one pleasurable experience of it. Yet, we often want to hear such pieces again and again, although perhaps not right away. How is this different from our desire to have more pieces of chocolate candy, although not right away?

(2) The concept of beauty should not be excluded from everyday aesthetics. Kant defines beauty in terms of play of the imagination and the understanding. It is true that everyday aesthetic objects do not typically generate such play, even when they generate pleasure. But why should judgments of beauty *require* such a play? For example, it is not clear that such play exists in the ap-

preciation of the beauty of the tone of a bell or of a minimalist painting. When Kant excludes things like "the smell of a rose" from beauty, he recognizes that he is recommending a revision of language (surely, it is all right to say "that is a beautiful smell!"). Such a revision is not warranted if we no longer accept a radical distinction between the agreeable and the beautiful.

(3) Even if we stuck to Kant's use of the term *beauty*, it would still be wrong to exclude it from everyday aesthetics. Kant ties "beauty" with the aesthetic pleasure we get from appreciation of good design and pleasing form. This kind of pleasure is surely not absent from the dinner party, the garden, or the use of tiles in the bathroom. Kant clearly includes such things as costumes and wallpaper under the category of beauty, rather than that of the agreeable. Since we would generally want to include these in the field of everyday aesthetics, Kant's distinction may not be useful for defining that field.

(4) It is arguable that what Kant calls the agreeable is not exclusively a matter of sense, and that there is an imaginative element in the experience of the agreeable. For example, although the pleasures of sexual intercourse would seem to fall under the agreeable, it would be wrong to ignore the role that imagination typically plays in that realm.

Nonetheless, Kant's work is still helpful, when modified. I recommend maintaining a rough distinction between the agreeable and the beautiful. The agreeable is primarily a matter of the play of sense and imagination. The beautiful is primarily a matter of the play of imagination and understanding. Yet, the agreeable may contain, in part, some play of imagination and understanding, and sense should not be excluded from the beautiful.

Everyday Aesthetic Properties

Perhaps we can talk about everyday aesthetics in terms of the notion of everyday aesthetic properties. What then are aesthetic properties? Some philosophers tie the concept of them closely to the arts. However, there is another tradition that sees aesthetic properties simply as characteristics of objects and events that give us pleasure in the sensuous or imaginative apprehension of them. I accept the latter view, although I would insist that "property" not be understood in an objectivist way. The properties appreciated in everyday aesthetics are neither wholly objective nor wholly subjective. They are properties of experienced things, not of physical objects abstracted from our experienced world.

My own view is that *both* sensuous and imaginative apprehension are aspects of aesthetic experience, both at the level of "the agreeable," and at the level of "the beautiful" (using these terms in the modified Kantian sense suggested above). There is always a sensuous *and* an imaginative dimension of aesthetic experience.

This position has a long tradition. It may be found for example in Bullough's description of an aesthetic experience of a fog at sea.[5]

We should not forget the other side of aesthetics: the feeling of *displeasure* that arises in connection with the sensuous/imaginative apprehension of certain things. Whereas the first side comes under the category of "beauty," using that term very broadly, the second comes under the "ugly," also broadly used. As we develop lists of properties relevant to everyday aesthetics, we should not neglect the negative properties: for example, "harsh" with respect to sound, or "dull" with respect to color. At the same time, we should not assume complete symmetry in our handling of positive and negative aesthetic qualities. Priority goes to positive aesthetic qualities: aesthetics has to do primarily with pleasure, and only secondarily with pain.

Is there a distinct set of everyday aesthetic properties? One thinks initially of properties that are either not of much importance in art or nature appreciation; or are important, but have not been much noticed because they have strong associations with everyday life. Examples of these are "neat" and "messy," which I have discussed in a previous paper.[6] The quality of neatness is closely related to the qualities of "ordered," "orderly," "organized," "tidied," and "straightened." We like to have ordered files and straightened rooms (although not always!). This liking often involves some pleasure in the apprehension of these things. Therefore, it makes sense to call these everyday aesthetic qualities.

Perhaps even more fundamental than these is the quality of "rightness," as in "sounds right," "looks right," and "feels right." Nelson Goodman has drawn our attention to the aesthetic quality of rightness and "good fit" with respect to architecture.[7] These terms also relate to everyday aesthetics. For example, if a particular arrangement of furniture in my living room does not look right to me, this may be an aesthetic matter. A good massage feels right, and this is part of what we mean by saying that it is good.

However, we should distinguish between the aesthetic sense of "right" and other senses, for example, epistemological and moral senses. There is also a *practical* sense of "right," where "practical" is used in the everyday sense of the term. The satisfaction of rightness is sometimes ambiguous between the aesthetic and the practical. If a wooden joint looks right to a carpenter, this may give him a sense of aesthetic satisfaction. This would be especially true for an expert in Japanese joinery. However, we often take the *look* of rightness as a mere indicator of *actual* rightness, by which I mean nonaesthetic practical rightness. Such rightness is a matter of fitting some explicit standard, and is not a matter of aesthetics. It might give some small aesthetic satisfaction to an electrician that all of the wires *look* like they are hooked up right, but this will be of little value if they are not *actually* hooked up right. Sometimes the expression "looks right" is intended to mean simply that something appears to be right (in a nonaesthetic sense) but may not be. Recognition of nonaesthetic practical rightness may give satisfaction, but not in a sensuous/imaginative display.

Qualities like "ordered" and "right" are a base line in aesthetics. They come *before* such complicated qualities as "symmetrical," "proportional," "balanced," "integrated," and "harmonious." I say they are a base line for two reasons. First, they are learned earlier by children. Second, judgments of the more complicated qualities are generally based on prior judgments of the base-line qualities. We cannot know whether something is symmetrical until we know how to apply such terms as "ordered" and "straight."

The above-mentioned complicated qualities have been much discussed in the history of aesthetics and have been long applied to the arts. This is not to exclude them from everyday aesthetics. The home decorator may be as interested in harmony and balance as in organization and neatness. If so, then a list of everyday aesthetic qualities may end up being very similar to a list of aesthetic qualities, period. Does this mean that we should give up on delineating the field of everyday aesthetics? I do not think so. We may learn much about everyday aesthetics simply by focusing on aesthetic qualities as they are applied in everyday life. Some qualities will be more prominent in everyday aesthetics than in other aesthetic domains, some less so.

Another item to add to the list of qualities that are relevant to everyday aesthetics is "clean," also discussed in the above-mentioned paper.[8] I now think that the aesthetic quality we are interested in is not simply "clean" but "looks clean," and such related qualities as "smells clean" and "feels clean."[9] Something can *be* clean without looking clean (a floor with a design that makes it look dirty, for example). Something can look clean without *being* clean (a floor that hides invisible germs). Although we might be disgusted or upset to find that a clean-looking object is not really clean, it is doubtful that this is an aesthetic matter.

To "smell clean" should be added such related qualities as "smells nice," "smells good," "smells delicious," and their opposites. These have a great importance to everyday aesthetics, in the home, the restaurant, the streets, and in our erotic lives. This is one area in which the aesthetics of everyday life departs from the aesthetics of fine art. Discussions of the aesthetics of smell are rare in fine arts texts, although smells can be refined and organized to the point where they are a medium for an artform.

Richard L. Anderson has noted that in the United Arab Emirates there is an informal ritualized gathering of women called the *fualah,* which involves the hostess bringing out a glass-lidded box that holds various bottles with perfumes and incenses.[10] I do not know enough about this practice to say whether it is an art form. However, the example does show how aesthetic experiences of smell can be of great interest and complexity.

Let me give another example closer to home. I am not a lover of shopping centers. However, through years of accompanying others who are, I have gained some pleasure in working my way through the various smells made available in soap, perfume, and scented-candle shops. Although these smells are not currently organized in a way that could make them a medium of fine art, the experience of them can afford aesthetic pleasure. Smell analysis and evaluation can be as complicated and sophisticated as the analysis and evaluation of wines, cheeses, and coffees. Perfume experts speak of various levels of smell experience and are able to make extremely subtle distinctions. Smell also has a strong imaginative dimension, often evoking powerful memories.[11]

It might be argued that the field of everyday aesthetic experience discussed is *not* aesthetic precisely because it is not amenable to judgments based on appreciation of complex fields of ordered elements. Early in the twentieth century David W. Prall argued that smells, tastes, and "vital feelings," are not materials of beauty in the sense that colors, sounds, and even textures are.[12] This is because "they are obviously not contents of typical aesthetic judgments." Prall, however, goes on to undercut this position dramatically. First, he admits that such qualities may be perceived with sensuous delight, that attention may be focused on them as specific qualities directly apprehended in sense perception, that they can be contemplated aesthetically, and that they can have specific and interesting character. He just thinks they are "not usually pronounced beautiful." He admits even that they can be *elements* of aesthetic experience and that much of the beauty of nature is made up of these elements. The problem, as he sees it, is that our grasp of such elements, while aesthetic, is a grasp of something specific and nonstructural in which there are no necessary orders of relation (unlike the orders of relation found in the laws of musical harmony, for example).

Yet, as Emily Brady observes in this volume, smells and tastes are arranged in various arts in much more complex ways than Prall imagines. Moreover, few critics today would agree with Prall that the arts based on sound and sight are necessarily governed by strict structural or critical principles. Prall's point would be more plausible if weakened: for example, to say that smells and tastes are somewhat less amenable as elements in complex art compositions than sights and sounds.

Also, Prall could not have anticipated developments in the contemporary visual and aural arts in which interesting juxtaposition of elements took on a greater significance than systems of formal relations between lines and colors, tones and rhythms. In recent times the differences between the visual and aural arts, on the one hand, and the arts of smell and taste, on the other, have become considerably less dramatic. Moreover, given environmental art, installation art, and other current trends in the visual arts, the difference between the aesthetics of art and the aesthetics of nature is also lessened (as Arnold Berleant has often observed).

Prall begins to undercut his original point when he observes that smells and tastes are "still beauties" insofar as they are elementary materials of certain limited aesthetic experiences. He further notes that natural beauty is similarly less organized. Nature, he says, "assumes lovely aspects, unintelligibly composed and unreasonably fine." He even admits that much of what we know of color combinations has been learned from perceiving such natural combinations as rocks under sunlight or hills beyond a running stream, and other such "happy accidents." In addition, he observes that combinations of smells, colors, and sounds can in nature "make up a rare beauty." The point is summed up in a lovely way worth quoting at length:

> If there is a beauty of August nights, or beauty in the rareness of a June day, or the fresh loveliness after rain, if there is ripe and languorous beauty in the mist and mellow fruitfulness of autumn, or a hard, cold beauty of glittering winter frosts, such beauty is not all for the eye and ear, and if we do not ourselves know how to blend smells and tastes with sound and form and color to compose such beauties, we need not foist our limitation upon nature. The saltiness of the breeze is as integral to the beauty of the sea as the flashing of the fish or the sweep of the gulls or the thunder of the surf or the boiling of the foam. If we know no modes of arranging smells or tastes or vital feelings or even noises in works of art, nature does not hesitate to combine the soughing of pines, the fragrance of mountain air, and the taste of mountain water or its coolness on the skin, with dazzling mountain sunlight and the forms and colors of rocks and forests, to make a beauty intense and thrilling in an unexpected purity and elevation, almost ascetic in its very complexity and richness. The greatest beauties of nature are concrete and full. Nature appears to have no aesthetic prejudices against any sort of elementary aesthetic materials, nor to lack insight into the principles of their combination in the greatest variety. Only human limitations may miss some of these elements and human insight fail to recognize any principles of structure or form to hold them so firmly together to make them often so transcendently beautiful. . . . But what happens in nature is not, of course, art, and an artist must work with materials that have relations, degrees of qualitative difference, established orders of variation, structural principles of combination. (55)

Nothing seems left of his original assertions that smells and tastes cannot really be subjects of judgments of beauty, and that they are not contents of typical aesthetic judgments. A space has been opened not only for natural aesthetics but also for everyday aesthetics, even for profound and complex aesthetic experience in everyday contexts. Moreover, as I suggested earlier, the rigid distinction between fine art aesthetics and everyday aesthetics dissolves when one considers that such central artists of our time as Joseph Beuys and Robert Rauschenberg did not work with materials that have degrees of qualitative difference worked out in established orders of variation.

Double Terms

Part of my strategy has been to allow double terms, two-word combinations, into our list of aesthetic terms. This allows us to expand the domain of aesthetic terms. For example, although the term *good* is not by itself aesthetic, the situation is quite different with "looks good," "sounds good," "tastes good," "smells good," and "feels good." The same can be said for similar terms, such as *great*. Here are some more examples.

Consider the term *new.* "Looks new" is often a term of aesthetic approval, and perhaps one of the most important. Along with this, again, comes "smells new," "sounds new," and "feels new." Although "tastes new" is not often used (except, perhaps, when we speak of a new cuisine or food-fashion), we do have the phrase "tastes fresh." The quality "looks new" may be appreciated mainly because that which looks new also tends to be shiny and well ordered.

Related to the concept of "new" are such concepts as "original," "authentic," "novel," and "real." "Sounds real," "looks real," "tastes real," and "smells real" are generally terms of positive aesthetic approval. We can add to this "genuine" and "actual." However, as before, I stress that among certain people on certain occasions the opposites of these can also be terms of aesthetic approval, for example "sounds unreal" when referring to certain avant-garde music. It should also be remembered that all of these phrases can be used in nonaesthetic contexts where the concern is not with the way something is experienced. For example, we might use "looks real" as evidence for the possibility that a hundred-dollar bill is not a fake.

Another word that operates aesthetically when combined as a double term is *fun.* "Fun" has virtually never been mentioned as a term of aesthetics. One of the main reasons of course is that *fun* is not generally considered a valuable term of praise for art (although we do sometimes say of an artwork, "that was a fun piece"). Nor do we use it to refer to the aesthetic phenomena of nature (although one can certainly have fun in nature, as in skiing or fishing). Application of the term *fun* is generally limited to everyday entertainment. This would place it in the domain of everyday aesthetics.

There is, however, a problem with such double terms as "looks fun" or "sounds fun." Unlike "looks good" and "sounds good," these may just be predictions of delights to come, rather than evaluations of something immediate. That is, to say that something "looks fun" is to say, "it looks like this will be fun in the future," or "it looks like it would be fun if I did it too." Actually, "looks good" can have this predictive meaning too. The difference is that "looks fun" seems to be merely predictive, whereas "looks good" can be directly evaluative as well.

Perhaps "fun," just by itself, is an aesthetic quality. After all, it is a quality of an activity that involves pleasure. Someone might reply that it does not involve pleasure in its apprehension, but rather in its experiencing. However, it does involve pleasure in the experiencing of *something*, for example, an amusement ride. So, to say "That amusement ride was fun" might well be an aesthetic judgment.

Against Supervenience Theory

Here I need to make a general observation. It is commonly said that aesthetic features depend on nonaesthetic features. This point has usually been made about art, but may also be applied to everyday aesthetics. However, as I would argue (somewhat controversially, I admit) aesthetic judgments are *never* supported by reference to nonaesthetic features.[13] The point is similar to Hume's idea that we cannot derive "ought," or value statements, from "is," or factual statements. My point is based partly on a claim about word meaning. If I say that this house is beautiful partly because it is a big house, I am using *big* in an aesthetic sense. Mere bigness (in some nonaesthetic sense) is not enough to provide a reason for aesthetic goodness in a house. Using the term *big* in this instance draws on our experiences of other things as "big" in an aesthetic way. This point covers all other attempts to defend aesthetic attributions in terms of so-called nonaesthetic properties.

Arnold Isenberg famously argued that one cannot give a set of reasons that deductively prove an aesthetic verdict.[14] He observed that even though someone might support the verdict that a painting is good by reference to a curving line in the painting, one could draw the same line on a blackboard and it would not be aesthetically good-making. Although I agree that one cannot deductively prove an aesthetic verdict, I disagree with Isenberg on one point. I believe the line on the blackboard cannot be the *same* line as the one in the painting (although it can symbolize it). In particular, it cannot have the same aesthetic properties. The critic who refers to the line in the painting is referring to something aesthetic: he or she is not referring to a nonaesthetic feature of the painting in order to support an aesthetic judgment.

Here is another example. Someone might say that a painting is beautiful because of its radiance, and then insist that radiance is something that can be determined scientifically. However, it is not radiance in this scientific sense that is aesthetically good-making. The radiance of the work is an aesthetic feature of that work, and is aesthetic because of its relations with several other features of the work. We could not abstract this radiance from the work and then apply it to something else in such a way as to make the other object aesthetically valuable in the same way. ("She is so beautiful because of her radiant eyes. I will make this chair beautiful too by transferring the radiance of her eyes to the chair!" Right!)

My position should be distinguished from that of F. N. Sibley. Sibley holds that no nonaesthetic features are sufficient conditions for applying aesthetic terms, and that we do not apply aesthetic terms based on rules. He also holds that aesthetic features depend on nonaesthetic features. Thus, he believes that if critics draw attention to certain nonaesthetic features they may get people to see aesthetic qualities. I agree with his first claim, which follows logically from my own. I disagree, however, that aesthetic features depend on nonaesthetic features and that we can see aesthetic qualities by having our attention drawn to non-aesthetic features. It is nonetheless true that critics may get us to see more complex, higher level aesthetic features by referring to simpler, lower level aesthetic features.[15]

This attack on the traditional distinction between aesthetic and nonaesthetic terms opens the field of aesthetics dramatically. For example, although *radiance* already belongs to that field, *big* typically does not (i.e., it does not belong to it in traditional aesthetic theory, although it does belong in language). That field now includes a whole array of predicates once relegated to the nonaesthetic realm. The domain of everyday aesthetics is no longer limited by the traditionally conceived set of aesthetic terms.

It might be thought strange to have distinctive aesthetic and nonaesthetic meanings of virtually all terms; for example, an aesthetic and a nonaesthetic meaning of *big, radiance,* and so forth. It is not strange, however, when we remember that meaning is a function of use, and that there are aesthetic uses for almost all terms. If a term is being used to support an aesthetic attribution, then that term is being used aesthetically, and has an aesthetic meaning.

"Nice," "Kitsch," and "Tasteful"

Consider the term *nice*. This is an important, perhaps even a central, quality in everyday aesthetics: "nice tie," "nicely written," "nice walk," "nice night," "nice feeling." "Sounds nice," "looks nice," and "feels nice" are also positive aesthetic qualities. "What do you think of the sound of the fountain in my garden?" "Nice." This is an aesthetic judgment, although at a very simple level.

Note that if we speak of a person as "nice," this is not an aesthetic claim. This is so, even though aesthetics may enter into our judgment about the person's niceness. "Nice" is a moral quality when applied without qualification to a person. However, it is not usually a moral quality when applied without qualification to a house or a garden, and scarcely ever when applied to an umbrella.

There is conflict between the lovers of art and lovers of niceness in everyday life. What the average person sees as nice is often abhorrent kitsch to the art sophisticate. Thus, within the artworld, the term *nice* can be a put-down when applied to a work of art (a case of damning with faint praise). The term *nice* may even be inconsistent with such terms as *powerful* and *intriguing.* On the other hand, what the art novice considers nice may not even be thought worthy of that term by the art expert. Although the motive for *Muzak* may be the promotion of something nice, it is truly awful to most music-lovers. None of this, however, makes the quality of niceness less important than other aesthetic qualities. Its importance rests on its pervasiveness: just about everyone wants aesthetic niceness on some level.

Consider the common exclamation: "What a nice day!" Any survey of every-day aesthetics should include the aesthetics of "the day." Some days are good, aes-thetically, and some are not. Typically, we refer to an aesthetically bad day as "dreary" or "depressing." A good one can count as "beautiful," "pretty," or "pleas-ant." The reference may be to the skies, or more broadly, to the weather. "Nice" can also refer to aesthetic pleasures of the day not related to weather. When peo-ple say, "Have a nice day!" they are expressing (albeit, often in a purely *pro forma* way) the wish that we enjoy the events of the day to come.

While speaking of niceness and *Muzak,* it is appropriate to say something general about kitsch. There have been several efforts to define kitsch, but none has focused on the actual terms of praise used in kitsch. When kitsch is admired, the appropriate terms are taken from the aesthetics of everyday life: e.g., *cute, cud-dly, charming, pleasing, thrilling, pretty, colorful, happy, joyous, sad-looking,* and *beautiful.* (Think of late-night television shows that sell ceramic "collectibles.") These are not usually terms of praise for serious works of art. By contrast, kitsch-haters often use words like *sentimental, bombastic,* and *banal,* to describe kitsch. If we focus exclusively on these terms, we may fail to understand an important aspect of kitsch.

Makers of kitsch exploit the aesthetics of everyday life. For example, we nat-urally gain a kind of everyday aesthetic pleasure from the cuteness of babies.[16] This is drawn on by the makers of cuddly dolls. Many other kitsch products par-take in cuteness, for example those based on cats. I do not want to suggest that the qualities referred to by terms like *cute* and *cuddly* cannot be appreciated aes-thetically. In fact, they seem to have particular importance for children, and may provide an initial training for aesthetic appreciation in adult life.[17]

Let us not forget the very important aesthetic quality of "tasteful." "The tasteful" is not to be confused with something that is beautiful strictly-speaking, or even with that which is in accord with taste (in the old eighteenth-century sense of the term). "The tasteful" is culturally emergent and constantly changing: turtlenecks may be tasteful one year and not the next. The quality of "tasteful" is generally ignored by contemporary aesthetics mainly because people confuse it with that which is considered aesthetically good by someone who has taste.

"The tasteful" is central to home decoration, clothing, and food preparation. It is also often associated with quality of materials and workmanship, as well as principles of formal organization and color coordination. Generally, the tasteful can only be afforded by those who have the money for quality craftsmanship, and the time to attend to such matters. The tasteful is also opposed to content that is jarring, disturbing or extreme in some way. One can have a taste for the war scenes of Goya, but it may not be considered tasteful to have these in the dining room. This is not to say that everyday aesthetics is exclusively or predominantly a concern of the upper classes. "The tasteful" has its place in everyday aesthetics, but should not dominate the field.

Related to the quality of the tasteful are such qualities as "artistic," "creative," "poetic," "imaginative," and "expressive." These are often attributed to things that are not works of art, for example, to hats, pillows, hairstyles, and car decoration. They might be metaphorical, as in "poetic," or literal, as in "this decorated room is imaginative and expressive, too!"

Superlatives

An interesting question is whether certain superlatives may also count as everyday aesthetic qualities. For example, where do we place the phrases "looks great" and "looks fantastic"? Similarly, how do we classify such terms as *wonderful, awe-inspiring, marvelous, amazing, extraordinary,* and *perfect* when used in conjunction with such sense-related terms as *looks, sounds,* and *feels;* as in "looks amazing," "sounds wonderful," and so on? For that matter, what about *beauty* and *beautiful?* Is beauty too rare to be considered "everyday"? If it is, then the example of the video of a fluttering bag from *American Beauty* falls out of everyday aesthetics.

Such terms are more likely applied to works of art, and to natural phenomena, than to a made-up bed or a cleaned room. We more readily say that a painting or a landscape is marvelous than we do a household appliance or a pair of shoes. Still, there are high-points in the various concerns of everyday life, and we mark these with high praise, although perhaps with some irony or exaggeration. We say that someone "looks great" or "fantastic" in a certain outfit, or that a dinner was "wonderful." Moreover, there are various crafts that sometimes transcend the ordinary. I once had the pleasure of trying on some very expensive Bally shoes. These were marvelous things: so soft, so malleable, and yet beautifully proportioned and finely worked. In wearing them, I seemed to float a bit above the floor. These shoes went far beyond ordinary shoedom.

Perhaps such terms take us too far outside of the ordinary to be closely associated with something called "everyday." Even more problematic are the phrases *deeply moving* and *powerful.* Although these are terms of high praise in the aesthetics of art, it is difficult to come up with examples of their application in everyday aesthetics. Although we might speak of paintings as powerful, the use of that term in everyday life tends to be more literal: for example, a powerful shower is one that generates a lot of water.[18]

The term *powerful* sounds strange when applied to flower arrangements and dinner parties. Still, when we do speak of real-life experience as "deeply moving" or "powerful" we do so in much the same way we speak of a theatrical performance as such. Therefore, although it seems odd to include such things in everyday aesthetics, I am inclined to do so. After all, it is not required that an aesthetic experience be a low-level one to count as part of everyday life: only that it not fit into one of the traditional aesthetic domains, and that it not be so extraordinary as to leave the domain of the everyday.

When we think of everyday aesthetic properties, we need also think of their complex dialectical relations to the noneveryday. "Shiny," for instance, may appear to be just an everyday aesthetic quality, but in fact, it has a profound relation to the more complex concept of beauty. This has been recognized by many philosophers. For example, Hegel defines beauty as "the sensible *shining* of the idea" and the sensible in the artwork is elevated to pure shining.[19] Heidegger refers to beauty as "a way of shining."

Zen Buddhist Monks, Schopenhauerian Artists, and Japanese Vernacular

There are also what I will call the problems of the Zen Buddhist monk and the Schopenhauerian artist. Each of these seems to be capable of transforming everyday aesthetic experience into something extraordinary. In the case of the Zen monk, the distinction between the aesthetic and the spiritual dissolves. Even a crack in a rice bowl can have great aesthetic/spiritual significance. For the Schopenhauerian artist, an ordinary apple can manifest the realm of Platonic Forms.[20] In both of these cases, the realm of everyday aesthetics appears to reach beyond its ordinary limits: and a flower arrangement *could* be powerful or deeply moving. Similarly, those who have argued that there is such a thing as "the aesthetic attitude" have sometimes claimed that anything can be appreciated under the aesthetic attitude, and hence become aesthetic. Such a position dissolves the distinction between everyday aesthetics and every other form of aesthetics.

Monroe Beardsley similarly describes what he calls the LSD problem.[21] Although he thinks an ordinary flower arrangement could be deeply moving if one viewed it under the influence of LSD, he believes that such an experience is illusory. He gives an example of a psychiatrist who described his experience of Beethoven's *Eroica* as causing him to simultaneously feel insatiable longing and total gratification, and replies, tongue-in-cheek, that we *know* he was on LSD when he said this. What he probably means is that the psychiatrist was describing an impossible experience. Beardsley concludes that for an object to have aesthetic value it must provide aesthetic gratification when *correctly* experienced.

I do not know what Beardsley means by "correctly," and I think it would be hard for him to come up with a clear account of it. Would he hold that Van Gogh incorrectly experienced his small bedroom in Arles when he painted it? Doesn't he exclude the transformative experiences that artists may have of the world during the creative process with the same argument that he excludes LSD experience? Perhaps the psychiatrist incorrectly *described* his experience. Perhaps there was nothing incorrect about the experience itself. (There is something odd about saying that experience of something under LSD is "incorrect.") Beardsley simply did not wish to be forced into the position of saying that everything has equally high aesthetic value since everything can provide intense aesthetic gratification under some circumstances.

It would seem that we need to make some sort of distinction between the aesthetics of everyday life ordinarily experienced and the aesthetics of everyday life extraordinarily experienced. However, any attempt to increase the aesthetic intensity of our ordinary everyday life-experiences will tend to push those experiences in the direction of the extraordinary. One can only conclude that there is a tension within the very concept of the aesthetics of everyday life.

Japanese aesthetics provides a constant source of reflection on the relationship between art and everyday aesthetics, and between the ordinary and the extraordinary within everyday aesthetics. Drawing on Japanese examples, Barbara Sandrisser has criticized the contemporary notion of "the commonplace" as something ordinary, characterless, and mediocre.[22] She notes that the term *commonplace* originally comes from the Greek for place where people met to exchange ideas. She then refers us to an older Japanese craft-oriented view of the everyday. In Japan, there is a special interest in unadorned wood, not only in fine art and religious contexts but also in vernacular building practices. Sandrisser encourages us to accept the vernacular, artistic, and even agricultural roots of our contemporary sophisticated culture: an admirable culture is one in which people gain emotional delight from their everyday environments. She admits that the traditional shaping of the environment carried out, for example, by Japanese carpenters has mythical and spiritual dimensions that are difficult to accept or appreciate today. For example, in the tradition of Japanese woodworking, the wood is seen to have a soul, a benevolent *kami,* which needs to be respected. The master carpenter in ancient temple grounds is expected to respect each log within the context of its destiny within a sacred space (204). Although this approach to the aesthetics of wood-working may seem overly romantic or superstitious, Sandrisser notes that it helped to create the vernacular elegance so admired today in Japanese aesthetics (203). Here again, we have reached a point where the commonplace is transcended, exceeding the mundane and the banal. Architecture, at its best (for example, in the contemporary work of Tadao Ando), gathers together the delights of everyday aesthetics, in the gentle perfume of wood, in the feel of textures, in our appreciation of weather, foliage, and other natural phenomena.

Relation to the Aesthetics of Art

The relationship between everyday aesthetics and the aesthetics of art is a persistent problem. Some may believe that the aesthetics of art is distinctively different because it contains institutional standards and a historical tradition. Although this does not distinguish the aesthetics of art significantly from the aesthetics of fashion or such aesthetically oriented sports as gymnastics, it may distinguish it from other sorts of everyday aesthetic experience in which evaluation is not standardized.

It is true that everyday aesthetics does not give as much a role to evaluation and interpretation as one finds in the aesthetics of art. It seems that one does not need special training in order to experience everyday aesthetic pleasures, although special training enhances our everyday aesthetic experience. As I have argued, constant viewing of contemporary art helps us appreciate our contemporary everyday environments.

Someone might argue that the domain of everyday aesthetics should be understood as completely subjective, and that Kant's point about the agreeable is also appropriate here: there is no disputing tastes in everyday aesthetics. On the other hand, there are regions within everyday aesthetics in which taste does not seem that subjective. (One *needs* special training to aesthetically appreciate the complexities of perfume as an art.)

One ideal of everyday aesthetics is the aesthete: someone who constantly extends her aesthetic skills to objects and events of everyday life. Moreover, there are communities of aesthetes. It may seem to some that Sei Shonagan's list of elegant things is strange. But it probably did not seem strange to her friends. Otherwise her book would not have been circulated and admired. That there are communities of taste in everyday aesthetics does not imply that the properties perceived exist independently of experience. The properties, as I suggested above, are emergent on interaction between the communities and their surroundings.

Conclusion

The field of everyday aesthetics covers the domains of everyday life not covered by such previously existing fields as the aesthetics of art, the aesthetics of nature, and the aesthetics of mathematics. Although Kant's notion of the agreeable was not exactly equivalent to the aesthetics of everyday life, at least he did not limit aesthetics to nature and art, as did many later writers. A more fruitful way to explore the aesthetics of everyday life is through discussion of aesthetic terms. It turns out that most of these are applied throughout the field of aesthetics. Some have special importance for everyday life, whereas others are seldom found in that domain. There are also certain terms that, although applicable across the field of aesthetics, have been neglected because of an overemphasis on the aesthetics of art in our attempts to understand aesthetics in general. These include "neatness," "messiness," "looks good," "smells nice," and many others. The field of aesthetic terms is broadened further by recognizing that aesthetic judgments can never be supported by referring to nonaesthetic properties. I observed an interesting conflict between the aesthetics of everyday life and the aesthetics of art, where certain terms that appear positive in one appear problematic in the other: the most important of these being "nice." This conflict between the aesthetics of art and the aesthetics of everyday life may be part of the reason for the neglect of the latter. Finally, the issues of ordinary everyday aesthetic experience versus extraordinary and highly intense everyday aesthetic experience were discussed.

Notes

1. There is not a large tradition of work on everyday aesthetics. A classic source of inspiration is John Dewey, *Art as Experience* (New York: G. P. Putnams, 1934). Recent examples are Joseph H. Kupfer, *Experience as Art: Aesthetics in Everyday Life* (Albany: State University of New York Press, 1983) and David Novitz, *The Boundaries of Art* (Philadelphia: Temple University Press, 1992). Kupfer includes sports in everyday aesthetics. I am inclined to exclude sports since it typically involves a set of formal institutions much like the arts. Novitz, as the title indicates, is more concerned with the boundaries of art (particularly between fine and popular art) than with the notion of everyday aesthetics, although he does have interesting things to say about the aesthetics of grooming, friendship, and character. In his effort to dissolve the boundaries between art and everyday life, Novitz draws our attention to such things as landscape gardening, tree pruning, debating, cooking, and living-room décor. However, his conception of everyday aesthetics seems limited to what can be conceived of as skilled arts, thus excluding appreciation of everyday phenomena that are not in any sense crafted, for example, the wonderful piles of garden clippings placed every week outside of houses in my town for recycling. See also Richard Shusterman, "Somaesthetics: A Disciplinary Proposal," *The Journal of Aesthetics and Art Criticism*, 57:3 (1999), 296–313. Somaesthetics might be a subspecies of everyday aesthetics as I describe it. Shusterman also draws our attention to Alexander Baumgarten's founding text of modern aesthetics, *Aesthetica* (1750/1758), which proposed an aesthetics of greater scope and practical importance than what we recognize as aesthetics today, going beyond the theory of fine art and natural beauty.
2. Arnold Berleant, *Living in the Landscape: Towards an Aesthetics of Environment* (Lawrence, Kans.: University of Kansas Press, 1997). Berleant's approach is fairly typical. See also Allen Carlson, "Environmental Aesthetics," in David Cooper (ed.), *A Companion to Aesthetics* (Cambridge: Blackwell, 1995), 142–144. Carlson insists, with good reason, that environmental aesthetics focuses on total surroundings. Here, we are immersed in the object of appreciation. However, Carlson, unlike Berleant, allows for the possibility of framing acts that isolate aspects of the environment for appreciation.
3. Allen Carlson, "Appreciation and the Natural Environment," *The Journal of Aesthetics and Art Criticism* 37:3 (1979), 267–275; Yuriko Saito, "The Aesthetics of Unscenic Na-

ture," *The Journal of Aesthetics and Art Criticism* 56:2 (1998), 101–11. Saito correctly observes that Carlson has not shown how and why cognitive considerations should outweigh such considerations as enjoyment, amusement, and entertainment accompanying the aesthetic appreciation (102).

4. Immanuel Kant, *The Critique of Judgment*, tr. James Meredith (Oxford: The Clarendon Press, 1928), 44.

5. Edward Bullough, "Psychical Distance," in Kathleen M. Higgins (ed.), *Aesthetics in Perspective* (Fort Worth: Harcourt Brace, 1996). See also Yuriko Saito's incisive and sensitive discussion of Bullough in "The Aesthetics of Weather," this volume.

6. See my "Everyday Surface Aesthetic Qualities: 'Neat,' 'Messy,' 'Clean,' and 'Dirty,'" *Journal of Aesthetics and Art Criticism* 53:3 (1995), 259–68. See also Kevin Melchionne, "Living in Glass Houses: Domesticity, Interior Decoration, and Environmental Aesthetics," *The Journal of Aesthetics and Art Criticism* 56:2 (1998), 191–200.

7. Nelson Goodman, "How Buildings Mean," in Nelson Goodman and Catherine Z. Elgin, *Reconceptions in Philosophy and Other Arts and Sciences* (Indianapolis: Hackett Publishing, 1988.)

8. See Kevin Melchionne, *Living in Glass Houses,* for further discussion.

9. Think of Sei Shonagon's list of "Things That Give a Clean Feeling": "An earthen cup. A new metal bowl. A rush mat. The play of the light on water as one pours it into a vessel. A new wooden chest." This is from Sei Shonagon, "The Pillow Book," selection in Kathleen M. Higgins, *Aesthetics in Perspective*, 619. Shonagon is not only listing things, she is listing aesthetic experiences.

10. Richard L. Anderson, *Calliope's Sisters: A Comparative Study of Philosophies of Art* (Englewood Cliffs: Prentice Hall, 1990), 273–74.

11. See "Sniffing and Savoring: The Aesthetics of Smells and Tastes" by Emily Brady, this volume, for an excellent discussion of this topic.

12. David W. Prall, "Aesthetic Surface," in John Hospers (ed.), *Introductory Readings in Aesthetics* (New York: The Free Press, 1969), originally Chapter 5, "Aesthetic Judgment" (Thomas Y. Crowell Co., 1929), 57–75.

13. A full defense of this would have to be made elsewhere, especially with respect to the aesthetics of art. Marcia Muelder Eaton provides an excellent critique of supervenience theory in her "Intention, Supervenience, and Aesthetics Realism," *British Journal of Aesthetics,* 38:3 (1998), 179–293. "Even if we could identify the set of base properties [on which aesthetic properties are supposed to supervene], it is possible for two things to be exactly alike with respect to base properties and for it still to be the case that one is F and one is not-F" (290). Also, see her "The Intrinsic, Non-Supervenient Nature of Aesthetic Properties," *The Journal of Aesthetics and Art Criticism* 52:4 (1994), 383–406.

14. Arnold Isenberg, "Critical Communication," in W. E. Kennick (ed.), *Art and Philosophy* (New York: St. Martin's Press, 1979), 658–67.

15. F. N. Sibley, "Aesthetic Concepts" (1959), reprinted in Joseph Margolis (ed.), *Philosophy Looks at the Arts: Contemporary Readings in Aesthetics,* rev. ed. (Philadelphia: Temple University Press, 1987), 29–52. My position escapes David Novitz's criticism of Sibley, that it is difficult to see why pointing to nonaesthetic qualities should be thought genuine reasons for regarding works of art as elegant or serene, David Novitz, *The Boundaries of Art,*

72. I agree with Novitz that Sibley wrongly left out the evaluative dimension of aesthetic features, and failed to realize that aesthetic properties are culturally emergent as well as physically embodied.

16. See John Morreal's excellent "Cuteness," *British Journal of Aesthetics,* 31:1 (1991), 39–47.

17. James Kirwan's unpublished "The Institution of Kitsch" given at the 1999 Pacific Division meeting of the American Society for Aesthetics has provided stimulus on this point.

18. An alternative way to talk about everyday aesthetics would be to stress that which is ordinary—distinguishing, as it were, between major and minor league aesthetic phenomena. For example, Stan Godlovitch in "Evaluating Nature Aesthetically," *The Journal of Aesthetics and Art Criticism* 56:2 (1998), 113–25, talks about distinguishing the local and little from the great and big. He suggests that "it is out of place to judge with the same ear the struggles of the Red Deer Civic Orchestra and the effortless perfection of the Berlin Philharmonic." On this view (not actually advocated by Godlovitch), my appreciation of a short glimpse of Coyote Creek over a bridge on my walk to work would be an example of small-scale appreciation of nature—nature in the little league. My appreciation of student fashions is small-scale in relation to the major league of high fashion appreciation. On this view, once experience becomes extraordinary it is no longer a part of the everyday.

19. I owe this information to John Sallis, *Stone* (Studies in Continental Thought) (Indiana University Press, 1994).

20. Arthur Schopenhauer, *The World as Will and Representation,* 2 vols., tr. E. F. J. Payne (New York: Dover, 1969).

21. Monroe Beardsley, "The Aesthetic Point of View," in John W. Bender and H. Gene Blocker (eds.), *Contemporary Philosophy of Art: Readings in Analytic Aesthetics* (Englewood Cliffs, N.J.: Prentice-Hall, 1993), 384–96.

22. Barbara Sandrisser, "Cultivating Commonplaces: Sophisticated Vernacularism in Japan," *The Journal of Aesthetics and Art Criticism* 56:2 (1998), 201–10.

CHAPTER 2

Ideas for a Social Aesthetic

Arnold Berleant

BEAUTY AND OTHER AESTHETIC SATISFACTIONS have long been valued as inveterately personal matters. Persons, of course, are at the center of experience, and our pleasures and our pains are personal, even though they occur as part of situations that involve other things and perhaps other people. We can recount them to others, recommend the occasions that evoked them, and form judgments of taste. But as Kant reluctantly concluded, any claim for universality is logically only an assumption and volitionally but a hope.

> There can be no rule according to which anyone is to be forced to recognize anything as beautiful. We cannot press [upon others] by the aid of any reasons or fundamental propositions our judgment that a coat, a house, or a flower is beautiful. People wish to submit the object to their own eyes, as if the satisfaction in it depended on sensation; and yet, if we then call the object beautiful, we believe that we speak with a universal voice, and we claim the assent of everyone, although on the contrary all private sensation can only decide for the observer himself and his satisfaction. . . . The judgment of taste itself does not *postulate* the agreement of everyone . . . ; it only *imputes* this agreement to everyone.[1]

Aesthetics, moreover, has long concerned itself with the arts, with the theory of the arts, that is, and with understanding beauty in nature. And that understanding, as Alexander Gottlieb Baumgarten, the originator of modern aesthetics, thought of it, lies in the perfection of sensory awareness. It is easy to see how this can relate to the various arts and to our appreciation of nature. These are preeminently sensory, embracing the full range of perceptual experience in all its modalities, not only by means of the senses but also in the sensory aspects of experiences that are imaginative, that involve recollection, or that may even be predominately cognitive. So understood, perception is broad, indeed, and necessarily so, since it is important to recognize how completely and thoroughly sensation pervades all experience. Traditionally, then, aesthetics is the province of the arts, in that attempts to understand the arts lead us to aesthetics. Or, more strictly speaking, the arts, and certain aspects of nature, are the province of aesthetics.

This is the heart of the traditional view, essentially true to the course of its long and respectable history. The personal domain of perceptual experience, especially in the arts, seems to have little to do with the social world. To think, then, of a social aesthetic would seem to be mere wishfulness in emulating Kant by sacrificing reason to desire. Yet where else might we locate the ground and scope of aesthetic value? As with so many philosophical problems, however, this one is less a true opposition than what Marvin Farber called a methodogenic problem, one that originates from the method being used rather than in the subject matter itself.[2] Assigning aesthetic value a subjective locus seems to render a social aesthetic impossible.

Some, however, have tended toward finding a social basis in aesthetic experience itself. Exploring this direction can lead us not only to its possibility but to its plausibility. Let me begin by recalling Schiller's intriguing insight in his *On the Aesthetic Education of Man:*

> Though it may be his needs which drive man into society, and reason which implants within him the principles of social behavior, beauty alone can confer upon him a *social character.* Taste alone brings harmony into society, because it fosters harmony in the individual. All other forms of perception divide man, because they are founded exclusively either upon the sensuous or upon the spiritual part of his being; only the aesthetic mode of perception makes of him a whole, because both his natures must be in harmony to achieve it.[3]

Apart from Schiller's imaginative claim, relating the theory of the arts to social thought has rarely been attempted. There have been tangential associations of the aesthetic with the social, as in the growing interest in aesthetic education. The growing interest in the intersection of art and morality brings the two together in a different context, since morality always implicates human relations. Moreover, the arts and their practices suggest the expansion of aesthetics in both interesting and important ways. The connection of the aesthetic and the social may even provide the basis for a philosophy of culture. To show how this is so, how an aesthetics of the arts leads us beyond the arts, let me start with the customary account of the aesthetic situation.

The distinctive pleasure we associate with the arts involves an aesthetic of objects—an aesthetic of art objects and sometimes of objects in nature. These stand at the theoretical center, and most discussion concerns the distinctiveness of such objects, their properties, qualities, and other features, their form and order, and how they transfigure the world beyond in ways that render it aesthetically enjoyable. Complementing this aesthetic of objects is a distinctive way of appreciating them. Once these art objects have been singled out and identified as paintings, sculptures, musical works, theatrical productions, or dance performances, aesthetic theory postulates a distinctive response, a way of appreciating these objects that matches their special character with an equally special kind of reception. Balancing this aesthetic of objects is an attention that is essentially passive and contemplative, a response that delights in those objects for their own sake, without any concomitant application or other purpose—in the usual terminology, disinterestedly.

Curiously enough, this traditional aesthetic of objects and their appreciation itself leads to the possibility of a social aesthetics. One can develop a sequence of arts that proceeds from a simple, delimited art object and its correlative response, to an integral aesthetic-social situation: a painting, as the paradigm of a single, delimited object, can easily be circumscribed by two dimensions. Enclosed by a frame, this art of the surface is clearly set off from what is around it and offers a clear and convenient focus for the appreciative eye. To these two dimensions, the related art of sculpture adds another. Sculpture resembles painting only superficially, for it does not simply thicken the surface and bend it around to achieve a third dimension but incorporates mass, and mass takes its position among other things in the world. Sculpture is unlike painting in still another respect: it not only fills the space as mass but charges the space around it, creating an aura that the beholder enters in the act of appreciation.

When we turn to architecture, we find this enlarged space extended inward as well as outward. Mass opens within to enclose space, and this interior volume is designed for people and invites them to occupy it. At the same time, architecture reaches far beyond the aura of sculpture into the surrounding space of its site, incorporating that space into an ensemble with its physical structure. Such an enlarged space may extend beyond the site and adjoining grounds to contiguous or nearby structures. Artists who construct environments that we can enter and inhabit for a brief time render the enlargement of art more explicit yet. Environments add to the two dimensions of painting and the third dimension of sculptural mass and architectural space a fourth, temporal dimension. For time enters into the art work explicitly and consciously, along with the appreciative observer, who is obliged to become a participant and activate the environment by moving through it.

Despite the theoretical and perceptual constraints of traditional aesthetics, then, we find ourselves well on the way to a social aesthetics, for it is but a short step in this sequence of arts to the social environment. An environment devised by an artist is a fabricated perceptual construct that concentrates features found in every environment. Yet even if a human environment does not originate specifically with an artist, it is a culturally constructed context. And since people are implicated in all experienced places, we end with situated human relationships, that is, with a social environment. Not only does an aesthetics of art objects lead to the possibility of a social aesthetics; we arrive at the same point if we start from the appreciator. Appreciative experience is never entirely passive but demands at the very least attention that is alert and focused. By introducing an active human contribution, then, aesthetics has again acquired a social dimension.

Although a traditional aesthetic of circumscribed objects and disinterested appreciators leads eventually to the social domain, when aesthetic theory is developed contextually, the social relevance of the aesthetic is more pronounced still. Let us see how this is.

Aesthetics as Contextual

In a contextual theory no single or dominant feature establishes an aesthetic situation. Instead, a number of factors combine into an inclusive situation.

Acceptance

In the aesthetic encounter, appreciation involves an openness to experience while judgment is suspended. It takes deliberate effort to set aside selective, restricted attention, the tunnel vision of ordinary life, which centers on specific objects and particular goals. This kind of attention is easily transferred to works of art, setting them apart from other objects and activities. Even Kant retains the teleological form of practical interest, but without a practical object, in his famous "purposiveness without purpose."[4]

The twentieth century fought successfully for the expansion of art against such a limitation. Given the appropriate conditions, anything whatever can now become art, whether it be a conventional art object or one that possesses practical utility. At the same time as the realm of art has expanded, so, too, has the range of aesthetic appreciation. Nothing is excluded a priori, and we must be willing to enter into appreciation with an open mind. This applies to the situation as much as to the object, especially since the art object has proved dispensable and has sometimes been replaced by concepts, programs, found objects, and even philosophy.

Perception

Perception is basic in all experience. What makes it important here is its predominance in aesthetic appreciation. Baumgarten established this when he adapted the Greek word *aisthēsis,* perception through the senses, as the name of this new discipline, defining aesthetics as the science of sensory knowledge directed toward beauty.[5] Sensory experience, however, is never pure sensation as the psychology of perception and social psychology have long known. Many factors shape our sensory awareness, from the physiology of the brain and other organic functions, to the formative influences of education and the other cultural institutions and practices that inform our belief system, affect our responses, and contribute to the many-layered complexity of perception. Sensation, nonetheless, lies at its center, making perception different from other modes of awareness, such as intellectual cognition, mystical bliss, and intense physical activity. Aesthetic perception, often considered peculiar to the arts, has always been at the heart of our appreciation of nature, from small objects of special beauty, such as a blossom or a stone, to monumental ones in the form of a waterfall, a canyon, or an entire landscape. Indeed, nothing in the character of aesthetic perception precludes its appropriateness for other objects and situations. Perceptual experience may also dominate certain social occasions, such as moments of affection between parents and children or between friends or lovers, and also times of quarrel or hatred.

Sensuousness

The senses lie at the heart of perceptual experience, and the pleasure they provide gives them special importance here. Traditional aesthetics has been constrained by its intellectualist premises from accepting the full scope of sensation. From Plato to Hegel, sight and hearing were declared the sole aesthetic senses, in large part because they are distance receptors and so conform to the contemplative model of knowledge that separates its object and sets it at a distance.[6] Yet all the senses can provide aesthetic satisfaction, including the proximal receptors of tactual, olfactory, gustatory, and subcutaneous kinaesthetic perception. Moreover, the common belief that experience flows through separate sensory channels distorts their actual synthesis in perception. In perceptual experience the senses fuse inseparably, and synaesthesia is especially pronounced in aesthetic appreciation.[7]

Discovery

From the central place of perceptual awareness, aesthetic experience is, at least in principle, unconstrained by preconceptions about what can be taken aesthetically. Ordinary experience is guided by signs or cues that often reduce its perceptual content to a mere vestige, sufficient only for recognition, and when experience becomes habitual or routine it loses its aesthetic character. In aesthetic experience, however, the usual order of significance is inverted. Perceptual qualities and experienced meanings are the center of attention, and those features that were once unnoticed or ignored become important. This opens the field of aesthetic experience to unexpected objects and events. And because aesthetic perception is focused and selective, novel and creative ideas and relationships may emerge.

Uniqueness

Every experience is perceptually unique, different in some respects from every other. This takes on special importance in aesthetic appreciation because of its emphasis on perception. Even repeated objects or events never actually duplicate each other, since each repetition resonates with its predecessors, while at the same time projecting its influence on the repetitions that will follow.

Reciprocity

The interplay that develops among the factors in an aesthetic situation is sometimes overlooked, yet this invariably occurs in an intense engagement with art. The experience of an art object is deeply affected by the knowledge and attitude of the person who joins with it.[8] At the same time the object acts on the beholder and subtly alters the character and quality of awareness.

This interplay between art and its appreciator overlaps with similar exchanges involving the other active factors in the aesthetic situation or field, such as the artist and the performer. These may sometimes be different persons but at other times simply the re-creative, activating attention of the audience. All these factors may contribute information, interpretive judgment, and other kinds of cognitive content, yet in this context they always assume a perceptual mode. The recent emphasis on interactive art makes the dynamic exchange of object, audience, artist, and performer in the aesthetic field explicit and prominent.

Continuity

Not only do these participating factors interact and overlap, but they also blend into one another in the living experience of an aesthetic situation. The distinctions we draw from a reflective distance between the constituent elements of the aesthetic field fade away, and the divisions and separations that we impose on experience to help us grasp and control it melt into continuities. This is the primary milieu of aesthetic experience and secures its contextual character.

Engagement

The concept of engagement encapsulates these features of a contextual aesthetic. Aesthetic engagement renounces the traditional separations between the appreciator and the art object, the artist and the viewer, and the performer and these others. The psychological distance that traditional aesthetics imposes between the appreciator and the object of art is a barrier that obstructs the participatory involvement that art encourages. Similarly, the divisions we are in the habit of making among these various factors introduce constraints and oppositions. In aesthetic engagement boundaries fade away and we experience the continuity of these factors directly and intimately. Those who can set aside the preconceptions of aesthetic distance and the dichotomizing metaphysics that underlies traditional aesthetic theory may discover that the fullest and most intense experiences of art and natural beauty reveal an intimate absorption in the wonder and vulnerability of the aesthetic.

Multiplicity

Because the aesthetic concerns the character of experience itself and is not confined to a particular kind of object or place, it knows no external or a priori restrictions. Thus the occasions on which aesthetic appreciation can develop are unlimited and can involve any object whatsoever. Further, aesthetic involvement need not be a rare or restricted event. It is limited only by our perceptual capabilities and our willingness to participate. At the same time, aesthetic experience does not dominate every situation. Often an aesthetic character is subordinate to other demands and interests, such as religious, practical, technological, or cognitive ones. Sometimes the aesthetic supervenes on our usual expectations, as when the Bible is appreciated for its literary art and not its religious significance, or when the design of a sewer facility becomes the opportunity for creating a tidal sculpture, re-creating a habitat for endangered species, and establishing a public-access bay walk.[9] And the practice of a craft may fuse aesthetic values inseparably with functional needs, as in throwing a clay bowl, building a wooden cabinet, or designing a sailboat or an airplane. In such ways as these, aesthetic values pervade the entire range of human culture.

These features of the aesthetic situation both establish and reflect its contextual character. Discussions about art often center on a single trait, most often the art object but sometimes the appreciator or the artist. Yet they err by synechdoche, taking part of the situation as if it were the entire domain. Even when the appreciator and the object are regarded as related to each other, they are usually still considered basically self-contained. Furthermore, if we do not also include the creative, re-creative, and performative aspects of such experience, the same error of partiality occurs and the account remains fragmentary. For this reason, discussions about expression, representation, formalism, and feeling are likely to misrepresent art. The concept of the aesthetic field is useful here because it reflects in an inclusive and convenient way the interweaving, indeed the fusion, of the objective, perceptual, creative, and performative dimensions of what is actually experienced as integral.[10]

Social Aesthetics

Although this account of a contextual aesthetics has focused mainly on art and nature, human relations bear a remarkable resemblance to its situational character. How can this be?

Some of the arts suggest that possibility. Consider architecture. To regard architecture merely as the art of building distorts the way in which it actually organizes an entire environment. The design of a building determines not just its own features, it also affects the site on which the building rests and our perception of the structures that stand nearby. Sometimes, in fact, a building casts its character over an entire neighborhood, for buildings are not self-sufficient objects but places for human activity, determining the patterns of movement toward, into, and out of them, as well as within them. This fact transforms our understanding of architecture from an art of physical structures into an art of complex social and environmental organization.

Theater also embodies a social aesthetic. Although theater design, sets, and costumes obviously exert a strong influence on the audience, the heart of theater does not lie in its physical properties. Theater's special contribution emerges most vividly in its depiction of social situations, especially of particular human relations. Because theater creates an environment that is predominately social, the aesthetics of theater must take this as central. Film and television harrow the same field but into different textures, for the nature of these media determines and shapes the qualitative character of the experiences they generate. Although film genres and styles vary enormously, cinema tends to focus on personal situations with a visual range and intensity that replace the bodily presence from which so much of theater's special power derives. As the eye of the mind, the camera becomes a virtuoso performer in its own right, invisibly directing both conscious and subliminal awareness. Television exhibits a similar process, but it tends to work best in small-scale situations, where its proximity to the viewer and frequent close-ups combine with the intimacy of quiet speech to create social situations that have their own distinctive quality.

Each of these preeminently situational arts—architecture, theater, film, and television—exemplifies a distinguishable mode of aesthetic engagement. Together they constitute a sequence of essentially social aesthetic situations. Each implicates and relies on human participants in a different way, and each contributes to our understanding of how aesthetic perception carries social significance. To give an adequate account of this, the usual categories and principles, especially those that focus on the aesthetic object and its properties, will not do. In their place we need a social aesthetics.

What would an aesthetics of the social situation look like? Perhaps it would resemble the aesthetics of environment, where many contributing factors come together to establish its aesthetic character and give it a distinctive identity: participants, physical setting, social conditions, along with time, history, and the powerful influence of culture and tradition, all join in the perceptual character of aesthetic experience. Moreover, no environment that we can know and speak about is without a human presence, for such a thing is empirically impossible. Social aesthetics may, then, *be* a kind of environmental aesthetics.[11]

Social aesthetics is, then, an aesthetics of the situation. But what identifies this particular kind of situation? Like every aesthetic order, social aesthetics is contextual. It is also highly perceptual, for intense perceptual awareness is the foundation of the aesthetic. Furthermore, factors similar to those in every aesthetic field are at work in social aesthetics, although their specific identity may be different. While there is no artist, as such, creative processes are at work in its participants, who emphasize and shape the perceptual features, and supply meaning and interpretation. There is certainly no art object here, but the situation itself becomes the focus of perceptual attention, as it does in conceptual sculpture or in environments. And at the same time as its participants contribute to creating the aesthetic character of the situation, they may recognize with appreciative delight its special qualities, and perhaps work, as a performer would, at increasing and enhancing them. In such ways, a social situation, embodying human relationships, may become aesthetic.

When Schiller attributes the source of social character in human beings to beauty, he finds in that experience the ability to harmonize the disparate qualities that, especially in Western culture, compete and conflict with other. The usual opposition that Schiller identifies as the source of this is psychophysical, "the sensuous [part]" and "the spiritual part of [our] being," as he calls it. Social harmony is achieved through taste, by which he means a developed aesthetic sensibility. This is not just a state of mind: a harmony of the sensuous and the spiritual demands full participation of all aspects of human perception, since the sensuous is as much body as the spiritual is consciousness.

A social situation, then, displays the characteristics of an aesthetic situation when its perceptual and other characteristic aesthetic features predominate: full acceptance of others, heightened perception, particularly of sensuous qualities, the freshness and excitement of discovery, recognition of the uniqueness of the person and the situation, mutual responsiveness, an occasion experienced as connected and integrated, the abandonment of separateness for full personal involvement, and a relinquishing of the restrictions and exclusivity that obstruct appreciation. A social aesthetic, then, is full integration, integration equally of the personal and the social, a goal as much social as it is aesthetic.

It is important not to leave this argument in the abstract, for many common social occurrences lend themselves to aesthetic experience and analysis. Each of these invites a fuller discussion of how it may take on a predominately aesthetic character. Nor is that character exclusive, for these settings also fuse moral and social values with aesthetic ones. Let us consider some cases.

Aesthetic Social Situations

Proper etiquette is ordinarily interpreted as rule-governed behavior, as conventions that are devoid of any real content but that serve to facilitate social interaction by establishing regular patterns. Yet there are occasions when the cultivation of such behavior assumes a certain grace, when the participants delight in the skills involved and at the same time manage to introduce genuine human content into what is usually empty ritual. When this occurs, discovery, perception, reciprocity, and the other aesthetic features overcome the sterile formalism often associated with etiquette. In much the same way, other rituals, whether religious or social, may turn into aesthetic situations. Religious rituals sometimes become full-fledged theater, and living drama often occurs at other ceremonies, celebrations, and festivals.

There are entire societies that seem to possess the harmony Schiller spoke of. One such culture is the Foi, a tribe living in Papua New Guinea. Foi society is constituted aesthetically, with close connections between language and movement, both in relation to their dwellings and to the overall territory. No boundaries exist between mind and body or the being of life and the being of death; these have a continuity that Foi sung poetry reveals as the basic conditions of spatial and temporal life. Furthermore, this poetry is fundamental in the discursive life of their communally lived world.[12]

Such aesthetically integrated societies are undoubtedly rare, but many kinds of social situations exist in less favored societies that at times exhibit the qualities of an aesthetic situation. Relations with small children, for example, often take on an aesthetic character when our judgment is suspended and perception becomes heightened by a special delight in sensory qualities, qualities of the sort Rubens depicted in the drawing of his son, Nicholas, as a child. On such occasions one can easily discern other aesthetic features: discovery, uniqueness, reciprocity, continuity, engagement, and the possibility of multiple occurrences of the same sort. These traits of an aesthetic situation occur in much the same way in close friendships, and Aristotle included some of them when he described perfect friendship as resting on mutual trust, providing for each other's good in a situation where the friend's good is inseparable from one's own.[13]

It may be, however, that the deepest and most intense occasions of a social aesthetic occur in the many forms that love can take. *Love* is an overused word in human relations but until recently it has been uncommon in philosophy. On the other hand, "beauty" is a common term in philosophical aesthetics but not in describing human relations. Can we pair their rarities and write a philosophy of love about beautiful relationships and, at the same time, a philosophy of beauty about the relationships of love? For both beauty and love are relational ideas and not formal features of objects. Better still, they denote the character of a situation. Of the many ways to pursue their connection, little has been said of how love can be illuminated through the traits of an aesthetic situation as a manifestation of beauty.[14] Let me comment on just a single feature of that situation, perhaps its key feature and the one that implies the others, as well: the idea of aesthetic engagement.

Although there are obvious differences between art and love, their resemblances are striking. Consider their common affective character. Shakespeare was hardly the first to recognize that music may be an aphrodisiac. Plato, long before, had found its seductive power distressing.[15] Yet whether stimulus or threat, art does more than excite amorous passions and it goes beyond being only a cause or an accompaniment of love. To treat art in these ways is to think of it as separate from love. Cannot a more intimate association hold between the arts and the passions, between art and love, a relationship that involves more than one being simply an occasion or condition of the other?

I believe that there is, but it is no thread joining externals, no curious connection of separates. It resembles, rather, a relationship of consanguinity, of siblings rather than of parent and child. What art and love have in common are the characteristics we associate with the aesthetic. What is different is more the participants than the occurrence, more the kind of activity than the kind of experience we enter into. Love concerns human relationships, although, like Thoreau, a person may love a landscape, a place, a home, or an object.[16] Aesthetic experience joins appreciator, object, artist, and activator. Surely some kinds of love reflect a similar fusion.

Whatever else may be involved in art, dwelling on the features of the object occupies a central place. In full appreciative engagement, what often develops is a sense of personal exchange with the image in the painting or with its pictorial qualities; a sharing of the dynamic progression of the work, as in the unfolding of a musical composition; an intimate involvement in the sequence of movement in a dance and the dramatic raveling and unraveling of a play or a novel; and in theater, a human situation that may evoke a strong feeling of kinship or human empathy or the intensity of an epiphany.

Yet these are the very signs of love, the common strand in its multitude of forms and instances: a personal exchange, a sharing of dynamic progression, perhaps a sense of dramatic development, the awareness of a rare human situation, a feeling of empathy or identity. In both art and love we may have a sense of being in place, of a dissolution of barriers and boundaries, of communion. Such connectedness, such continuity, such engagement lie at the very center of the aesthetic, occurring with the greatest intensity on the most powerful occasions.

Others have recognized such a bond. In her essay on "Human Personality," Simone Weil speaks of "a type of attention, converging upon love, that enables the attender to commune with an object (or person) at the level of the impersonal—seeing it with acuity, understanding, and affection."[17] Communing with an object characterizes aesthetic engagement, while the impersonal here refers to the loss of a discrete, separate sense of self. In an oddly parallel fashion Thoreau likened the aesthetic relation to nature to a loving friendship: "As I love nature, as I love singing birds, and gleaming stubble, and flowing rivers, and morning and evening, and summer and winter, I love thee my Friend."[18]

The general resemblances of love to aesthetic contact, continuity, participation, and engagement suggest a structural similarity, an isomorphism between these two most human of experiences. We can, indeed, describe both art and love as aesthetic situations. Both involve acceptance without judgment and, at their best, both exhibit free value. Once we discard the negative elements of possessiveness, exploitation, insecurity, egoism, jealousy, and power, much of what is left in relationships of love is its aesthetic character, whether with friends, with children, or with partners. A lesson for morality lies here in recognizing the importance of free value, rare and fleeting though it be.[19] Love and art dwell, too, in the perceptual domains of sense, imagination, and memory, and both focus on the sensory qualities of the situation. A rich love relation, like good art, holds new and surprising awareness, cognition, and re-cognition, as the peculiar individual features of the art or love object become the focus of attention. It is ultimate particularity.[20]

Further, both art and love evoke an awareness of mutuality among the factors and forces in the aesthetic situation. The various arts and the different modes of love exhibit reciprocity in ways that are similar, as the participating factors blend into each other.[21] Divisions and separations disappear and are replaced by a feeling of empathy. These connections are personal ones, for both art and love produce a sense of shared living, a certain continuity and oneness, an intimacy in which divisions disappear. Love, indeed, is a binding force that melts boundaries, something that Empedocles recognized as far back as the fifth century B.C.E., when he described love as the attracting and unifying force in the universe.[22] Finally, both possess uniqueness without exclusivity, for various and diverse occasions and relationships are possible. This is not love of the beautiful or love as the path to the beautiful, which Plato's Socrates learns from Diotima in *The Symposium*. It is rather love *as* beauty, both of them manifold and irreducible.[23]

The Politics of Social Aesthetics

This confluence of the aesthetic and the social carries us eventually to that domain in which the social formalizes itself in political patterns. Here a social aesthetic has significant and powerful implications. Schiller again points the way:

> No privilege, no autocracy of any kind, is tolerated where taste rules, and the realm of aesthetic semblance expends its sway. . . . In the Aesthetic State everything—even the tool which serves—is a free citizen, having equal rights with the noblest. . . . Here, in the realm of Aesthetic Semblance, we find that ideal of equality fulfilled which the Enthusiast would fain see realized in substance.[24]

Is "the Aesthetic State" merely a metaphor for the aesthetic situation or does it, in fact, have genuinely political implications?[25] Could it perhaps be both? If it is in some sense political, then what is it that is equal in the aesthetic state? Does the aesthetic suggest a different sense of equality from the many meanings and practices that have been urged since the Stoics and early Christians? Let us consider these questions by uncovering some of the parallels and implications that an aesthetic model holds for political order and other social institutions.[26]

The social equivalent of the willing acceptance of the object in an aesthetic situation lies in recognizing the intrinsic value of every person. Like the readiness to engage aesthetically in all kinds of experience, the fundamental acceptance of each person is the precondition of a social ethics. No one is excluded a priori. No classification stands between a person and his or her inherent worth, not race, religion, ethnicity, private history, level of cultivation, or any other category by which we lose the person in the generality. This accords with the ethical ideal that holds all people as morally equal, irrespective of other differences.

The aesthetic emphasis on perception suggests that judgments of worth, whether they apply to actions, practices, laws, people, or institutions, be based on the immediacy of the experience to which they lead, on their empirical manifestations and not on rules, principles, or other substitutes for experience. The sensuousness in aesthetic awareness has its parallel in the fact of human embodiment in the political order. People are flesh and blood creatures, not statistics, blocs, classes, districts, or votes. The political equivalent of discovery lies in an openness to new ideas and to change that comes from wide participation in social decision-making. The idea of aesthetic uniqueness provides a special meaning. Equality is not exhausted by the notion of a common moral standing, although ultimately this is crucial. It suggests, in addition, that human beings are incommensurable, and that whatever generic features they may exhibit, individual people possess ultimate and irreducible particularity.

Reciprocity lies at the heart of the democratic process, for it takes the essential interplay and fusion that develop in aesthetic experience as a model for social and political order. This means that an aesthetic state must be nonauthoritarian and nonhierarchical, and that the imposition of force or power in any form must be rejected in the social dynamic. Genuine reciprocity transforms all parties to the process, as difficult to achieve as it is desirable. Yet how else can true reconciliation and collaboration take place? Reciprocity turns aesthetic continuity into a social ideal promoting cooperation, not conflict, and it dissolves class divisions and other such separations that impede continuity. By reconciling oppositions and enhancing humane connections within a social group, the social equivalent of aesthetic engagement encourages intimacy in personal relations and rejects formalized structures that separate people and form them into oppositions. Further, the openness and readiness to enter into multiple aesthetic occasions becomes a basis for the social pluralism to which free association freely leads.

We may ask, finally, what claim the aesthetic can make as a social model. It is easy to dismiss the aesthetic state for being as naive as it is noble. Perhaps it does exceed the grasp of our faulty institutions and the flawed people who run them.

Yet maybe its rarity has more to do with cynicism, narrow purposes, and an ignoble spirit than with any inherent impossibility. For such an aesthetic community does in fact exist in more limited forms, imperfectly and impermanently, perhaps, but nonetheless actually, in art, in love, in societies like the Foi, and in many small, intentional groups and communities. It may be that a modest scope is the precondition for an aesthetic social order, a necessary corrective to the overpowering magnitude of mass culture.

The idea of a social aesthetic offers a distinctive, fresh, and illuminating approach to human relations, whether in the form of friendship, family, or the state. It is flexible and adaptable to different kinds of situations and looks at the need for some kind of ordering in society with a positive eye. The usual social dynamic is one of conflict and societies provide various mechanisms for resolving it, from legal and judicial systems to police power and open repression. However these be administered, the ethos of opposition remains. Whatever euphemism is used to mask it—competition, the free play of the market, individualism—conflict is essentially a repressive standard. It rests on a social dynamic of power that is really a model of violence, however cloaked in benign language or pious ideology. A social aesthetic replaces the pattern of conflict with a model of mutuality and support and is really a model of love. Ultimately and best, in giving new meaning to tolerance, reciprocity, and equality, a social aesthetic offers the basis for a truly humane community. Is this what Schiller was leading us to see?

Acknowledgment

This is a revised version of "On Getting Along Beautifully: Ideas for a Social Aesthetics" that appeared originally in A. Haapala and P. von Bonsdorff (eds.) *Aesthetics and Everyday Life* (Lahti, Finland: International Institute for Applied Aesthetics, 1999), 12–29.

Notes

1. Immanuel Kant, *Critique of Judgment,* tr. J. H. Bernard, (New York: Hafner, 1951), §8, 50, 51.
2. Marvin Farber, *Basic Issues of Philosophy: Experience, Reality and Human Value* (New York: Harper & Row, 1968), 85ff.
3. Friedrich Schiller, *On the Aesthetic Education of Man,* ed. and tr. by E. M. Wilkinson and L. A. Willoughby (Oxford: Clarendon, 1967), (27th letter, para. 10), 125.
4. Immanuel Kant, *Critique of Judgment* (1790), §10.
5. Alexander Gottlieb Baumgarten, *Aesthetica* (Frankfurt a. o., 1750), vol. I.
6. Hegel follows Plato's restriction of the sensuous aspect of art to the aesthetic (theoretical) senses of sight and hearing, since the work of art is halfway between the directly perceived material object (and thus retains sensuousness) and the ideal universal of pure thought.

The aesthetic senses should have no direct physical relation to (connection with) the object. G. W. F. Hegel, "The Philosophy of Fine Art," in A. Hofstadter and R. Kuhns (eds.), *Philosophies of Art and Beauty* (New York: The Modern Library, 1964), 409.

7. See, for example, Maurice Merleau-Ponty, "Phenomenology of Perception," tr. Colin Smith, (London: Routledge & Kegan Paul, 1962), 228–29. See also A. Berleant, "The Sensuous and the Sensual in Aesthetics," *The Journal of Aesthetics and Art Criticism*, XXIII, 2 (Winter 1964), 185–92. Reprinted in *Philosophical Essays on Curriculum*, R. S. Guttchen and B. Bandman (eds.), (Philadelphia: Lippincott, 1969), 306–17.

8. Wolfgang Welsch, "Aesthetics beyond Aesthetics: Toward a New Form of the Discipline," *Literature and Aesthetics*, Oct. 1997, 17ff.

9. I am thinking here of Patricia Johanson's "Endangered Garden" in San Francisco.

10. See A. Berleant, *The Aesthetic Field: A Phenomenology of Aesthetic Experience* (Springfield, Ill.: C. C. Thomas, 1970), re-publication forthcoming as electronic text by Cybereditions (http://cybereditions.com/spis/runisa/dll?SV:cyTheBooksTmp.). Chapter 1, "Surrogate Theories of Art," is also a critique of partial theories.

11. See my *The Aesthetics of Environment* (Philadelphia: Temple University Press, 1992), esp. chapters. 1 and 3. See also *Living in the Landscape: Toward an Aesthetics of Environment* (Lawrence, Kans.: University Press of Kansas, 1997), chapter 1. Chapter 9, "The Aesthetics of Community" (135–55), complements the present chapter.

12. James F. Weiner, *The Empty Place: Poetry, Space, and Being among the Foi of Papua, New Guinea* (Bloomington: Indiana University Press, 1991), 8.

13. Aristotle, *Nicomachean Ethics*, VIII, chapters 4 (1157a) and 5 (1157b).

14. An important exception is Guy Sircello's rich exploration in *Love and Beauty* (Princeton: Princeton University Press, 1989). He and others have illuminated the subject from perspectives other than the one taken here.

15. Plato, *The Republic*, III. 400–03, X. 602–07.

16. Henry David Thoreau, in Carl F Horde et. al. (eds.), *A Week on the Concord and Merrimac Rivers*, (Princeton: Princeton University Press, 1980), 285.

17. "Human Personality" in Sian Miles (ed.), *Simone Weil: An Anthology*, (New York: Weidenfeld and Nicolson, 1986). I am indebted to Professor Hilde Hein for this reference.

18. See note 12.

19. "Even with Tomas she was obliged to behave lovingly because she needed him. We can never establish with certainty what part of our relations with others is the result of our emotions—love, antipathy, charity, or malice—and what part is predetermined by the constant power play among individuals. True human goodness, in all its purity and freedom, can come to the fore only when its recipient has no power. Mankind's true moral test, its fundamental test (which lies deeply buried from view), consists of its attitude towards those who are at its mercy: animals. And in this respect mankind has suffered a fundamental debacle, a debacle so fundamental that all others stem from it." Milan Kundera, *The Unbearable Lightness of Being* (New York: Harper & Row, 1984), 289.

20. "To love everyone is a noble enterprise. Unfortunately it denies one a certain faculty of discrimination." Anita Brookner, *A Family Romance* (London: Jonathan Cape, 1993).

21. If this is true, then one-sided love is a misnomer, much as Fromm interprets self-love as selfishness. Narcissism and subjective self-indulgence fail in the same way. Erich Fromm,

Man for Himself, an Inquiry into the Psychology of Ethics (New York: Holt, 1947), chapter IV, 1.

22. Empedocles, *On Nature*, in K. Freeman (ed.), *Ancilla to the Pre-Socratic Philosophers,* (Oxford: Blackwell, 1952), fragments 18–21.

23. Plato, *Symposium*, 210–12a.

24. Schiller, *On the Aesthetic Education of Man,* para. 11.

25. Josef Chytry, in *The Aesthetic State* (Berkeley: University of California Press, 1989), draws his title and much of his inspiration from Schiller. For Chytry, the " 'aesthetic state' . . . stand[s] for a social and political community that accords primacy . . . to the aesthetic dimension in human consciousness and activity. . . ."

26. "Environmental aesthetics does not concern buildings and places alone. It deals with the conditions under which people join as participants in an integrated situation. Because of the central place of the human factor, an aesthetics of environment profoundly affects our moral understanding of human relationships and our social ethics. An environmental aesthetics of engagement suggests deep political changes away from hierarchy and its exercise of power and toward community, where people freely engage in mutually fulfilling activities. It implies a humane family order that relinquishes authoritarian control and encourages cooperation and reciprocity. It leads toward acceptance, friendship, and love that abandon exploitation and possessiveness and promote sharing and mutual empowerment." Arnold Berleant, *The Aesthetics of Environment* (Philadelphia: Temple University Press, 1992), 12–13.

CHAPTER 3

On the Aesthetics of the Everyday
Familiarity, Strangeness, and the Meaning of Place

Arto Haapala

ONE OF THE MOST RECENT developments in philosophical aesthetics has been the extension of the field of inquiry. Not long ago, the term "aesthetics" was being used as a synonym for "philosophy of the arts," and even now, when reading recent introductions to aesthetics, the emphasis lies so firmly in the problems of art that other areas of aesthetic interest—nature and everyday objects—are hardly even mentioned.[1] The dominance of the high arts is still obvious, and considering the tradition of aesthetics and problems of art during our century, it is understandable. In the history of aesthetics, however, it is clear that before Hegel the domain of aesthetics was broader than it has been more recently. In Kant's aesthetics, for example, nature played a significant role. And going much further back, we find the same tendency—in *Peri Hupsous,* composed about 50 A.D., nature was a significant source of sublime experience.[2]

In contemporary aesthetics, when philosophers have wanted to expand their field of interest, it has mainly been in two directions, popular culture and the aesthetics of human life. In the former, the distinction between the high arts and the popular arts has often been put into question. Richard Shusterman's account of rap-music—"The Fine Art of Rap"—is well-known by now,[3] and David Novitz has also problematized the distinction.[4] The most systematic account so far of the "lesser arts" is by Noël Carroll.[5] A clear step away from the arts orientation, whether high or popular, is that by Ossi Naukkarinen whose emphasis is on human appearance.[6]

Naukkarinen's account deals also with issues of the aesthetics of human life, but most often this has been in the context of pragmatism. John Dewey, with his interest in aesthetic experience as a factor in everyday life, is one of the founding fathers of this line of thought. Shusterman relies partly on him, partly on more recent pragmatist accounts, especially on Richard Rorty.[7] But also Novitz—who does not proclaim himself as a pragmatist—draws on Dewey and Rorty when considering the aesthetic aspects of human life.[8] What I am doing in this paper is, however, something very different compared to the approaches of the scholars mentioned above. I shall put forward an existential account of the phenomenon of the everyday and its aesthetic character. In this context, I am not interested in the popular arts, nor shall I look at the problems of the aesthetics of living or the aestheticiation of everyday life.[9] I shall not consider aesthetic objects that attract our attention and stand out in our normal daily routines, but exactly the opposite—what is the aesthetic relevance of the everyday per se?

Reflections in this paper rely on some Heideggerian considerations, although I cannot go into any details of Heidegger's philosophy. Heidegger has inspired a number of philosophers studying the problems of the everyday, especially the role that technology has gained in the present world.[10] Heidegger's concept of "poetical dwelling" has also offered points of departure for analyzing human relations, especially toward nature: "Voll Verdienst, doch dichterisch wohnet der Mensch auf dieser Erde" ("Full of merit, yet poetically, dwells man upon this earth"), is a well-known Hölderlin line that Heidegger uses.[11] Although in passing I shall touch upon the issues of dwelling when developing the concept of place, I set aside all the connected Heideggerian ideas, like that of the fourfold (the earth, the sky, mortals, and gods). Instead I draw ideas from *Sein und Zeit,* which are all centered around the concept of being-in-the-world, and Heidegger's existential ontology of the *Dasein,* human beings.[12]

I shall enter the problems of the everyday through an analysis of the concept of place. Place in the sense I am developing below is the "area" in which the everyday is realized. I define the key terms—what I mean by *place,* what I mean by *placing,* and by *sensing.* What does it mean to identify a place and to become rooted into it? The concepts of place and the everyday are further linked to the idea of familiarity. Place and the everyday objects and events that constitute a place are marked by familiarity. I try to show how these concepts can be understood by reference to the existential structure of the human being: we are in the world in such a way that we create familiarity around ourselves, and in this way also construe a place. Familiarity and the everyday are at the very heart of place.

The aesthetics of the everyday differs considerably from traditional aesthetic considerations. Traditional aesthetics has been much more interested in what I call "strangeness." Art is the paradigmatic example of a phenomenon that is supposed to be something special and not ordinary or everyday. Philosophers have paid hardly any attention at all to the gray colors of the everyday, even the popular arts are supposed to stand out from the stream of the everyday. The issue in this paper is, what is the aesthetic character of the everyday, in particular in relation to place, which structures our everyday dealings. To get to the specific meaning of "place" I shall delineate, we need to look at some other usages of the term.[13]

The Concept of Place

Let me begin with a quote from Edward S. Casey:

> A tree stands in its own place. Its life is sedentary. It is a life in one place, a life without anxiety. Not only is a tree in its place; it actively contributes to its place, filling it up with its own organic substance. It knows no menacing void, even though to move from its own place is to risk the death of the organism.[14]

Casey goes on to animals and humans to distinguish them from plants: in contrast to plants, animals and humans are mobile, they move from one place to another; and he stresses the distinction between space and place. Places are culturally formed and defined by reference to the human body.[15] What interests me in this paper, however, is not the immobility of plants, but the idea that plants have a place. Place does not involve or require anything more than physical location. A tree has a place, a house occupies a place, a pen has a place on the table, etc. Movement means physical movement; I have come to a new place when I come to a new city. Again, my office is a different place from, say, my home or other rooms of the university. To have a place is to fill physical space. Some kind of stability is required—if something or somebody is in constant movement, it does not have a place. A balloon in the sky is placeless; flowing water does not have a place either. This is a very concrete idea of place: simply to be planted in, to find oneself a space. This is also the geographical concept of place: you can pinpoint the coordinates of your place from the map.

There is another usage and meaning of the term *place*. This can be heard from the widely used expression "sense of place." What is place in the expression "sense of place"? It is obvious that place is no longer just physical residence; when talking about the "sense of place," we are assuming a "senser," somebody who is "sensing." A place cannot have a sense without a person perceiving and understanding it. It might be possible to extend the meaning of the word "sense" to cover animal life: cats seem to have a sense of place in the meaning that they recognize places, that they have their favorite chairs they lay in, that they seem to be frightened or nervous in surroundings they have not visited before, etc. Cats and dogs, probably many other animals too, certainly recognize places; it matters for them whether an area is familiar or not, and in this sense they make a distinction between familiar and strange places. Humans and at least some animals can have a sense of place.

Genius loci is originally a Roman concept referring to the guardian spirit every independent being and place supposedly possesses.[16] It captures the other side of the expression "sense of place." The "spirit of the place" puts emphasis on the nature of a place, not on the person who is sensing it. When a place has a *genius,* a spirit—both words we understand metaphorically rather than literally—then we assume a much larger and a very different context than the mere physical space. A place in this sense does not necessarily have to be a cultural milieu, although it often is. Big cities have their distinctive atmospheres: New York differs from Paris and London. We can also talk about the sprit of smaller geographical units: London's chinatown has its own spirit; *Quartier Latin* in Paris its own, and so on. But also natural areas have their distinctive atmospheres: a deep green forest with old pines has a very different feel to it compared to the open moors of Scotland or Lappland.

Let me quote an illuminating passage from Norberg-Schulz in which this meaning is obvious:

> A place is a space which has a distinct character. Since ancient times the *genius loci,* or "spirit of place," has been recognized as the concrete reality man has to face and come to terms with in his daily life. (5)

And further:

> What, then, do we mean with the word "place"? Obviously we mean something more than abstract location. We mean a totality made up of concrete things having material substance, shape, texture and colour. Together these things determine an "environmental character," which is the essence of place. In general a place is given as such a character or "atmosphere." A place is therefore a qualitative, "total" phenomenon, which we cannot reduce to any of its properties, such as spatial relationships, without losing its concrete nature out of sight. (6–8)

A sense or spirit of a place is something possessed by the place; the place is characterized by its spirit. To realize or understand it, we must have a sense for it, a sensibility of some kind.[17] But still we could ask, what is it that constitutes the spirit of a town or a city? A very general answer would be to refer to the cultural history: French and Parisian cultural history constitute the *genius* of Paris, and it is manifested, not only in the architecture but also in people and their customs. Those who have grown into the culture exemplify the spirit because it is part of their nature; as cultural creatures each of us manifest some cultural tradition. When an outsider enters the place, she or he feels its distinctiveness because it is different from her or his own background. An outsider sees the distinguishing marks from a distance because they do not constitute her or his identity in the same way as they constitute that of the insiders. This is an issue to which I shall return later in this chapter. When we are talking about nature and her *genius,* then we normally refer to different landscape types and their effects on humans experiencing them. An open space feels different compared to a dark forest. A sense of place in the context of nature has to do with geological and ecological specifics of an area.[18]

Strangeness and Familiarity

There is still a third meaning of *place* that is perhaps not as widely used as the two aforementioned. This is a sense that gives place a more personal flavor; personal in the sense of defining place by referring to particular individuals. This meaning also puts more emphasis on certain aspects of interpretation in our encounters with environments. I shall delineate this meaning in more detail because my analyses of our being rooted to an environment and of our aesthetic responses to it are based on this particular meaning. I should add that I do not see the different meanings I have outlined as competing or conflicting. My purpose is not to give a better theory of place compared to some previous views. To a great extent the matter is only terminological: there is nothing wrong in the other two usages. Still I think that the meaning I give below adds something important to our understanding of our being in the world, and, further, to the aesthetic character of the everyday.

The process of making sense of the world can be analyzed in the terms of strangeness and familiarity.[19] This is the very basic distinction that does not in itself attribute any particular meanings to objects but puts them in existentially significant categories. In a new environment the objects and events we see and hear are mostly strange. They are not necessarily strange in any ontologically radical sense—when coming to a city we have not visited before, we are not Martians unable to make any connections between the various things encountered. In my usage "strangeness" does not mean or imply "being an alien," literally. Strangeness means rather that we are not used to seeing and hearing the sort of things and events we occasionally face. Strangeness is the experience of going to Florence, Paris, London, or New York for the first time and trying to orient oneself in these cities both in the concrete sense of finding one's way to a certain area, to a certain hotel, and in the psychological sense of being in the midst of unfamiliar buildings and people. Strangeness is the very basic experience we all have in new environments. These environs do not have to be man-made—being in the Alps for the first time, or camping in the wild areas of Finnish Lappland create the same kind of experience. We experience the surroundings as unfamiliar.

The process of getting visually and through other senses acquainted with the environment could be called "sensing." I am far from being satisfied with the term—it is being used in so many ways—but for the time being it will have to do. When we face something unfamiliar, we pay special attention to it. We observe the thing, we try to categorize it, we may think as to what to do with the object, whether it is of any use for us or not. We are also particularly attentive to its aesthetic potentiality. Let me return to the experience we have in a foreign city. We pay attention to the most trivial-looking things—like the color of public transport vehicles, the color of telephone boxes, the sound of the metro cars, the smell of the sea, etc. We are much more sensitive to these sorts of features in a strange surroundings than at home. In one sense of the word *aesthetic*, strangeness creates a suitable setting for aesthetic considerations. Our senses are more on alert in a strange milieu than in our home region. We can judge the aesthetic character of an area without being biased by the preferences that define our normal surroundings. This is the outsider's gaze, visitor's curiosity, which has been very much in the forefront in aesthetics.

In a very concrete sense we are sensitive to the looks of things. They seem to require our attention much more than in familiar surroundings. As we are not yet embedded into the milieu, as we have not yet made it part of our existence in terms of the meaning I shall develop below, we have a certain distance to, for example, a foreign city, and judge it on different grounds compared to those who live there. Our perceptions and judgments are not any more objective than the judgments of those who see the environment as familiar. Foreign visitors bring their own background, or in Gadamer's terms, *horizon,* with them; a foreign city looks and sounds strange precisely because we are used to something else; our own place is different from the new surroundings we now find ourselves in. But it is easier for us to concentrate on the looks of things as we have not yet taken an interest in the functional aspects of the surroundings. We are seeing them "fresh," and this is what was traditionally often required from aesthetic considerations. The distinction could also be put in terms of different sets of values: an outsider puts emphasis on the recreational values, including aesthetic values, the local on everyday functional values.

Familiarity and Place

Strangeness is temporally prior to familiarity, but it cannot be a continual state. While we are living in the lifeworld, doing and making things, acting in different ways in different situations, we create ties to our surroundings, and in this way familiarize ourselves with it. We make the environment "our own," we create relations that are significant for us and serve our purposes and interests. Our personal likings often play a role in this: we prefer particular kinds of art, for example, classical music to cinema, and accordingly concert halls are a significant factor in our everyday surroundings rather that cinemas, or vice versa. The network of the significant-things-for-me can be complicated and surprising in the sense that a person may make connections that do not make sense to someone else. I may take a particular route from the office back home because I find it more beautiful, or because there is a particular grocery store in which I want to do my shopping.

Let me elaborate the nature of familiarity through a personal example. Being my home city, Helsinki is familiar to me; certain routes I take everyday from home to office have become dear to me in the sense that I feel very much at home when walking there. None of the buildings I pass calls my attention because of its strangeness. Normally I do not pay any particular attention to them; I certainly notice buildings I find particularly beautiful or ugly, but most of the time I do not pay any special attention to my surroundings in my neighborhood. The situation is analogous to Heideggerian analysis of the tool, *das Zeug*.[20] As long as my shoes function as shoes, as long as the computer I write with operates without problems, I hardly pay any attention to them. Only when my computer starts to create problems, or when I do not know how to use a particular feature in my word processing program, only then I start to look at the computer as an object. Until then it is only a means to an end; something that is looked through rather than looked at. In familiar surroundings things call attention mostly then when something has changed. When a building has been demolished, repainted, when a new building has been built, and so on. When familiarity has been broken by something new, then we start to look at things.

When we have settled down into an area, not only do we recognize the buildings and sites, we also have a more personal relation to them. We make the environ our own. In *Sein und Zeit* Heidegger introduces the notion of *Jemeinigkeit* to characterize *Dasein*'s way of being, human existence.[21] Similarly we could say that settling down means making the area *jemeinig*, one's own. Depending on our interests—understood here in the widest sense of the word—we form different kinds of bonds to the same physical objects. Each of us has very different interests in the surroundings in which we live. These interests have been formed in the course of our lives, our profession, hobbies, habits, friends, colleagues, enemies, etc. In this sense of the word "place," place is something that we have made significant and meaningful for ourselves. We have our roots in a place in the very concrete sense that our way of being, our existence, is determined by the bonds we have formed. We are very much engaged in the milieu in which we have made our home. It is part of my existence, and accordingly part of my essence, that I live in a particular city rather than in another. Not only is it a very different kind of life in New York compared to Helsinki; we ourselves would be different. The fact that we would have had to adapt ourselves to the hectic rhythm of a metropolis would alone force our existence into new tracks. But if we were able to do it, a big city like New York, or at least a section of it, could become familiar to us, and in this sense become our place.

I have already dealt with the question of how we place ourselves into an environment—we start to construe connections that are significant for us. We spread our network over matters that are of relevance for our everyday life. In terms of the existential ontology I am relying on, we could also say that we spread our existence over certain parts of the cultural world in which we are. When we have created enough familiarity, when things do not appear as strange any more, when the region is our home region, *Heimat,* then we have concretely rooted ourselves into the milieu. This rootedness is something that can take place several times in one's lifetime. Every time we move somewhere else we have to create new connections. Sometimes this happens easily, without any particular effort; sometimes one really has to work in order to find one's place in a milieu. If the change between one's previous place and the new one is considerable—from the hectic city life of New York to the solitude of Scottish moors, or vice versa—one's effort can understandably be fruitless. A person's existence cannot change totally overnight.

"Placing" is the process of "home building." Familiarizing oneself with the environment is home building in the sense that home is by definition of utmost familiarity. Home is a place where everything is familiar. Home is something where most of the matters are under control. If not anywhere else, at least at home we have a say as to what it should look like, how it should be organized, etc. We create our homes and know them thoroughly. The familiarity and control obviously diminishes as one steps outside the front door, but still one is on top of things in the sense that she or he does not have to face strangeness. Strangeness is an attack on our home building nature, our desire for familiarity. Even though familiarity may be nothing else but a visual habit—that is, that I am used to seeing certain buildings without knowing any details about them—it still is an apparent control over things, things are in their places; they are there where they should be, where I am used to seeing them.

Interpretation and Place

In one sense of the word "interpretation," the third meaning of the place is an interpretation of the two previous ones. It is an interpretation in an existential sense—when entering a new environment we start immediately to interpret it. This interpretation is not necessarily, not even primarily a conscious and deliberate searching for meanings. It is interpretation in the hermeneutic sense of living in an environment and making sense of it by acting there, by doing various things in the environment, by creating different kinds of connections between matters seen and encountered. In this sense interpretation is very much a matter of action—it takes place on the level of praxis rather than theory. It is interpretation that takes place in the process of being-in-the-world; it is something that we are engaged in all the time while engaged in our daily practices.[22]

The first step in the process of interpretation is making the strange surroundings familiar. As I said, this is something we start to do as soon as we enter a new environment. Perhaps it is more appropriate to say that it starts to happen; first on a purely sensuous level—what we see and hear is not as striking as it first was; we get used to the visual and auditory features of the surroundings. We also start to recognize the functions and meanings of different buildings and sites: there is a shop, there is school, kindergarten, police station, church, these are residential buildings, the market is there, the harbor further away, etc. If we decide to stay longer in the area, we start to settle down. It is the process of settling down that finally makes the surroundings familiar to me, and at the same time makes the surroundings my place.

In the third sense, place is interpretation of an environment by an existence. I want to emphasize the existential quality of the relation of a place and a person. In understanding the existence of a particular individual, it it crucial to know about the individual's past. Historicity is built into human existence. I cannot thow my past experiences away, I cannot neglect my university training and the ways of thinking into which I have been educated even if I wanted to. My interests are dictated by my training and education. Similarly, the places that have constituted my identity in the past influence the way I am presently connected to my surroundings. Our existence is formed through our past and it interprets the surroundings each of us faces and makes it meaningful for us. We pick up from the environment things that are in accordance with our existence, or at least that are not in clear contradiction with it, and in this way make the milieu accessible.

Lifeworld and Place

Living in the lifeworld is creating relations, and these relations constitute our existence, how we are in the lifeworld. How we exist determines our identities. As Heidegger pointed out, the different kinds of relations we are tied to in our ordinary everyday existence—for example, being with other humans, *das Mitsein*[23]—finally constitutes what we are. That a person is a husband or a wife, a father or a mother, a brother or a sister—these sorts of features are at the core of one's identity, and all of them are relational features, defined by a particular kind of tie to another person. And the other person is in turn determined by her or his relation to me—which is a different relation from that which I have with her or him. But also relations to nonhuman entities and events are part of my existence, or to use other terms again, constitute me as a cultural entity. That I have lived in certain towns and cities, studied at certain universities, read a number of books, written articles and monographs, all these relational features constitute my existence too. This is what it means to say that place is a part of human existence. The present place and its familiarity are obviously dominant in the present moment, but also past places, sites to which I have once been attached to, play a role when I start to think of what I am. I still have a relation, however weak presently, to all the surroundings that were primary places of identification for me in the past. They are in the past but the past is present in the present.[24]

It is often small, and from somebody else's point of view, insignificant things that matter in one's life. Let me take an example from literature, a novel by a German contemporary writer Bernhard Schlink entitled *Der Vorleser, The Reader,* published in 1995. It is an extremely well-written and well-structured story about an affair between a schoolboy and a middle-aged woman. As the story develops, the boy, who is also the narrator of the story, finds out that his lover Hanna was a member of the SS and worked in Auschwitz during the war. One of the themes of the novel is the relation of an individual to an existing set of norms and values. Let me use once again Heidegger's terminology, and call an existing set of norms and values a "world." The Nazi world consisted of values very different from ours; we live in a very different world now compared to the German world during the Second World War. But once you are in a world, once the basic values have been determined, what then really matters are "small" things, not metaphysical systems. Hanna is not educated, she is not particularly reflective about her activities. Working in Auschwitz was for her only work; she did not define the rules that led to the deaths of millions of people, nor did she question them. She wanted to have a work and to organize her life in other ways as well: to have a home and beautiful things around her. What she did was immoral by most standards, and she was subsequently sentenced in the novel. But the point I want to raise is exactly the importance of everydayness over metaphysics, sometimes even over morality. In Husserlian terms, matters of the *Lebenswelt* precede those of science and philosophy.

Place and the Everyday

In a familiar environment we often have to make a special effort to really see the visual features of things surrounding us. We see the surrounding buildings through their functionality rather than as objects to be visually contemplated. When we have made the surroundings our place, practical everyday activities are in the forefront—going to work, going to the grocery store, going to the library. When we go into our habitual library our action is obviously determined by the function for which the library has been built—to read there, to get the books we need. We may every now and then pay attention to the building itself, especially if it is visually striking in some sense. I would say that this is a conscious effort on our part to decide that, at the moment, what we really want to observe are its aesthetic qualities.

I have already referred to the analogy of Heideggerian tools and the everyday familiar surroundings. A hammer is defined as hammer by the structure to which it belongs, the *Zeugganzes,* a network of other tools and their functions.[25] An individual tool disappears into its function as Heidegger says.[26] A tool is something in between the user and the purpose, and as long as it functions properly there is no need to pay attention to it. This is how objects in our familiar surroundings function in a general sense: they have a practical function, and as such they disappear into their function. To see them as objects, or aesthetic objects in the traditional sense, they have to be digged up from their functions. For many, perhaps even for most of the objects in our familiar surroundings, their function is simply to be present; for example, to me most of the houses on my street are just houses on my street. They are simply there as a kind of background; something that I have been used to. This kind of function is still a function in a weak sense; but these objects "do a service for us" just by being part of the familiar surroundings, by not being strange. Obviously, for those who live in the houses, they serve a much more substantial function: these are places in which to live, their homes.

The emotional relation we have to our place is attachment. The concept of attachment is key for understanding the aesthetics of place.[27] Our place is dear to us because it constitutes a part of our essence. It is not a negligible fact that a person lives in a particular area. Although we are not always able to choose the town, or area, or house we would mostly like to live in—for example, due to obvious economic reasons—we are always at least to a certain extent attached to the area we happen to live in. It would be impossible to live in a constant state of strangeness, of not creating any significant ties, of not getting rooted to any degree. And once one becomes rooted to some degree, one becomes attached to the surroundings. We may like a particular building because there exists a shop in which we do our shopping, or because the building serves some other function important to our normal routines. Although sensing sometimes plays a role in our home region, it is of minor importance.

There has been a discussion going on in Helsinki about a particular building designed by Alvar Aalto that lies at the very center of the city. It is a typical functionalist building: simple, ascetic, and white, a big cube without any additional decoration. The shape and the color are why this particular building facing the harbor and the main market is called the sugar cube, or the sugar block. I agree with those who find this building ugly. It is ugly mainly because it does not take into account the surrounding architecture; it looks extremely arrogant across from an old Orthodox cathedral, and next to the former presidential building. It is very much an attack on the sense of place in the second meaning I have given, disregarding completely the earlier architecture around it, even though, taken in isolation, the building might satisfy a functionalist's definition of beauty.

I would imagine that this kind of building is something an outsider cannot help noticing; its strangeness in a strange city is very striking. I have to face the building almost on a daily basis. It never gives me any satisfaction, but on the other hand it does not bother me on a continuous basis either. Most of the time, what I considered the unsuccessful Aalto creation does not particularly bother me. As a visual image I have grown used to it. However, I am still irritated by the sight of it when, after having been abroad for a long period, I return and look at Helsinki again with a stranger's eyes. It is safe to say, however, that if a bold decision were made to have the building demolished, I would welcome such a decision, despite the feeling of strangeness that the disappearance of the building would cause for awhile.

The Aesthetics of the Everyday

What is, then, the aesthetics of place? As I have pointed out, strangeness creates a basis for sensitive aesthetic appreciation.[28] In the state of familiarity, being in our place, surrounded by everydayness, we tend to lose this kind of sensitivity. The aesthetic standards differ when considering strange versus familiar surroundings. One major difference stems from the ontology, or from the existential structure of the place. Place in the third sense I have delineated is part of our existence and constitutes our way of being, whereas strange surroundings do not. By definition there is less distancing, less possibility for appreciation in the traditional sense of the word. However, place has its own aesthetics. The aesthetics of place is stamped by our existential structures; in one sense of the word, it is more subjective than the aesthetics of unfamiliar surroundings. It is more subjective exactly in the ontological sense I have given. This does not make the aesthetics of the everyday less satisfying than the aesthetics of the strange. Ordinary everyday objects lack the surprise element or freshness of the strange, nevertheless they give us pleasure through a kind of comforting stability, through the feeling of being at home and taking pleasure in carrying out normal routines in a setting that is "safe."

Although we are embedded in the structures of the everyday and see things most of the time through functionality, every now and then we take some distance from the concerns of the daily activities. When doing so, we do not see familiar objects surrounding us as strange, rather we start to enjoy their visual and auditory features. I develop Heidegger's well-known and controversial analysis of the van Gogh painting a step further to illustrate this.[29] Through the pair of peasant shoes depicted in the painting, Heidegger emphasizes how the life of a peasant woman is determined by numerous practical demands: to work, to get food, etc. But we need to add something to this conception: the peasant, and this is something Heidegger does not say, can from time to time sit down and set aside the needs and demands of the everyday, and enjoy the familiar scene—the fields, the sky, birdsong. This reveals another aspect of the aesthetics of the everyday. This aspect is not distinct from the pleasure that we take in fulfilling the daily routines, but rather dependent on them. We enjoy scenes familiar to us because we know them well and because we are deeply rooted into them.

The aesthetics of everyday familiar surroundings and the aesthetics of the strange have their own roles in human life, and I do not want to rank them. Still there are good reasons to argue that recently the emphasis in aesthetics as a discipline is on the strange as a phenomenon, and art has been closely tied to strangeness. Consider huge museum buildings, theater constructions, and music halls, the purpose of which has been to create a setting distinctive from everyday life. Art is presented in contexts that create strangeness, and the tendency in aesthetics has been to maximize strangeness and to minimize familiarity. The Western tradition of the visual arts confirms this; the key term for understanding the development of nineteenth- and twentieth-century art is "innovativeness." The aim has been to go against the tradition. This tendency for maximum strangeness reached its peak in avant garde art, and dada in particular, but to a lesser degree it can also be found in contemporary music and literature.

There have been movements especially in the visual arts where the *quotidien* has been used as a subject matter. Also, photography is often about the everybody. For example, Henri Cartier-Bresson's pictures are about the very basic events of human life. But my point is that in the context of art the everyday loses its everydayness: it becomes something extraordinary. When taken out of the context of day-to-day living and put into an artistic context, a picture such as Cartier-Bresson's *A Bank Executive and His Secretary* (1960) becomes an object of wonder.[30]

All this has contributed to the neglect of the aesthetics of the everyday. It might look as though this kind of aesthetics leads to complete subjectivism: I have my place, you have yours, and they are by definition different because our background and interests differ. But we can consider the structures of familiarity at a more general level, as I have done in this paper, without entering the problems of subjectivism and objectivism. Central in understanding the aesthetics of the familiar at this level is the concept of attachment. Because of the ontological connections that exist between our existential structures and the environment that we make our place, we have the kind of bond that can be called "attachment" to our home region. Attachment most often involves a positive emotional connection, but not necessarily. As I have pointed out above, we may feel strongly for a particular building in the area in which we live simply because of our interests, but on the other hand our attitude to many other buildings and things is often that of indifference. We notice them if there is a change, only after the normalcy has been broken in some way. So the aesthetics of familiarity does not always involve a positive reaction to something. What I find most important in the habitual surroundings from the point of view of aesthetics is the contrast to strangeness, the relevance of the everydayness. We take pleasure in being in the surroundings we are used to, and fulfilling our normal routines. The aesthetics of everydayness is exactly in the "hiding" of the extraordinary and disturbing, and feeling homey and in control. One could paradoxically say that the aesthetics of the familiar is an aesthetics of "the lacking," the quiet fascination of the absence of visual, auditory, and any other kinds of demands from the surroundings.

How is it that the everyday can be aesthetic without having to be strange? We have seen that the tendency to link aesthetics with strangeness has been strong and even when the everyday has become a matter in art, the context of art has created an aura of strangeness. I think we should simply become more aware of the pleasurable aspects of the everyday without making them objects of aesthetic appreciation in the traditional sense. Perhaps we could give new meaning to the phrase "the aesthetics (or the art) of living," that is, to value the particulars of the everyday. This adds a new dimension to our aesthetic thinking, a dimension that is indeed dominant in our daily life. Aesthetics does not have to be only about the extraordinary; it can also be about our daily routines.

When we are talking about everydayness, its aesthetics, in this sense, it is difficult to draw any strict line between the ethical and the aesthetic aspects of life. I have tried to outline two existential structures through which we relate to things. Especially in familiarity and accordingly in the concept of the place, ontological, ethical and aesthetic considerations are intertwined with each other. Someone might want to use the term "ethics" rather than "aesthetics" in considerations I have developed—we are talking about a way of living and its structures as essentially ethical. My using the term "aesthetics" rather than "ethics" is that "aesthetic" sets the tone of our everyday life, an important reason to start paying attention to those things that appear under the category of the familiar, those things that define our everyday life.

Notes

1. See Gordon Graham, *Philosophy of the Arts: An Introduction to Aesthetics* (London and New York: Routledge, 1997); Colin Lyas, *Aesthetics* (London: UCL Press, 1997); Dabney Townsend, *An Introduction to Aesthetics* (Malden and Oxford: Blackwell Publishers, 1997).
2. See James J. Hill, "The Aesthetic Principles of the *PERI HUPSOUS*" and Dabney Townsend, "From Shaftesbury to Kant—The Development of the Concept of Aesthetic Experience" in Peter Kiry (ed.), *Essays on the History of Aesthetics,* (Rochester: University of Rochester Press, 1992).
3. Richard Shusterman, *Pragmatist Aesthetics: Living Beauty, Rethinking Art* (Oxford and Cambridge, Mass: Blackwell, 1992), chapter 8.

4. David Novitz, *The Boundaries of Art* (Philadelphia: Temple University Press, 1992), especially chapter 2.

5. Noël Carroll, *A Philosophy of Mass Art* (Oxford: Clarendon Press, 1998).

6. Ossi Naukkarinen, *The Aesthetics of the Unavoidable: Aesthetic Variations in Human Appearance* (Lahti: International Institute of Applied Aesthetics, 1998).

7. Shusterman, *Pragmatist Aesthetics,* chaper 9, and *Practicing Philosophy: Pragmatism and the Philosophical Life* (New York: Routledge, 1997); Richard Rorty, *Contingency, Irony, and Solidarity* (Cambridge: Cambridge University Press, 1989).

8. Novits, *The Boundaries of Art,* 8–9, and chapters 7, 8, and 10.

9. See Wolfgang Welsch, *Undoing Aesthetics,* tr. Andrew Inkpin, (London: Sage Publications, 1997), 1–102.

10. See Albert Borgmann, *Technology and the Character of Everyday Life* (Chicago: Chicago University Press, 1984); Michael E. Zimmerman, *Heidegger's Confrontation with Modernity: Technology, Politics, Art* (Bloomington and Indianapolis: Indiana University Press, 1990); Don Ihde, *Technology and the Lifeworld: From Garden to Earth* (Bloomington and Indianapolis: Indiana University Press, 1992).

11. Martin Heidegger, ". . . dichterisch wohnet der Mensch . . ." and "Bauen Wohnen Denken" in *Vorträge und Aufsätze* (Pfüllingen: Neske, 1954). A Heideggerian account based on the concept of poetical dwelling is offered by Bruce V. Foltz, *Inhabiting the Earth: Heidegger, Environmental Ethics, and the Metaphysics of Nature* (New Jersey: Humanities Press, 1995).

12. I shall not translate the term "Dasein." Heidegger uses it to refer to one particular kind of being, human existence, or persons. See *Being and Time,* tr. John Macquarrie and Edward Robinson, (Oxford and Cambridge, Mass.: Blackwell, 1997), 27, translators' note 1.

13. The term "place" has become a kind of catchword in recent studies of the human environment. There are book-length studies of the topic, Edward S. Casey's, *Getting back into Place—Towards a Renewed Understanding of the Place-World* (Bloomington and Indianapolis: Indiana University Press, 1993) and *The Fate of Place: A Philosophical History* (Berkeley: University of California Press, 1997) are the latest, and Christian Norberg-Schulz's *Genius Loci—Towards a Phenomenology of Architecture* (London: Academy Editions, 1980, first published in Italian under the title *Genius Loci—paesaggio, ambiente, architettura* in 1979) has gained a wide reputation and become a sort of classic. Many present writers have also sought inspiration from Gaston Bachelard's *Poetique de l'espace* (Paris: Presses Universitaires de France, 1957), *The Poetics of Space.* The originator of the present discussion about place is, however, Martin Heidegger. Heidegger's early investigations of the concept of being-in-the-world, *das In-der-Welt-Sein,* and later deliberations on dwelling, *Wohnen,* have given a solid foundation for phenomenologically oriented studies. One can go back to the Greeks, and to the concept of the *topos,* but Heidegger is certainly much more relevant in the present discussion.

One should also mention Kevin Lynch's numerous studies in relation to the experience of architecture, for example the early work *The Image of the City* (Cambridge, MA: MIT Press, 1960) and *Managing the Sense of a Region* (Cambridge, MA: MIT Press, 1976). Norberg-Schulz gives credit to Lynch in developing his theory of place (*Genius Loci,* 201). The concept of place has figured also in Yi-Fu Tuan's work, e.g., *Space and*

Place (Minneapolis: University of Minnesota Press, 1977), and the list of authors could be continued considerably. The term "place" has also been mentioned in discussions clearly addressing the issues of environmental aesthetics. See, for example, J. Douglas Porteus, *Environmental Aesthetics: Ideas, Politics and Planning* (London and New York: Routledge, 1996), 154 and 252–53, and Arnold Berleant, *The Aesthetics of Environment* (Philadelphia: Temple University Press, 1992), 75, 92–94, and *passim*. See also Charles Taylor, "Heidegger, Language, and Ecology" in *Heidegger: A Critical Reader* (Oxford: Basil Blackwell, 1992). An excellent account on Heidegger's notion of the being-in-the-world is Hubert L. Dreyfus's *Being-in-the-World: A Commentary on Heidegger's Being and Time, Division I* (Cambridge, Mass.: MIT Press, 1991).

14. Casey, *Getting Back into Place*, xi–xii.

15. Casey's concept of the place is more sophisticated than this, but for my argument, it is more relevant to use his initial formulations rather than go into details of his view. See Casey, xvii, 30–31, 58–59, 65, and *passim*. See also his article tracing the history of the concept of place, "Smooth Spaces and Rough-Edged Place: The Hidden History of Place," at http://www.sunysb.edu/philosophy/faculty/papers/casey2.htm.

16. Norberg-Schulz, *Genius Loci*, 4.

17. This might be comparable to the aesthetic sensibility, taste, in Frank Sibley's sense. Although I am not going to develop the issue in any detail here, it is worth noticing, however, the analogies between sensing the spirit of a place and seeing or hearing the aesthetic qualities of an art work. Also in the former case, we could make a distinction between first-order properties and second-order properties that are somehow dependent on the first-order properties, but not reducible to them. This was Sibley's conception of the relation between nonaesthetic and aesthetic properties. In the quotation above, Norberg-Schulz made a distinction very similar to that. That is, the spirit of Paris is constituted by her cafés, by certain kinds of architecture, by people, noises of cars, by the metro, etc., but it is not reducible to any of these single factors or even to their abstract collection. In the same vein one could continue that if one does not possess the sensibility for the sprit, one is not able to "see" and "hear" it even though he would see and hear all the particulars mentioned and even more. The relation of the two sets of properties, non-aesthetic and aesthetic, or perceivable and the spirit, could, for example, be analyzed with the help of the concept of supervenience. See John Benson, Betty Redfern, and Jeremy Roxbee Cox (eds.), *Approach to Aesthetics: Collected Papers on Philosophical Aesthetics* (Oxford: The Clarendon Press, 2001).

18. See Casey, *Getting Back into Place*, 227–70.

19. I have developed the concepts in more detail in an article titled "Strangeness and Familiarity in the Urban Environment," in Arto Haapala (ed.), *The City as Cultural Metaphor—Studies in Urban Aesthetics* (Lahti: International Institute of Applied Aesthetics, 1998).

20. Heidegger, *Sein und Zeit* (Tübingen: Max Niemeyer Verlag, 1979), 68–72; Heidegger, "Der Ursprung des Kunstwerkes," in *Holzwege* (Frankfurt am Main: Vittorio Klostermann), 22–25, 50–52.

21. Heidegger, *Sein und Zeit*, 52–53.

22. I should note that I am not taking a stance in the present problems of interpretation,

although I am aware of using the term in a very broad sense. Still I am not claiming, for example, that "everything is interpretation" in the sense of hermeneutic universalism. What I am saying is that when we face things not familiar to us, we start to make sense of them not only rationally but also in terms of action, and that this process can be called "interpretation." See Richard Shusterman, "Beneath Interpretation," in his *The Interpretive Turn: Philosophy, Science, Culture* (Ithaca: Cornell University Press, 1991).

23. Heidegger, *Sein und Zeit,* 117–25.

24. Arto Haapala, "Art and Time: Towards the 'Analysis of Time in Art'," *The End of Art and Beyond: Essays after Danto* (New Jersey: Humanities Press, 1997)

25. Heidegger, *Sein und Zeit,* 68–72.

26. Heidegger, "Der Ursprung des Kunstwerkes," 50.

27. See Yi-Fu Tuan, *Topophilia—A Study of Environmental Perception, Attitudes, and Values* (Englewood Cliffs, N.J.: Prentice Hall, 1974), 99–100.

28. See Tuan, *Topophilia,* 93–95.

29. Heidegger, "Der Ursprung des Kunstwerkes," 18–20; also Tuan refers to a similar case: "We are well aware of how a person can become deeply attached to old slippers that look rather moldy to an outsider." (*Topophilia,* 99.)

30. See E. H. Gombrich, "The Photographer as Artist: Henri Cartier-Bresson" in *Topics of our Time—Twentieth-Century Issues in Learning and in Art* (London: Phaidon Press Limited, 1991).

CHAPTER 4

Danto and Baruchello
From Art to the Aesthetics of the Everyday

Michael A. Principe

> *If you want to find a history for him, or a place in history for him, the history you have to review isn't so much the history of art, but rather the whole history of thought.*
>
> —Gianfranco Baruchello on Marcel Duchamp, *Why Duchamp*

IN THIS CHAPTER I will examine the aesthetics of everyday life by beginning from the perspective of art and the artworld. Two very different figures will play important roles in this discussion. One is Arthur Danto. Specifically, I will argue that reflection upon the aesthetics of the everyday will allow us to see the limitations, both conceptual and political, of his well-known neo-Hegelian reading of the history of art. Danto's thesis with regard to the end of art history, involving the idea that art is finally liberated from its exile by philosophy, is richly suggestive of an aesthetics of the everyday, for it would seem that such liberation would make art in some way a significant or relevant part of the world. However, the development of an aesthetics of the everyday is almost entirely lacking in Danto. When he does venture into this theoretical domain, his attitude is thoroughly negative. Indulging in Danto's own Hegelian metaphors for a moment, I am tempted to employ a relevant Marxian one: that is with Danto, art history, insofar as it is dissolved into philosophy, seems to be standing on its head. It needs to be placed on its feet. Toward this end I will call upon the writings of Italian painter Gianfranco Baruchello, especially his book *How to Imagine,* a narrative account filled with various ruminations, speculations, and philosophical reflections on his attempt to run his farm as an artwork. This is a text in which Baruchello directly confronts issues of the aesthetics of the everyday. I will show furthermore that it provides a helpful setting for the examination of Danto's theses. Baruchello serves as a particularly helpful example insofar as many of his themes are identical to Danto's, especially as he considers the issue of indiscernibles. Baruchello, though, uses this notion to emphasize art's entrance into the everyday world rather than the everyday's entrance into the artworld. His work will help us to see both the limitations and possibilities of Danto's position.

Among the many interesting theses that Danto puts forward in developing his account are two that are in some tension with each other. First, he sees his own analysis of the philosophical disenfranchisement of art as contributing to reenfranchising art, that is, the liberation of art from "repression" by philosophy.[1] Second, he holds that this liberation marks the end of art history, bringing with it an age of pluralism which is itself a mark of art's aimlessness (*PD*, 111–15). Danto seems to regard this second claim as following from the first. I will attempt to show that it does not. In fact, the kind of liberation of which Danto speaks might well revitalize the *directionality* of art. Baruchello and his farm will help us see this, as well as pointing us toward a more fruitful conception of the aesthetics of the everyday than that found in Danto.

To begin, let us consider how Danto comes to his theses. Of course, his view that art history has come to an end with art's self-consciousness, that art has in this way become philosophical, is well known. Crucial to his project is the claim that an artwork's essential identity is not constituted by its sensory qualities. Rather, such works as Duchamp's ready-mades and Warhol's Brillo Boxes illustrate the importance of particular art-theoretical contexts. In fact, Danto reads works such as Duchamp's and Warhol's as explicitly rendering problematic the distinction between artworks and real things. Such works raise a philosophical question about the nature of art, and as such, represent art's attaining a kind of self-consciousness. Art becomes its own subject. At one point Danto, consciously echoing Hegel, goes so far as to claim that insofar as art ultimately becomes philosophy, Danto's own essay may represent art's final stage, for example, be the last work of art. As he puts it, when the line between art and reality informs the production of artworks, "the boundaries between art and reality become . . . internal to art itself."[2] This concern about the nature of reality is, though, the traditional domain of philosophy. A transformation has thereby occurred.

Let us move now a bit closer to my concern regarding Danto's project. While Danto's story about the history of art is extraordinary and even dazzling, there is a sense in which *it too* suffers from the kind of original sin that Danto discusses in the context of both the history of art and the history of aesthetics. This is the relationship of philosophy to art as established by Plato. That is, for Danto, the tradition has followed Plato in removing art from the city, of rendering art useless. For many aesthetic theories, this is to place art on a pedestal. In a helpful analogy, Danto compares this to placing women on pedestals.[3] What looks like elevation is actually not. Talking about the fine arts is much like talking about the fair sex. In both cases, something is removed from the clamor and dirtiness of the everyday within which it turns out it has no business. Its virtue is that it is useless. Pursuing the analogy further, Danto describes art as doing something that looks like it might be for something, but isn't really. This, he says, is much like many "women's" activities such as embroidery or knitting. One can, according to Danto, as a woman or an artwork try to reject the game by making oneself ugly. But even so, one is still a useless sort of thing whose value lies in appearance. For the artist, one does not escape judgments rendered regarding appearance by producing ugly art. For women, one isn't liberated by moving from a sex-object to an anti sex object. In both cases, one hopes, instead, to avoid objecthood altogether. And so with real things that enter the artworld, essence must be more than skin deep. This is the only way for real things to become in some essential way artworks, that is, for them to escape their identity as real things. Here then is art's self-consciousness and the key to seeing art as philosophy. And so we find ourselves at the end of art history. And what is an artist to do at the end of history? Whatever he or she wants. Danto compares this situation to a stock reading of Hegel and Marx: "Post-historical life, for Hegel as for Marx, will have the form of a kind of philosophical *Club mediterranee*, or what used to be known as heaven, where there is nothing left for us to do but—in the phrase of our adolescents— hang out" (*PD*, 113). For Danto, nothing can any longer be new. For him, this is not exactly a moment for celebration. He says "that it has been an immense privilege to have lived in history" and that now "the age of pluralism is upon us. It does not matter any longer what you do, which is what pluralism means. When one direction is as good as another direction, there is no concept of direction any longer to apply" (*PD*, 114–115).

This is a credible critique of pluralism. Its relevance does depend upon art history having ended. Here is where my claim a moment ago about Danto being subject to the same sense of the aesthetic as he criticizes becomes important. For Danto is not claiming as he construes Hegel and Marx to claim or predict that history per se is over or will end, but simply that art history has ended. But *art history* can only end, in a context where *history* does not end if art is *separated* off from the world in a crucial way, that is, precisely in the manner that Danto shows has occurred in the history of aesthetics from Plato onward. Because we have not broken through to heaven, we still operate, to use a Marxian turn of phrase, within the realm of necessity. Within this context various human projects both individual and collective are developed and pursued. Here Danto's lack of social/political engagement clearly emerges. For he seems not to recognize the possibility of art's history continuing as part of the rest of history. If art is part of the world, and we still live in history (contra Fukuyama),[4] then art will not partake of the directionless pluralism that he suggests is its face. Art's coming off the pedestal would then mark art's entrance into real history, rather than into directionless pluralism. Artists, like the rest of us, are likely to struggle to find direction, but this will be a struggle that still makes sense, where it does not on Danto's account where one direction is as good as any other. Here we see clearly the tension between the two theses of Danto's mentioned earlier. The kind of liberation of art described by Danto does not represent its return from Platonic exile.

Against this background I wish to introduce the writings of Baruchello. A painter of some note, his writings take up some of the issues raised by Danto at precisely the point where Danto's own account leaves off. In his rather unusual book, *How to Imagine,* Baruchello chronicles his attempt, as an artist, to run his farm "Agricola Cornelia" as a work of art.[5] Duchamp is a recurring figure in Baruchello's meditations, as he is in Danto's. Baruchello remarks, though, that he has always been concerned with Duchamp's apoliticism, Baruchello's own concerns being ones that touch regularly on the political. Here we start to have the ingredients for a fruitful engagement with Danto. To read the work's opening pages is to become clearer that such an approach makes sense. Baruchello begins by describing in some detail one of his paintings of the farm. This is one of the many art objects (paintings, films, recordings, narrative accounts) made possible by the farm. As he looks at the painting he begins to tell the story of Agricola Cornelia. But what kind of story will it be? Well, as with Danto, this will be a response to Plato, though Plato is nowhere mentioned. Baruchello is but an artist who has voluntarily left the city for the country. By beginning his account with a description of a painting of his farm, he is initially placed right where Plato located the artists, twice removed from reality. There is a farm, something of which he tries to capture on canvas (here we are once removed), which he then tries to capture with words (now we are twice removed). Baruchello is an artist struggling to get off the pedestal. That is, he is not just an artist-painter and artist-writer, these standing at some remove from the farm, but also an artist-farmer. He aspires to move into this reality while maintaining his role as an artist. But what does this mean? What does it mean for Baruchello to run his farm as an art project? How does his growing of vegetables differ from similar projects carried out by his neighbors? One can't necessarily tell by looking. These questions touch the central themes of Baruchello's text. Note, that Baruchello does take as part of his project the liberation of art from its exile from the world. This fits with Danto's conception of certain sorts of contemporary art. By looking at his project, we will be better able to see the way in which art is still subject to Platonic exile within Danto's own account.

For Baruchello, his farm is crucially both a context for generating works of art, and as such a context is itself a kind of artwork. Initially, the first role is easier to understand. Any space surely can serve as a context for producing poems, plays, films, and so forth, but for Baruchello, providing such a context is precisely what constitutes some works of art as works of art. Speaking of Duchamp, his friend and mentor, he says, he would find it difficult and beside the point to own any of his work. When confronted by a work like *Bicycle Wheel,* he says that instead of having any desire to own it, he imagines having Duchamp as a room-mate, where Duchamp would be creating *Bicycle Wheel* while Baruchello was off in another part of the house doing his own work.[6] *Bicycle Wheel* has aesthetic import precisely when it is a context for further creative work. Baruchello cru-cially links the importance of Duchamp's work to ongoing activity rather than to a narrowly construed artworld. Part of the meaning of Baruchello's farm is that it is a resource for all kinds of creative activity. To anticipate for a moment, we can already begin to see that Baruchello's aesthetics of the everyday is connected to the ability to experience the world as such a resource, for example, as the appropriate sort of context for creative thought and activity. This is indeed what he hopes to get at when he reflects upon "how to imagine." In fact *How to Imagine* (*HI*) itself is but one instance of the kind of creative activity that Baruchello sees emerging from the farm.

One way to open up Baruchello's project is to think about it in the context of other aesthetic appropriations of nature. Allen Carlson provides a theoretical framework designed to facilitate our understanding of aesthetic *appreciation* of nature, with which we can begin.[7] Carlson notes that, unlike art, which is a human creation made under particular circumstance for a particular purpose, it can be very unclear what we are to appreciate in nature. So Carlson distinguishes three modes of appreciation; these involve what he calls the object model, the scenery model, and the environmental model. Briefly, the object model regards the objects of nature (rocks, driftwood, seashells) as akin to nonrepresentational sculptures. But Carlson tells us that this is not to appreciate nature, but rather to either turn the objects of nature into art or at best to *remove* certain objects of nature from nature so as to enable appreciation. Next is the scenery model where we in essence look at nature as if it were a landscape painting or picture postcard. This requires us to be at a distance from nature and again serves to separate out a part of nature from the rest. Carlson advocates the third approach, the environ-mental model, that "involves recognizing that nature is an environment and thus a setting within which we exist and which we normally experience with our com-plete range of senses as our unobtrusive background. But our experience being aesthetic requires unobtrusive background to be experienced as obtrusive fore-ground."[8] We must notice those dimensions of our environment that are nor-mally background.

Here we draw closer to Baruchello, who often includes in his paintings a fig-ure that looks somewhat like a butterfly, which he calls "the corner of the eye." He says of it that "it's a figure concerned with all the things that are in the corner of the eye where you don't really see them. It's an image where everything that's cen-tral to vision has been eliminated, and what's left is this corner of the eye and the things that are there are all the things of which you don't usually have any clear realization" (*HI*, 14). It is precisely in this way that the farm in its everyday functioning can be a context for creation and constant occasion for meditation on life, sex, and death. Baruchello's project, however, goes beyond Carlson's environmental model. This is because the concept of nature is broader. Baruchello isn't attempting to appreciate his environment, but to creatively live with it. His is a nature that includes human beings, and so this background against which one lives includes, for example, one's own mortality, which is an important source of reflection for Baruchello. That Carlson's scheme doesn't quite account for Baruchello's approach points to what makes him interesting for our purposes. He is specifically interested in blurring the lines between the aesthetic and everyday life in a way that nothing in Carlson's scheme is intended to do. Baruchello is not just interested in noticing that which is background, but rather living with his environment in such a way that something new, whether it be an artwork or a way of thinking, is brought into the world.

We begin, then, with the artist in the world. Baruchello tells us at the very start that he is "interested in the idea that farming this land could also be considered a work of art" (*HI*, 35). So in the style of a kind of Kantian transcendental argument, Baruchello explores the grounds for this being the case, though like Duchamp's *Bicycle Wheel,* its aesthetic status comes largely from its being an occasion for other aesthetic statements. But just as *Bicycle Wheel* has the status of art, so Baruchello claims the same status for his farm. To make this claim is, indeed, to make a statement, and surely a statement that is more than a problematizing of the concept of art (as in Danto), though Baruchello is aware that it is this latter thing as well. But Baruchello is trying to move in the opposite direction of Danto. In contrast to Danto, Baruchello's reflection on indiscernibles leads him to the world and its problems.

In the course of his essay, Baruchello alludes several times to some of the sorts of statements he hopes his farm can make. He tells us that a return to the earth is "an almost polemical reply to the exploration of space" (*HI*, 25). In addition, he regards the farm as a political response to the meanings he takes to be embodied in land art (Christo being Baruchello's named foil here, though he seems also to have in mind works such as those by Walter Demuria and Robert Smithson). Both of these dimensions of Baruchello's project implicate it in social and political realities not through explicit didactic means but through the power of the artist to make something into art, though importantly without carrying it off into the artworld, that is, without removing it from everyday experience. In this way, Baruchello enters into significant social and political terrain. Conceiving his farm as an artwork is intended as a reply to the exploration of space. Of interest to us in the context of our discussion of Danto is the fact that farming is not in and of itself essentially such a reply. The difference between two farms that look the same is that one embodies a kind of statement and has certain sorts of thoughts attached to it. This fits with certain things Danto says. When considering three hypothetical blue painted ties, one by Picasso, one by a forger, and one by a child, Danto notes that Picasso uses his tie to make a statement.[9] But we need not follow the Hegelian metaphor here, as Danto seems to, and think that most statements are about oneself, or that once one starts talking about oneself one will find there is really nothing else left to talk about. Conferring the status of art upon the farm functions as a statement, but a very different kind from those that Danto generally considers, Baruchello sees himself as engaged in *politics*. His aesthetic ties him to the world. Also, Baruchello sees the aesthetic status of the farm as an opening up of the possibilities of thought. Baruchello's political reflections are only a part of this. While Baruchello, as an artist, brings with him a kind of self-consciousness that makes the statement possible, his larger point is (unlike Danto) that one needn't be an established artist to have this self-consciousness. Baruchello's point in the end is that the imagination of his book's title is not the exclusive property of the artworld, being more connected with a way of life, an aesthetics of the everyday, in which imaginings play a regular and important part.

To carry on his political polemic with regard to space exploration via his farm-art may have particular advantages. One thinks of Hannah Arendt's prologue to *The Human Condition* where she describes Sputnik's flight into space. She calls this an "event, second in importance to no other, not even to the splitting of the atom" because an attempt to flee the earth is to place oneself in a domain in which the human condition would be permanently altered.[10] Arendt and Baruchello share a sensibility, but the point here is not to evaluate this sensibility. Arendt is helpful here in another way, for hers is a worldview in which communication or, to be consistent with the language so far employed, the "making of statements" is of central importance. Developing her reflections on space travel, she says, to the extent that science adopts a technical "language" of mathematical symbols that cannot be translated back into speech it becomes disconnected from the domain of human meanings: "Wherever the relevance of speech is at stake, matters become political by definition, for speech is what makes man a political being. If we would follow the advice, so frequently urged upon us, to adjust our cultural attitudes to the present status of scientific achievement, we would in all earnestness adopt a way of life in which speech is no longer meaningful."[11] The artist, then, can attempt to enlist all of the resources of speech to issue a rejoinder. This is clearly Baruchello's goal. It is a political project that is advanced by conferring the status of art upon the farm. By becoming a statement it attains political significance. Words need a context in order to be meaningful, so Baruchello gives a context to his farm by calling it art. This is to enlist art in the human projects that constitute history. He does this by turning the farm into a kind of speech.

Important for Arendt is the fact that speech is linked with action; speech and action mutually implying each other. With such a view, art, to the extent it makes a statement, is a kind of action, and furthermore, the entrance of something new into the world. For Arendt, action is precisely the giving birth to the new in public, which in turn is politics. That the world can be this kind of an occasion for creativity is crucial to Baruchello's aesthetics of the everyday. Baruchello does not want to embalm his farm. Essential to his project is that it continue to work on the imagination. His polemic with regard to space travel is one small element of this. The aesthetic with which Baruchello operates is one that is *enabling*. His art in having gone over into the world gives us an aesthetics of the everyday in which it is possible for us to act, create, and find direction. The point is to bring something new into the world.

That Baruchello's art is intended to generate further activity is crucial. Danto tends to neglect this notion. For example, in the essay "The Philosophical Disenfranchisement of Art," Danto begins by agreeing with Auden that poetry makes nothing happen.[12] He broadens the discussion by introducing Picasso's *Guernica* and arguing that it too has made nothing happen except promote an admiration for itself. Danto makes these points as an aid to showing that the supposed danger of art springs not from empirical observation, but from philosophical theory. Now, at one point he notices, as he should, that this account might actually contribute to the disenfranchising of art. In what amounts to an aside to the main presentation, he then reminds himself of his own view expressed earlier in *The Transfiguration of the Commonplace* that art shares the same structure as rhetoric.[13] He notes then in a summary way that, since rhetoric influences people, art must indeed be dangerous. That art may have such an influence seems right. It also follows from art's being a kind of statement, and a statement's being a kind of political action, as in Arendt. However, the main trajectory of Danto's presentation works in the opposite direction. Art is neutralized by being separated from the rest of history and by being condemned to directionless pluralism. Danto senses this problem, though he is only able to deal with it by way of asides to the main argument, which clearly does include elements of Platonic disenfranchisement.

The other political dimension that Baruchello reflects upon is the economic. This emerges in the text through a critique of such projects as Christo's. While stating that such works suggest humanity's domination over nature, he also says that, "The disturbing thing about land art is that it's so completely aesthetic, and all on such a terribly wrong scale. Anything that big should have other kinds of meanings altogether. Anything that enormous doesn't make sense any more if it's entirely without awareness of the social realities inside of which and all around which it operates" (*HI*, 21). He calls Christo's wrapping of the Pincian Gate "pure consumption," saying that "they'd have done better to hook up the electricity and the sewers in some of the abusively constructed parts of the suburbs, that would have been a real sign of culture" (*HI,* 27). Ultimately, he regards this kind of event as being about marketing, with a well-sustained media event followed by the marketing of emblems of the event. This is precisely a model of aesthetic involvement with nature that turns it into an object at a distance. In this way it is akin to Carlson's first two models of aesthetic appreciation discussed above. Furthermore, here art stays safely in its own economic domain, or as Baruchello puts it, "within the precincts of the market of art" (*HI,* 38). But, again evoking Danto's project, can art really come back into the city, remove itself from the pedestal now with regard to the economic sphere? Baruchello clearly thinks so. He says,

> I wanted to treat a truck of carrots or potatoes or whatever just the way (Duchamp) had treated his bottle dryer or the urinal called *Fountain.* . . . That was a gesture that had contained a criticism of all of the bourgeois culture of his epoch, and what I wanted to do was to go even beyond that with a gesture that also criticized the social and political aspects of bourgeois culture. It was a question of pulling aesthetics into economy and of pulling the most rudimentary and fundamental forms of agricultural economy into aesthetics (*HI,* 38).

He even momentarily imagines that artists and art critics (he doesn't mention aestheticians) everywhere might plant, grow, and sell potatoes, sugar beets, and so forth, hopefully creating an abundance of that which is needed for life. Here the artist's involvement with the land could be life-enhancing, unlike what he sees as happening with land art. We have, then, an illustration, resembling many of Danto's own in that we are dealing with indiscernibles. However, in this case art is pushed out into the world of the everyday, rather than the world of the everyday being pushed into art.

This last remark requires elaboration. Following the Hegelian model, it is of course hard to distinguish art's moving into the world from the world's moving into art. But Danto himself does make this distinction on several occasions. However, he is only able to see the negative consequences of pushing art into the world. Here we see a fundamental contrast between Danto and Baruchello with regard to an aesthetics of the everyday. For example, at the conclusion of "Artworks and Real Things," Danto briefly moves away from his consideration of real things in the artworld to consider the consequences of blurring the distinction between art and world for the world as a whole. He describes this as a moment where "the categories which pertain to art suddenly pertain to what we always believed contrasted essentially with art. Politics becomes a form of theater, clothing a kind of costume, human relations a kind of role, life a game. We interpret ourselves and our gestures as we once interpreted artworks. We look for meanings and unites, we become players in a play."[14] I am not interested in rejecting

Danto's critique of this manner of moving in the world. We must note, though, that this rather pessimistic characterization *is* the other side of the coin, for Danto, of real things entering the artworld. *This is Danto's aesthetics of everyday life.* Consequently his Hegelian synthesis is one-sided. For Danto, while the everyday can *fruitfully* enter the artworld, the reverse is not the case. Another instance of this, again rather negative, is when Danto refers to what he calls "disturbational art." Note the following definition: "So it is disturbation when the insulating boundaries between art and life are breached in some way the mere representation of disturbing things cannot achieve just because they are representations and responded to as such. It is for this reason that reality must in some way then be an actual component of disturbational art."[15] What Danto has in mind are such works as Chris Burden's *Deadman* of 1972 in which Burden was enclosed in a sack and placed on a California highway, thereby risking death. Danto also considers the possibility of exhibiting a bomb such that people would have to risk their lives in order to view it. Actually, one needn't use hypothetical cases here. Edward Keinholz's work *Still Live* is a chair, in which one is invited to sit, facing a loaded gun designed to go off once every several years. In these sorts of cases Danto holds that art is no longer at a safe distance from life. But why is it that the paradigm case of art scaling this boundary is the kind of case in which art becomes dangerous? Obviously Danto is talking about two different things when he talks about an aestheticized politics and artworks that pose a danger to life and limb. But these are the sorts of things that one finds when he considers art entering into life rather than life entering into art. This is the flip side of the world of readymades. Strangely in these examples art turns out to have very little to do with life, and whatever impact it has would seem to be negative (Danto himself admits that he doesn't care for disturbational art). Baruchello is working in this same sphere. But here it seems that ending art's seclusion and its entrance into life may be a positive thing for both art and life. Baruchello helps us see a conceptual possibility missing in Danto's work.

How to Imagine is the story of a process. It is the story of Baruchello's own reflections as he runs his farm. The reflections are tentative and revised in the course of the writing. In contrast to his fantasy of creating a political movement (he tells us that he did at one point write a pretentious manifesto) he ultimately becomes comfortable with a more humble task. For he does not think there is any way to exhibit the project without pulling it completely back into the artworld. As an artist of some reputation he knows that he has the power to unequivocally bestow the status of art upon his farm. He says,

> There'd be no question about having made art with it if I'd gone ahead and distributed that first press release I did or if I'd had an invitation printed and asked people to come out and visit the herd of sheep. I could have declaimed a

speech on agriculture and then asked everybody to put his finger up the ass of a sheep of his choosing and then to smell it, and they'd all have been saying, 'Well, he invited us out to this house in the country and did this very curious and very interesting event where everybody puts his finger up the ass of a sheep'; and that would be art, no question about it (*HI*, 134).

But, he asks, if this is the only thing missing between his farm as art and its not being art, surely this is not a difference that makes a difference. So, unlike Duchamp and his urinal, Baruchello will not exhibit his work. He refuses to turn it into a thing at a distance. It is to stay in the world of the everyday, serving as the occasion for imagining, speaking, and acting. In a certain sense, it remains as background highlighted in various ways by Baruchello's own statements, reflections, and artworks. Baruchello is, though, as one such occasion for reflection, willing to tell us about his farm. "Our potatoes may not after all be intriguing, and nobody had shown any special interest in them, but making a certain kind of use of them, the way we talk about them, writing about them, having ideas about them, in that case things perhaps are a little different and the potatoes we've produced become disquieting potatoes after all" (*HI*, 154). The disturbance created here, in contrast to Danto's account above, is one that suggests social and political critique. Art has the possibility of moving in some direction. The point is not to show that art is a loose notion that includes anything and everything. For Baruchello,

> the point isn't still further to weaken the definition of art so that it can finally even include agriculture and driving a tractor across a field, or digging potatoes out of the earth, I'm trying to move in precisely the opposite direction. Whereas recent art history has tended to simplify art to make it accept certain minimal gestures, my own deepest interest is in seeing a possible aesthetic in Agricola Cornelia through a recomplication of the idea of art. The thinking that leads me now through the experience of Agricola Cornelia is in fact an extension of an idea of testing the power of art against the power of the much more potent social structures that stand adjacent to it (*HI*, 149).

Baruchello's "recomplication" comes in his attempt to situate his art relative to a particular project. That is, his art is a context for speaking and acting in the world. In fact, it contains potentially all of the complications of the world and all of the possibilities for direction to be found in the world. If there is history to be found, art can be a participant. This, much more than Danto's pluralism, marks art's return from exile. Baruchello imagines art having something to do with everyday life. In contrast, Danto, when he imagines this, comes up with an aestheticized politics and disturbational art. Mostly, though, he does not imagine it at all. Return from exile for Danto paradoxically isn't entrance into the world, but rather into meaningless pluralism.

Finally, let me consider a possible concern regarding my criticism of Danto. One might think that I have in some sense missed the point of Danto's view. Obviously, Danto doesn't doubt that people carry on with the activities that we call making art. His point is that art is no longer connected to any larger project. But perhaps the possibility for larger projects that I have sketched takes art out of art's characteristic domain so that it no longer finds direction *qua* art, but only insofar as it aligns itself with other nonartistic projects. But art has always done this, and, in fact, this is part of what has motivated the fear of art from Plato's time to ours. Consequently, this is an integral part of art's history, not something extraneous that can be shuttled off into another category. Furthermore, that works of art might in their own unique way intelligibly contribute to other perhaps profoundly significant projects accords with the idea of art's liberation from the pedestal. Danto claims that at the end of art, artists are free to pursue anything that they wish, it being impossible for them to orient themselves in any particular direction. This is what he means by pluralism and he is rightly unhappy with it. My point has been that it does not follow from Danto's attempt to liberate art from Platonic aesthetics that artists must be adrift within this pluralism. Statements can be made that are astute, wise, uninteresting, or objectionable. Such evaluations can be made against the background of larger social concerns and struggles, as seems to be Baruchello's main intent; or against the background of the more subtle personal and psychological issues to which he sometimes alludes. I have tried to show that the fact that Danto believes that his unhappy pluralism does follow betrays his own commitment to the kind of Platonic aesthetics that he seeks to critique. The end of the history of art only leads to directionless pluralism if the artist is forbidden from entering real history. With Danto real history has *not* ended, yet the artist is denied admission.

To sum up, Baruchello's concerns are Danto's concerns but with a difference. The difference is that Baruchello sees this puzzle not as an ending, but as a vehicle for art's going somewhere. Where? Well, Baruchello does not give us a full-blown theoretical account. The text he gives us instead is one filled with possibilities. There are social and political possibilities, as well as possibilities for the imagination itself. In contrast, this is the weakness of Danto's approach. By seeing the problematizing of the difference between art and reality as the fundamental issue raised by real things entering the artworld, he misses (at least sometimes) the fact that there is a polemical dimension to labeling such objects as art. There is a power to this labeling that can be used for a variety of purposes, a power that may best be harnessed when such objects remain in the world. That is, the world of the everyday becomes an occasion for creativity, reflection, and imagination. Baruchello describes his attempt to wield this power. While there are indeed many possible polemics, Baruchello focuses on a handful. But that he chooses the ones that he does helps us see something else about Danto's position. Baruchello's point is to reject the uselessness and irrelevance of art. In this he is like Danto. Danto thinks that by showing that art has become philosophical, art is in some sense liberated from the way it has been defined by philosophy, for example, as separate and irrelevant. But then Danto betrays his own commitment to the philosophical model by imagining that art history could end, without history itself ending, implying that art remains separate from the world. Baruchello, while working some of Danto's themes, suggests that art can move into the world and find a direction via other human projects. While Baruchello's project may have initially looked like just another instance of one of Danto's cases of indiscernibles, we find that Baruchello's notion of the aesthetic moves in the opposite direction of Danto's, that is, toward the world. In this he succeeds in pointing to an aesthetics of the everyday where the world becomes an occasion for speaking, acting, and imagining. In fact for Baruchello this sort of aesthetics of the everyday is precisely what gives art the possibility for purpose and direction. This is an idea that is consistent with Danto's idea of liberating art from philosophy, and as Baruchello suggests bodes well for the health of art. For surely it is not just Baruchello's farm art that can provide such a context. Many other works of art can as well. But Baruchello's farm art does help make the point that art can be such an environment, and further, that an aesthetics of everyday life need employ no particular or special way of seeing an environment that is out there and separate, but rather aspires to find a context for living that promotes speaking, acting, and imagining.

Notes

1. Arthur Danto, *The Philosophical Disenfranchisement of Art* (New York: Columbia University Press, 1986), 8–9. Henceforth *PD* where cited in text.
2. Arthur Danto, "Artworks and Real Things," *Theoria* 39 (1973):16.
3. Danto, *Philosophical Disenfranchisement of Art*, 12–13.
4. Francis Fukuyama, *The End of History and the Last Man* (New York: Free Press, 1992).
5. Gianfranco Baruchello and Henry Martin (interviewer, editor, translator), *How to Imagine* (New York: Documentext, 1984).
6. Gianfranco Baruchello and Henry Martin (interviewer, editor, translator), *Why Duchamp* (New York: Documentext, 1985), 62.
7. Allen Carlson, "Appreciation and the Natural Environment," *Journal of Aesthetics and Art Criticism* 37 (1979).
8. Ibid., 274.
9. Danto, "Artworks and Real Things," 7–10.
10. Hannah Arendt, *The Human Condition* (Chicago: The University of Chicago Press, 1958), 1.

11. Ibid., 4.

12. Danto, *Philosophical Disenfranchisement of Art*, 1–21.

13. Arthur Danto, *The Transfiguration of the Common Place* (Cambridge, Mass.: Harvard University Press, 1981).

14. Danto, "Artworks and Real Things," 17.

15. Danto, *Philosophical Disenfranchisement of Art*, 121.

PART II

Appreciating the Everyday Environment

CHAPTER 5

Building and the Naturally Unplanned

Pauline von Bonsdorff

IN THE CONTEXTS of planning and building, architecture is mostly approached as an intentionally designed body of objects, expressive of commissioners' and planners' views of society and of their aesthetic ideals. Legitimate as that approach is, it makes us forget those elements of the built environment that are not the result of decision-making. As experienced, the environment is also dependent on elements that are independent of human intentions, such as topography, climate, and weather. Although these are variable, they are always present, in one version or another. These "naturally unplanned" elements are not only present in the built environments between the buildings, they also have real effects on buildings, effects that are visually perceptible on the surface of the building or present in the quality of the air inside, as humidity or smells.[1] I would also include the way a building is "worn" through contact with human bodies as part of the naturally unplanned. On the whole, the naturally unplanned in the built environment is an effect of time, a way in which natural time, as opposed to historical, appears to us. By calling this dimension unplanned rather than contingent I want to stress that it belongs of necessity to any inhabited environment and is no less essential than the planned. It might also be noted that in addition to the naturally unplanned there is a socially unplanned dimension to the environment, comprising ways in which human life adapts to and remodels the environment in unforeseen ways. But this, I think, is of a different status and significance than the naturally unplanned, and a discussion would have to include questioning the priority of planners' views over inhabitants' actual use.

In this chapter, I focus on the aesthetic impact and existential significance of the naturally unplanned. I argue that in our time, a time of globalizing civilization, there is more reason than ever to address building through the interaction of culture and nature. This is because in certain respects, which I later point out, human life in the rich countries is characterized by alienation from both the concrete environment and from the organic processes that sustain and renew life.

I start by looking at the concepts of nature and culture and relate them to building, understood in the double sense, indicated by Aldo Rossi, of both objects and processes.[2] As a material and cultural entity, a piece of architecture is subjected to construction and reconstruction and is, thus, a process. On the other hand, at any particular moment it is experienced as a particular given, an object. I defend a view of culture as cultivation that answers to the understanding of building as a process, where building not only means creating new things, but also dwelling among what is given. Such building, which takes advantage of and adapts to existing climatic, topographic or historical features, and conditions, is nowadays more an exception than a rule. In the second part of this chapter, I point out how contemporary environmental management typically causes a "flattening" of the world as experienced, a loss of temporal and historical depth. However, the roots of the problem are not only in the world, but also in our modes of experiencing it. In the third part, I suggest that the notion of tacit knowing, as opposed to formal knowledge, can be helpful for an understanding of the world in depth. Finally, I point to the existential value of types of building that lets the naturally unplanned appear, and thus facilitates a reconciliation of the human being with himself or herself as a temporal, aspiring, and finite being: "an architecture responsive to our essential incompleteness."[3]

Building as Cultivation and Dwelling

The fact that buildings are planned is a reason to find them aesthetically interesting, since it means that questions about appearance, design, and symbolic content can be asked in a meaningful way. Buildings are suggestive of human intentions, meanings, and value, positive or negative. We often see the significance of building as belonging entirely to the realm of culture. But to disregard the other side, the unplanned, the workings of nature, would be a mistake. By acknowledging the presence of the unplanned we get a complementary perspective.

The word *building* is ambiguous, since it refers both to the activity of building and to an object which is the result of that activity. Neither the process nor the object have to be planned in detail from the start, but it is clear that both process and object are intentional in a general sense, as opposed to random. For example, even if the builder works without drawings, his work involves ongoing planning, and this is partly because unforeseen elements interfere. In a similar way buildings, as they exist and are experienced at any particular moment, contain both planned and unplanned aspects. The use and articulation of a certain material in a facade is planned, but the way the material reacts to the weather is not, although it can to a large extent be foreseen.

These observations pertain to the sum total of buildings, to the present built heritage. Unlike much of the past, contemporary building is often planned in detail from the start. This is part of the overall aesthetic problem I am trying to indicate. Even if this kind of building is not independent of nature, nature is present only as the laws of nature, as articulated in the natural sciences. Nature in the natural sciences is an object of knowledge, "brute" nature, mute material that is controlled and manipulated according to the demands of technology. Seen in this way, nature indeed has little cultural significance, and its significance for building is reduced to technical demands of construction, for example, in calculations of durability. Aesthetically, nature is absent; it is not seen as a resource for design.

Before proceeding, it must be noted that a discussion of nature is sometimes argued to be meaningless, because there is no concept of nature independent of a particular human culture. There is no "natural nature," no "nature as such." But the conclusion that we cannot, therefore, meaningfully talk about nature seems to be based on the false assumption that to use the concept "nature" implies an identification of the concept with particular appearances or, even worse, a certain essence. This is not necessarily the case: it is indeed possible to use the word nature without trying to define its essence or describe it.[4] It might even be necessary, for we cannot extract nature from the world, we cannot separate it and put our finger on it. Nature, as Spinoza's *natura naturans,* creative nature, generates life and change, not only in *natura naturata,* created nature, but also in cultural products. It is with creative nature, nature in the climate or in our bodies, we have to cooperate in practical matters and adapt to in personal life. What is true in the idea that there is no nature as such is that nature does not exist for us independently of ourselves. But this is no reason to stop reflecting on our relation to nature; rather, the contrary.

Whether the reduction of nature to material is part of a process of increased global well-being is, to say the least, open to doubt. I cannot go into economic and ecological questions here but shall instead concentrate on the potential existential value of confronting both the unpredictability of nature and the limits of our own knowledge. This confrontation can be staged and manifested in different ways in different cultural practices, among which, I think, building is not the least important. Building, if it is open to the unplanned, could provide a path toward a reconciliation of the finite human being and the world as an extending, continuing totality, an object of a knowledge that will always remain preliminary.[5]

These are reasons to let the unplanned enter our physical and mental spaces and to make room for nature as a significant element of building. But with this, what happens to our idea of culture? If nature is seen as process, does culture become more reified? Not necessarily, for the distinction between nature and culture does not demand that we think of them as polar opposites in every respect. We often speak of culture and nature as if they were opposed: nature is raw, while culture is cooked; nature is animal, while culture is human; nature is without sense, while culture is meaningful; nature is sensuous, while culture is spiritual. These statements, which are normally presented as descriptive are, to a high degree, evaluative. Their apparent factuality makes it easier to believe that in human existence progress consists in culture ousting nature, where these are separate phenomena.[6] Still, in our concrete lifeworld nature and culture can in most cases only be separated conceptually: we are ourselves both natural and cultural creatures. We forget too easily that concepts such as nature and culture, animal and human, do not denote separately existing entities, but instead articulate conceptual distinctions and perceptual differences by which we order the world, but which are not identical to the world.

In its etymological roots, the word *culture* refers to cultivation, to rural agricultural activities, like growing crops or raising animals.[7] In these activities, nature is worked upon, but also worked with. It is important to note that the success of the labor is dependent on the workers' knowledge of and adaption to natural processes, which take their own course and in the last instance decide when and how the work must be done. Nature is not only material; cooperation is a necessary condition of successful farming. The aim of farming is the maintenance and enhancement of human life in an evident and necessary interdependence with other species. The agricultural context also makes us more aware of the organic conditions of existence: growth, nutrition, birth, and death.

The above imagery can be accused of idealization, in combining a somewhat archaic conception of "traditional farming" with contemporary ecological consciousness, but I present it for the useful potential it contains. Values that have disappeared from much contemporary farming might not be irretrievably lost, nor are they lost everywhere. To summarize what is relevant to our theme in the rural excursus, we can note that in cultivation nature does not just change into culture. Nature and culture continue to exist side by side, intertwined[8] copresent in mutual influence, interdependent, but without either losing its own character. It would, for example, be an anthropocentric fallacy to think that animals or plants stop being nature if they move into new ecological niches, which are created as a result of human activities.

The idea of culture as cultivation makes it easier to perceive the simultaneity of nature and culture, where nature is present as those processes which, in Hannah Arendt's words, "come into being without the help of man" and that are "not 'made' but grow by themselves into whatever they become."[9] In contrast, the element of culture consists, on the one hand, of our intentional activities and, on the other, of the material and immaterial entities and structures with whose help we cope with the world.

There are architects who have defended the view that nature should not be thought of as being outside culture or its radical other. Among these is Alvar Aalto, who saw architecture's central tasks as making the most of what nature offers and protecting human beings from both natural and cultural evils and threats.[10] In combining with nature, culture is forced neither to destroy nor cover it. Martin Heidegger's notion of dwelling points to a related sensitivity to both site and situation as they are found. To dwell is to abide but, on the other hand, dwelling is also an activity, and so cannot preclude but has to include changes to the site as it is found or given.[11] The notion of dwelling also implies that human beings belong with places.[12] Dwelling, we are not outsiders to the place, but appropriate it and become appropriated. Part of my history and my possibilities are present to me through my places, and to dwell is necessarily to dwell meaningfully.

A central claim of Heidegger's is that building, which among other things is the construction of dwellings, should share the sheltering quality present in dwelling.[13] It is easy to agree with this, especially when we remember that dwelling includes attention to the site and its possibilities but also to the situation: the way a place is inhabited. The need for the kind of tacit reflectivity implicit in dwelling becomes evident through a concern for a better built environment, but also through the observation, which is both empirical and ontological, that no building is ever finished. A building cannot "stand as it is," and since the natural processes that are part of the very materials of building do not stop, it would be wise to note, adapt, and take advantage of them. Also, if we choose to see culture as cultivation, as a form of life rather than as a system of forms, we have reason to pay attention to those processes in building that, from the planners' perspective, are unintended. Building, in both senses of the word—verb and noun—becomes dwelling, but only if we acknowledge nature and understand culture as a process.

It must be noted that in using the words *nature, culture,* and *building* in this way, we point to dimensions and aspects of the world, not to separate realms or objects. Language may deceive us, but the limits of our language are the limits of our world only if we firmly believe so,[44] and the reverse idea, that the limits of our world are the limits of our language, deserves equal attention,[15] especially in a context of environmental aesthetics. That concepts frame our cognitive and, to some extent, practical dealings with the world does not mean that they draw a line which we cannot cross. The ongoing modification of language is rather a sign of its inbuilt perspectivism, which can be seen as a chronic insufficiency, but only if we demand everything. To see our patterns of life, material and immaterial, as containing elements of both nature and culture is not an objectively true view. It is based on a set of values and on a wish to find a livable balance "in-between" nature and culture, with both.[16] I shall give additional reasons for this in the final part of this chapter. Some reasons, I hope, will be found in what I now turn to, namely a criticism of Western civilization in terms of what happens to environmental experience.

Flattened Experience

Vehement criticism of modern industrialized society—today's globally dominant form of organizing human life—is to be found more than a hundred years ago, in texts of social utopians such as William Morris.[17] Perhaps the most thoroughgoing critique was launched by Max Horkheimer and Theodor W. Adorno in their classic *Dialektik der Aufklärung,* published in 1947.[18] Similar themes were taken up at the same time, though from a different philosophical standpoint, by Martin Heidegger.[19] This criticism is still of interest. Despite the talk of a postindustrial or information society, industrialized society has not disappeared, although production has been moved out of smelling distance from wealthier people. Further, the postindustrial emphasis on information brings with it an escalation of trends of industrial modernity.

Let me pick out some aesthetically important themes from the work of the Frankfurt School and from Heidegger's critique of culture. Relevant, with respect to the present discussion, is the gradual disappearance of individuality, of the concrete, of history, memory, and the human voice through the process of modernization. This goes for the physical, perceptible aspects of environment, for planning procedures, and for modes of experience. Reason becomes instrumental, and political discourse deals more and more with procedures and less with questions of value.[20] In both our self-understanding and in our patterns of life there is an increasing quantification of both time and space.[21] The past, says Karsten Harries, "becomes no more than a reservoir of materials that we may incorporate in our constructions as we see fit."[22] In Giorgio Agamben's words, experience is destroyed.[23]

There is even a sense in which cultural criticism is a misleading characterization of the above analyses, for the point is not so much that culture has taken a wrong turn as that culture, in the concrete and local sense, has given room to a worldwide and spreading, universalizing civilization.[24] Rather than a poor form of life this version of civilization represents no life-form at all. The technosphere, supported by anonymous, transnational corporations, is largely autonomous and on the whole politically immune to needs arising in the basic sphere of social life, human ideals, and political thinking.[25] But this does not mean that it exists separately from our everyday existence. On the contrary, the macrostructure conditions everyday life in many ways, where the general trend is toward an increasing separation of the person and other persons and the abstraction of human interaction, which is seen basically in terms of transmission of information.[26] Drawing on Lévinas's ideas, we may note that as a consequence of the weakening of the aesthetic sensuous dimension comes a weakening of the ethical dimension, since there are fewer occasions for that ethical moment of encounter with an expressive other where my responsibility for the others originates.[27]

Although the above picture overlooks existing alternative ways of life, it points to a trend that is undeniably with us. It is also worth emphasizing that the critical question here is to what extent the human-made environment produced by the processes of modernization affords spaces for interaction and attachment. Let me call attention to two examples, which in different ways exemplify contemporary relations of human beings and environment as mediated by the body. The first, the car, is the typical contemporary vehicle for physical movement. The other, the hospital, is the place where we cannot avoid realizing that we are bodily and finite creatures. Interestingly, in both the car and the hospital the body-environment relation is affected in a neutralizing way.

It has been claimed that walking is the optimal mode of human environmental experience, since our sensory system is best adapted for its perspective and pace.[28] For many people in the rich industrialized countries driving is, however, the natural and commonest way to move from one place to another, even over short distances. But although driving is not a poor experience in terms of sensuous engagement or perceptual interaction with the most immediate environment,[29] it gives a different and less multidimensional access to the environment as place than walking. This is emphasized when we are transported as passengers, where the interactive element of movement through driving is lacking, and a filmic view instead may be said to dominate.[30]

Alienation is due to the mode and speed of movement, but also to the degree and kind of engagement and identification between human being and landscape. With the risk of simplification I venture to suggest that I inhabit the landscape where I walk: my relation to it is intimate and extended over time, different times; whereas from the car, landscape and road often exist as obstacles, quantified stretches of distance to be overcome. We may also note the typical character of motorway and roadside, which are not hospitable to improvised stops. The urban automobile environment is rather designed as a billboard, where the landscapes behind the signs remain unseen.[31] In addition, the private car is, even for the driver, poorer in terms of social interaction than public transportation, since we are separated from people other than those we already know.

As a result of changes of this sort the landscape we pass through in a car is less accessible and has fewer dimensions than the landscape we walk in, both sensuously and from the point of experienced meaning. As Heidegger pointed out, the overcoming of distance does not create nearness.[32] Here it is interesting to observe, with Bernhard Waldenfels, that the visualization of landscape in modernity occurs simultaneously with the separation of nature from culture and natural landscape from agricultural landscape. Control of nature on the one hand, contemplation and enjoyment of nature on the other, are two sides of the same coin.[33]

In the other example, the modern hospital, organic processes like birth and conception, sickness and death are isolated from their context in everyday life. In the situations of entry into or exit from life, the human being is today dependent on complicated technical and medical equipment. The body and its processes are analyzed in functional and technical terms, and some processes are transferred to machines. The patient is deprived of authority over his or her own body: disintegrated from the exterior, which is different from an interior disintegration through illness. Cosmetic surgery is a striking example of a contemporary medical practice where the individual body and its history is neglected and abandoned. It is easy to see this as a caricature of Cartesian subjecthood, of the separation of mind and body and the emancipation of mind from body: I am what I think I am. But with the separation of identity and body comes a decrease in continuity, in relatedness, in the individual materials and narratives through which we exist and appear to ourselves and others. Today sickness, aging, death—processes that demonstrate the vulnerability of existence—are regarded as particular problems that should be solved and overcome through operations and therapy. But we should remember that if we deny these experiences, we shall also be less experienced.[34]

I do not deny the blessings of cars and hospitals but these blessings do not cancel disadvantages that have not, so far, been sufficiently identified and pointed out. The modern car and the modern hospital represent losses in concrete, sensuous experience. We are relieved of pain, but simultaneously of the integrity of our corporeal selves. Life becomes smoother, but loses touch with the material details of reality, with both environment and body as concrete, historically saturated places. Freedom and rootlessness come hand in hand, and the "attack on distance" is accompanied by a weakening of both place and community.[35] Losing touch with the environment is not primarily a diminuation of the amount of sensory impulses here and now. More importantly, it entails a disappearance of the subjective strata that give my environment(s) temporal depth. As Jean-Francois Lyotard puts it, "what merits attention is the disappearance of the temporal continuum through which the experience of generations used to be transmitted."[36] Here the loss in collective self-understanding comes hand in hand with a loss in our self-understanding as finite subjects of nature. That is a basis for the relevance, interest and reevaluation of the naturally unplanned.

Flattening of experience is one overall effect of modernization. The environment, experienced flatly, is not strange to me so much as insignificant, irrelevant, null and void, none of my business. It is a strange kind of alienation, for it does not increase distance but rather takes it away. The overcoming of distance is an abandonment of "place" as the qualitative and meaningful aspect of environment.

And if places are evolving as well as given, this can be expected to have consequences not only for our understanding of history but also for the ways in which we make and implement plans.

As a rule, contemporary planning is not very sensitive to the narrative character of places or to the natural and cultural continuities to be found in materials or techniques of construction. An important part of the problem is a lack of sensibility, an inability to attend to qualities where the naturally unplanned is present. One answer to this problem is perhaps education, to teach people to observe certain qualities and aspects. But probably more than words are needed: a facilitation of modes of experience that in ideal cases should be practiced as part of everyday life. I now turn to an account of what this might involve.

Temporal Depth and Tacit Knowing

Building is, among other things, a concrete articulation of a culture's relation to nature. A basic axiological and aesthetically relevant question of building is thus how culture meets nature, how it deals with it, and how it is able to receive, reflect, and react to it. The question can be approached from a technical and scientific point of view, in terms of transportation, energy, resources, biotopes. There is, however, also a perspective that focuses on the meanings and values embodied by constructive processes, fabricated objects, and styles of life as they appear to us. This perspective cannot be ignorant of science, but is in the end dependent on reflective and critical judgment. The questions are of the following kind: how do construction processes confront the site; how is the building related to site and climate; are the materials and scale of the building appropriate; what life-styles and what kind of social structures does the building propose?

In the above kind of questions, the difference between construction activities and built objects is not very sharp. Both in construction and habitational activities we perceive and appreciate patterns of behaviour, ways of dwelling. Further, it is the how, the style of human action, not site or climate, that makes a local culture seem brutal, gentle, or elegant. These aesthetic qualities, which are also human values, are dependent on how built culture meets nature. Aesthetically, it is the builders who are primarily in charge of how the inhabited environment appears, although its character is molded by the meeting and melting of natural and cultural elements.[37] An important part of the art of building is the ability to handle and confront the natural givens.

If activities present behind questions such as "how was this made?" and "how can one live here?" are a central dimension of the understanding of building, the move from a discussion of functional themes, related to human behavior on the macro- and microscales, to a discussion of values embodied in objects is smooth. A habitat is a place to live in, a home, but it also embodies behavioral patterns and habits. As an inhabited and particular place, the environment carries signs of how life is lived and how it could be lived, which are present even when human beings are not in sight. Perceptible habitational qualities demonstrate a potential of the environment. Their understanding requires, however, a familiarity with life-forms or culture. But this knowledge is not so much dependent on a particular culture as on an acknowledgment and familiarity with the tacit dimension of experience in general. That is, it is not important to belong to a particular culture to be able to realize how it feels to seize a certain door handle. The identification of habitational qualities is rather tied to basic experiences of bodily existence.[38] It is to these experiences that the tacit dimension of dwelling refers.

How the environment appears to us, embodies, and communicates is coexistent with what we know of it. Part of this knowledge is discursive, part is a knowledge by acquaintance. Michael Polanyi describes these two, interrelated kinds as formal and tacit, or personal, knowledge.[39] Interestingly, he argues that there is a tacit component in all knowledge because it is always dependent on what the subject is willing to accept. Here one could add that it is reasonable to think that tacit knowing, as performed by human beings, also always, to some degree, contains formal components. It is worth noting that Polanyi prefers the word *knowing* to *knowledge,* and thus emphasizes the active aspect. He describes knowing as an activity typical of all organisms, animals and humans alike. "The animal's intelligence is spontaneously alive to the problem of making sense of its surroundings."[40] The tacit component includes the importance of former experiences and a synaesthetic cooperation of all senses, both in relation to the world outside and to kinaesthetic feelings.[41] Tacit knowing is built up over time; it is cumulative, not because it piles new information on top of former information, but because it builds the new into the old, and thus makes experience denser.

The idea of tacit knowing is fruitful especially in dealing with uncoded types of meaning, to which expressive and aesthetic qualities of environments largely belong. In perceiving the environment the tacit component, to know how it would feel to do something or to be in a certain kind of place, is basic to understanding the character or atmosphere of a place as, for example, gentle, elegant, dynamic, or aggressive. To be aware of the tacit component also helps us to understand how phenomena such as traffic, smog, storm, and sunshine are met by us and appreciated.

That we should take tacit knowing seriously does not mean that it is always reliable. An environment might seem to be something it is not, where seemingness is based on irrelevant associations. However, when we have to deal with familiar environments it is more likely that tacit knowing can be trusted. It is also in this context that tacit knowing is related to the experienced temporal depth of the environment. My life is parallel to and embraced by certain environments—houses, streets, and physical objects—which as part of my life are part of experienced time and carriers of meaning. This meaning is subjective, but not in a privative way, since the experienced world, a continuum of time and place, implies from the start other people, companions, the social dimension.[42]

The possibilities of experiencing continuity in the environment and of experiencing the environment in a rich, multisensuous interaction, are related to the meaningfulness of environment and to our existential feeling at home, or homeless, on the earth. Under the habitational aspect, aesthetic issues are less than ever separated from ethical and cognitive ones.

When Space Appears as Place: A Eutopian Attempt[43]

R. W. Hepburn points out the metaphysical and existential dimensions of the aesthetic enjoyment of nature, where there is "mutual involvement . . . but also a reflexive effect by which the spectator experiences *himself* in an unusual and vivid way." This kind of experience is "not unknown to art, especially architecture," but "more intensely realized and pervasive in nature-experience—for we are *in* nature and part *of* nature."[44] At least to some extent, I think, the latter idea—that human beings are part of organic nature—can be suggested for us by architecture. It is also a quality worth seeking, especially if one agrees with the view that many tendencies of contemporary life produce discontinuities and fragmentation, and as a consequence a weakening of the sense of the particularities of time and space.

The theme of the final part of this chapter is the existential dimension of building, including the analogy between body and buildings. This analogy should not be understood visually, comparing facades with faces, but as referring to temporality as undergoing, as being subjected to processes that were not chosen and which therefore call forth ideas of fate and finitude.[45] The idea of fate is not meant to imply a "celestial" perspective, where the scripts of our lives would exist from the moment we are born, but is meant to be seen from an earthly, terrestrial perspective, as the experience of things happening to us without our volition, of accidents and coincidences that in particular ways become parts of a particular life.

Finitude, we must remember, is not only a condition of destitution. It is through being here that we can be at all. The built environment can remind us of this, and it happens, when it happens, largely through visual appearance. But what appearance conveys is more and other than visual. Among and between forms, parts and elements we can observe reflections, shadows and change, or tactile and tectonic qualities related to the materiality of building.[46] Buildings may also confront us "with some long-forgotten aspect of our past" and so "provide our dwelling with a usually obscured continuity."[47] Here we must note that the appearance of a building cannot be understood in terms of frozen images, but is constituted historically through repeated encounters of subject and environment. These do not form a fragmented series, for we are aware that there is continuity in the environment between my visit here today and yesterday, or three years ago. Further, we are aware that every appearance belongs to one possible perspective and situation, but that none is comprehensive. "There is absolute certitude of the world in general, but not of any particular thing."[48] The "thickness" of the world, which Merleau-Ponty alludes to, is a condition of its experienced depth.

Through an evocative symbolism buildings can acknowledge and address existentially significant issues. Among the loci of this kind of symbolism—which, as Douglas Davies describes it, is actualized in reflective experience—are the ways in which buildings react to and make perceptible certain natural processes or, which is a somewhat different matter, bring forth nature as earth.[49] Thus, in John Sallis's *Stone,* it is the very resistance of stone to spiritual meaning that makes it heavy with sense and significant also in a cultural context. "Like the earth to which it belongs, stone shows itself only when it is brought into the open *as* self-secluding, as closed off, as self-closed."[50] Sallis also describes a moment of Heidegger's visit to Delos where truth as *alétheia* "is no longer just intended but is encountered in the stone of the island itself."[51] The material is evocative in a nonarbitrary way but not, strictly speaking, symbolic.

Leaving these specific suggestions aside we might agree, in a more general context of building, with Karsten Harries who observes that "[d]ifferent materials are differently affected by the passage of time, they speak of different attitudes to time and thus of different ideals of building and dwelling."[52] The idea that the human-made environment as a whole embodies the values of a society is useful to keep in mind, but then it must not be forgotten that the embodied values are not identical to those that are verbally expressed. This is precisely the reason why the corpus of buildings, in its own way, so strongly suggests what kind of humans we are.

For example, the low quality, both in terms of construction and functionality, of much modern housing from the sixties and seventies is a well-known and worldwide phenomenon. Often these buildings are characterized as ugly. Their experienced ugliness is related to their technical and functional shortcomings, which I shall not discuss here. I shall only make some observations on what kinds of attitudes these buildings seem to demonstrate in relation to nature. Modern housing typically demonstrates an attempt to master existence in a formal and abstract way. But often the attempt fails, facades crack, apparently because what Ralph Waldo Emerson called our first environment, nature, has not been taken into account.[53] As a result of the inability of buildings to meet the challenges of the actual local environment, of changing seasons and weather, temperatures and humidity, buildings begin to look awkward, uncomfortable, "out of place." Building is thus easily experienced as both alienated and alienating already on a prereflective level, for the knowing it denies and the human import it denigrates is dependent, to a considerable degree, on our tacit acquaintance with very basic conditions of life: how it feels to walk on this earth, to act and move in a body that is itself subject to natural forces.

In contrast, less processed materials, such as stone or wood, show in their very texture, as traces, processes of nature such as growth or sedimentation. That these materials are generated by geological or organic processes can be perceived and is, in part, understood through their appearance. Natural materials also react more smoothly to natural processes and are likely to "cooperate" with these: they are receptive and interactive in relation to the climate. The surface of the building often emphasizes and brings out changes in light or humidity, which, in addition to their cognitive interest, are aesthetically pleasing in an immediate way.[54] Similar qualities may be found in buildings of different type and origin, but they are less usual in facades made of prefabricated elements, partly because of their flat and static surface. Compare that to traditional paint, which becomes transparent with time and allows us to be conscious of both painted material and paint, to follow the impact of climate on the building as a process that at some point urges us to begin again, with a new layer of paint. Such buildings demand our care, and tell us so.

That materials do not last forever is a technical problem, but that is not the only viable or important perspective. There is aesthetic and existential significance in aging, withering materials that show the interaction of nature and culture, with humans as mediators, belonging to both sides, erecting and wearing down.[55] This significance is especially important in a culture forced to seek sustainable patterns of interaction with the natural environment but infested with a technology that often becomes an end in itself. A wooden building can present us with a reconciliation of humans and nature, creation and finitude, in a silent and, for that reason, more powerful way than words. What the building embodies, in this respect, is something we can grasp, but it does not force itself upon us as a truth to which we have to surrender. Neither is meaning just projected upon the building. The elements we reflect upon and reflect with exist independently of ourselves as individuals, but in experiencing them, we bring them to life.[56] The parallels between the building, the trees, and our bodies are there for us to perceive. This does not mean, of course, that we necessarily pay attention to them.[57]

It could be objected that we do not really have to construct in wood, for example, in order to present these themes of reconciliation: a wooden cladding would be enough. But if knowledge frames the way we experience the character of a building, that is, the way it appears to us, then a clad building with a concrete skeleton will not, lastingly, present us with the same apparent and real reconciliation of nature and culture as a wooden construction. The same argument holds, *mutatis mutandis,* for the reconstruction of historical sites. There is also another, more directly sensuous reason for the difference, namely, that a building is not only a visual environment. Materials influence atmosphere, humidity, and the auditory and olfactory microclimate.

One of the parallels of the wooden house and the human body has to do with time, the influence of which is perceptible in a building made of natural materials. We cannot but see that no reparation is final; we shall always have to continue. There is much to take care of in a wooden house, which suggests that the wooden culture glorifies processes and dynamic continuity rather than single, completed accomplishments. Individuality is not threatened, but more closely connected to and interwoven with temporal and spatial tissues. Aesthetically, this is enriching.

The ability of a building to integrate natural processes in its appearance is an additional quality, compared to buildings on which the climate only produces clashes or cracks. This perceptual richness is partly due to a suggestion, presented by the building, on which we can reflect. But it works also on a more everyday, less reflective level. To be aware of what happens to a building, to follow how it reacts in time to different seasons and weather is to be simultaneously aware of oneself as an experiencing subject in a particular inhabited environment. As Mikel Dufrenne observes, experienced space is temporalized space, space made intimate.[58] It would seem reasonable to say that intimacy and habitation, or dwelling, come hand in hand. Of course, all spaces are potentially indwelt spaces, spaces of interiority and intimacy, but they are not equally apt for dwelling. The signs of the nature that moves us are among the elements which make it easier for us to dwell, silently, but not mutely, when space appears as place.

Concluding Remarks

Reasons to pay attention to the naturally unplanned in our built environment are found through diagnoses of forms of contemporary life. In a thoroughly planned, technocratic society, temporal depth and difference as well as the relating, non-privative individuality that this gives rise to are scarcity values. At the same time they are vital for the quality of life. The problem is that if we try to solve these problems through methods of planning alone, difference will probably stop making a difference: in thinking the other only as opposite to the known we cannot avoid its becoming swallowed by "the logic of the Same."[59] Another alternative, outlined here, is to step back at certain points and allow things to be and become, in their own ways.

Aesthetics helps us to focus on values that are central to the enjoyment of life, but we must also remember that axiology and politics are necessarily related in reflecting on the good life. Different answers and directions are possible. What is important is to realize that to choose one demands a response to the world and an acceptance of our situation as acting out of and in a finite, conditioned freedom, instead of clinging to an ideal of objectivism that represents alternative courses of action as abstractly displayed before us.[60]

Acknowledgments

Early versions of this chapter were presented at the conference "Architecture and Culture in Transition: Order and Chaos in Urban Context" in Tampere, Finland, 17–19 March 1995 and "Nature—Man-Made Environment," in Lahti, Finland, 7–12 August 1995. I thank participants in these for their comments. Special thanks go to Arnold Berleant and Emily Brady, who have helped me with perspicacious comments on the later version.

Notes

1. My idea of the naturally unplanned is differently focused but close to George Simmel's idea of nature as part of building in "Die Ruine," *Philosophische Kultur: Gesammelt Essais von George Simmel* (Potsdam: Gustav Kiepenhauer Verlag, 1923), 135–143.
2. Aldo Rossi, *The Architecture of the City,* tr. Diane Ghirardo and Joan Ockman (Cambridge and London: MIT Press) (first published in Italian 1966), 18.
3. Karsten Harries, *The Ethical Function of Architecture* (Cambridge and London: MIT Press, 1997), 363.
4. Both "nature" and "earth" are often used to refer to something that is outside conceptual mastery. This is an important point with these words, compare John Sallis, *Stone* (Bloomington and Indianapolis: Indiana University Press, 1994), 9. On various meanings of "nature," see Arthur Lovejoy, "'Nature' as Aesthetic Norm," *Essays in the History of Ideas* (Baltimore: Johns Hopkins University Press, 1948), 69–77. For two related but different notions of "earth" compare Holmes Rolston, III, *Conserving Natural Value* (New York: Columbia University Press, 1994), 203–36, and John Sallis, *Double Truth* (Albany: State University of New York Press, 1995), 37–55.
5. Compare Merleau-Ponty, who describes the world we perceive as an "open and indefinite unity," Maurice Merleau-Ponty, *Phènomènologie de la perception* (Paris: Gallimard, 1992) (first published 1945), 351. The limit of knowledge holds true for any particular individual. No matter how much information can be stored in a computer, *human* knowledge remains limited.
6. The evaluative polarization of nature and culture is today reversed by many, but this solves no problems. Among the most extreme is the Finnish author and fisherman Pentti Linkola, who has suggested the killing of humans in order that other species might live. Dichotomies blind us to real and concrete problems, which are typically complicated and need local solutions.
7. The Latin word *cultura* comes from the verb *colere,* to cultivate. This sense is still present in the French language, see, for example, *Grand Larousse Encyclopèdique en dix volumes,* (Tome troisième, Paris: Librairie Larousse, 1960), 709–10. This meaning is noted by Heidegger and integrated in his concept of building-dwelling as one of its central aspects, Martin Heidegger, "Bauen Wohnen Denken," in *Vorträge und Aufsätze* (Pfullingen: Günther Neske, 1954), 145–62: 147.
8. This is the model of Merleau-Ponty's *chiasm,* which in his latest, unfinished work is pre-

sented as a basic ontological structure, Maurice Merleau-Ponty, *Le visible et l'invisible,* Paris: Gallimard 1991 (first published 1964), 268, 316–19, 321–22, 328.

9. Hannah Arendt, *The Human Condition,* Chicago: University of Chicago Press 1958, 150. Compare J. S. Mill on nature as "what takes place without . . . the voluntary and intentional agency of man," quoted in Robin Attfield, "Rehabilitating Nature and Making Nature Habitable," in Robin Attfield and Andrew Belsey (eds.), *Philosophy and the Natural Environment* (Cambridge: Cambridge University Press), 45–57, especially 45.

10. Alvar Aalto (1941), "Euroopan j Alleenra Kentaminen tuo pinnalle aikamme rakennus-taiteen keskeisimmän probleemin" (The reconstruction of Europe brings up the most central problem of the architecture of our times), *Arkkitehti* (Finnish Architectural Review, 1941), 75–80, especially 78–79.

11. Heidegger, "Bauen Wohnen Denken," 146, 149.

12. Ibid., 157. Heidegger does not here claim that persons belong to particular places where they would have to spend the rest of their lives. His observation, at the end of the article, that homelessness summons us to dwell, instead supports the idea of dwelling as an activity and an ability, 162, 161.

13. Ibid., 146–48, 152, 161.

14. Ludwig Wittgenstein, *Tractatus Logico-Philosophicus* (Suhrkamp Verlag, 1963), 89 (section 5.6).

15. See M. C. Dillon, *Merleau-Ponty's Ontology* (Bloomington and Indianapolis: Indiana University Press), 265, note 61.

16. A development of "in-between" as a central epistemological and ontological notion relevant for this approach is found in F. G. Asenjo, *In-between: An Essay on Categories* (Center for Advanced Research in Phenomenology and University Press of America, 1988), esp. 44–60.

17. For an overview, see Kenneth Frampton, *Modern architecture. A Critical History. Revised and enlarged edition* (London: Thames and Hudson, 1985), 42–50.

18. Max Horkheimer and Theodor W. Adorno, *Dialektik der Aufklärung. Philosophische Fragmente* (Frankfurt am Main: S. Fischer Verlag, 1969).

19. See, for example, Martin Heidegger, "Die Frage nach der Technik," "Wissenschaft und Besinnung," and "Das Ding," all in *Vorträge und Aufsätze,* 13–44, 45–70, 163–81. The relations between critical theory and Heidegger are discussed by Fred Dallmayr, *Life-world, Modernity and Critique: Paths between Heidegger and the Frankfurt School* (Cambridge: Polity Press, 1991), especially 44–104.

20. A relevant reference here is Max Weber's analyses of different types of rationality, where modernity is characterized by the dominance of rule-governed rather than value-oriented action. Stephen Kalberg, "Max Webers Typen der Rationalität. Grundsteine für die Analyse von Rationalisierungs-Prozessen in der Geschichte," in *Max Weber und die Rationalisierung sozialen Handelns,* Hrsg. Walter M. Sprondel u. Constans Seyfarth (Stuttgart: Enke, 1981), 9–38: 31.

21. An influential example of time-space abstraction in architectural theory is Siegfried Giedion, *Space, Time and Architecture: The Growth of a New Tradition* (Cambridge: Harvard University Press, 1952; in German, 1941). Compare Sokratis Georgiadis, *Siegfried*

Giedion: An Intellectual Biography, tr. Colin Hall (Edinburgh: Edinburgh University Press, 1993), 115–21.

22. Harries, *Ethical Function of Architecture,* 210.
23. Giorgio Agamben, *Infancy and History: The Destruction of Experience,* tr. Liz Heron (London and New York: Verso, 1993).
24. Kenneth Frampton, "Towards a Critical Regionalism. Six Points for an Architecture of Resistance," in Hal Foster, (ed.) *The Anti-Aesthetic: Essays on Postmodern Culture* (Port Townsend: Bay Press, 1985), 16–30:17, 27–29. Frampton borrows the distinction of culture and civilization from Paul Ricoeur, whose view on the dialectic between these two is rather optimistic, "Civilisation universelle et cultures nationales," in *Histoire et vèritè* (Paris: Seuil/Esprit, 1995), 286–300 (first published 1961).
25. Admittedly, some corporations have funds for charity or environmental programs, but this is not the rule, and the reasons might be based on marketing research rather than altruism. For a discussion of the technosphere, see Georg Henrik von Wright, *The Tree of Knowledge and Other Essays* (Leiden, New York, Köln: E. J. Brill, 1993).
26. Ibid., 190–191.
27. See Emmanuel Lévinas, *Totalité et Infini. Essai sur l'extériorité,* (Dordrecht: Kluwer Academic/Le Livre de Poche 1994: section III, "Le visage et l'extériorité" (first published 1971), compare Lévinas, *Autrement qu'Ître ou au-delè de l'essence* (Dordrecht: Kluwer Academic/Le Livre de Poche, 1996), 116–29 (first published 1978).
28. For a concise argument, see Yi-Fu Tuan, *Topophilia. A Study of Environmental Perception, Attitudes, and Values* (Englewood Cliffs, N.J.: 1974), 5–12, 175, 189–91. In environmental aesthetics generally, the implied paradigmatic mode of environmental experience is the kind of direct, multisensuous human-environment interaction typical of walking.
29. For an account of automobile engagement verging on psychosis, see J. G. Ballard, *Crash* (London: Vintage, 1995) (first edition 1973) or David Cronenberg's film version of the novel.
30. Bernhard Waldenfels, "Gåladngar genom landskapet," tr. William Fovet and Björn Sandmark, *Nordic Journal of Architectural Research* 7:1, 57–65:63 (trans. from and first published in *In der Netzen der Lebenswelt,* Frankfurt am Main: Suhrkamp 1985).
31. Robert Venturi, Denise Scott Brown, and Stephen Izenour, *Learning from Las Vegas: The Forgotten Symbolism of Architectural Form.* Revised ed. (Cambridge, Mass.: MIT Press, 1988) (first edition in 1977), 3–72.
32. Heidegger, "Das Ding," 163.
33. Waldenfels, 58, 59.
34. The otherwise rich English language deplorably lacks the distinction of *Erfahrung* and *Erlebnis* found in many other languages (German, Swedish, Finnish). That there are two words reminds us of the fact that experience is not only here and now, but sedimented, and carries the there and then both backward and forward.
35. Harries, *Ethical Function in Architecture,* 168.
36. Jean-Francois Lyotard, "The sublime and the avantgarde," tr. L. Liebmann, G. Bennington, and M. Hobson, in Andrew Benjamin (ed.), *The Lyotard Reader* (Oxford: Basil Blackwell, 1989), 196–211.

37. "Criteria of judgment are used only when we reflect upon the human contribution in changing the natural environment. . . . Critical aesthetics focuses on the interaction of humans and nature." (my translation). Aarne Kinnunen, "Luonnonestetiikka" (Aesthetics of nature), in Aarne Kinnunen and Yrjö Sepänmaa (eds.), *Ympäristöestetiikka* (Helsinki: Gaudeamus, 1981), 35–56.

38. See Harries, *Ethical Function,* 215. Compare Björner Torsson, who argues that the mimetic element in architecture is related to the adaptation of space to the presence of a moving and acting human body, "Vad föreställer ett hus? Kring mimesistemats möjligheter i arkitekturen" (What is a house a representation of? On the applicability of *mimesis* in architecture), *Nordic Journal of Architectural Research* 7:1 1994, 49–56.

39. Michael Polanyi, *Personal Knowledge: Towards a Post-Critical Philosophy* (Chicago: University of Chicago Press, 1958), esp. chapter 5.

40. Ibid., 98, also 120. This can be compared to J. J. Gibson's or Merleau-Ponty's ideas of perception as an activity, James J. Gibson, *The Senses Considered as Perceptual Systems* (Boston: Houghton Mifflin Company, 1966), Merleau-Ponty, 1992.

41. An example of an "art of knowing" where the tacit component plays an important role is riding a bicycle, which cannot be learned formally, by learning rules, Polanyi, *Personal Knowledge,* 49–50. The only way to test this knowledge is through performance.

42. Compare Maurice Merleau-Ponty, *La prose du monde* (Paris: Gallimard, 1995) (first posthumous edition in 1969), 190–193.

43. I use this spelling to underline the meliorative element: eutopy refers to the best place rather than nonplace. See M. I. Finley, "Utopianism Ancient and Modern," *The Use and Abuse of History* (London: Penguin Books, 1990), 178–92, especially 178.

44. R. W. Hepburn, "*Wonder" and Other Essays: Eight Studies in Aesthetics and Neighboring Fields* (Edinburgh University Press, 1984): 13. The quotation is from the seminal article "Contemporary Aesthetics and the Neglect of Natural Beauty" (first published 1966). More reflections on the metaphysical and existential relevance of nature appreciation are found in the final chapters, 131–83.

45. I can only hint at the relevance of Lévinas' notions of passivity and proximity here, Lévinas 1996, 78–99, 129–55, 223; compare Elisabeth Weber, "Anamnèse de l'immémorial. A propos de *Autrement qu'Être ou au-delè de l'essence* d'Emmanuel Lévinas," *La différence comme non-indifférencethique et altérité chez Emmanuel Lévinas,* sous la direction d'Arno Munster (Paris: Éditions Kimé), 69–96, especially 72–73.

46. Compare Frampton's characterization of what he calls critical regionalism in architecture: "It is opposed to the tendency in an age dominated by media to the replacement of experience by information," *Modern Architecture,* 327. He emphasizes the tectonic and the tactile rather than the scenographic or the visual as primary aspects of building. Also in Frampton, "Towards a Critical Regionalism," 27–28.

47. Harries, *Ethical Function,* 209.

48. Merleau-Ponty, *Phenomenologie de la perception,* 1992, 344.

49. Douglas Davies, "The evocative symbolism of trees," *The Iconography of Landscape: Essays on the Symbolic Representation, Design and Use of Past Environments,* Denis Cosgrove and Stephen Daniels (eds.) (Cambridge: Cambridge University Press, 1989) (first edition 1988), 32–42, especially 33.

50. Sallis 1994, 114.

51. Ibid., 88–89.

52. Harries, *Ethical Function*, 122.

53. Ralph Waldo Emerson, "The American Scholar" (first published 1837), in Carl Bode in collaboration with Malcolm Cowley (ed.), *The Portable Emerson*. New edition. (Harmondsworth: Penguin Books, 1981), 51–71.

54. Compare Sallis 1994, 90, 104–5 (these pages refer to Martin Heidegger, "Der Ursprung des Kunstwerkes" in *Holzwege*, vol. 5 of *Gesamtausgabe* (Frankfurt am Main: Vittorio Klostermann, 1977).

55. This is also Simmel's point, "Die Ruine."

56. Davies, "Evocative Symbolism," 33.

57. These qualities are iconic if that, as Peirce describes, is a feature of a sign which represents its object "mainly by its similarity," and also in the sense that these qualities do not say anything about actual relations, in Charles Hartshorne and Paul Weiss (eds.) *Collected Papers of Charles Sonders Peirce*, vol. II (Cambridge: Cambridge University Press, 1932), 157 and 143–44.

58. Mikel Dufrenne, *Phénoménologie de l'expérience esthétique* (Paris: Presses Universitaires de France, 1992) (first edition 1953), 349–50.

59. Lévinas 1994, 21–45.

60. Compare Merleau-Ponty, *Phenomenologie de la perception*, 1992, 517–20.

CHAPTER 6

What Is the Correct Curriculum for Landscape?

Allen Carlson

The Central Question of Environmental Aesthetics

IN HIS CLASSIC WORK, *The Sense of Beauty,* aesthetician, philosopher, and poet George Santayana characterizes the landscape as follows:

> The natural landscape is an indeterminate object; it almost always contains enough diversity to allow the eye a great liberty in selecting, emphasizing, and grouping its elements, and it is furthermore rich in suggestion and in vague emotional stimulus. A landscape to be seen has to be composed . . . then we feel that the landscape is beautiful. . . . This is a beauty dependent on reverie, fancy, and objectified emotion. The promiscuous natural landscape cannot be enjoyed in any other way.[1]

With these few words, Santayana sets the stage for the central question of environmental aesthetics. The landscape, he says, is indeterminate and promiscuous. To be appreciated it must be, as he puts it, composed. But yet its appreciation is dependent upon all that is vague and whimsical, upon reverie, fancy, and emotion. Thus, the problem posed, the central question of environmental aesthetics, is that of *how* the landscape is to be composed in order to facilitate its appreciation. And furthermore, among all of the vague and whimsical stuff upon which this composition might depend, *what* is really relevant to a landscape's appropriate aesthetic appreciation?

In this chapter, I address this central question of environmental aesthetics as an issue in aesthetic education. The question is that of exactly *how* to appropriately appreciate a landscape and of exactly *what* is relevant to such appreciation. If aesthetic education is the business of teaching appropriate aesthetic appreciation, then, concerning the landscape, the key question is that of what to teach those in whom we wish to instill the appreciation of landscapes. What skills, what talents, what information, what knowledge must we give to our children, and indeed to our peers and even to ourselves, in order to engender a rich, appropriate appreciation of landscapes? To put it in another way: What is the correct *curriculum* for teaching the appropriate everyday aesthetic appreciation of landscapes? In what follows, I approach this question by working through a number of topics each of which might be considered a candidate for such a curriculum. I consider eight different items, inquiring of each what role, if any, it should play in the curriculum. The eight items are the following: 1. form, 2. common knowledge, 3. science, 4. history, 5. contemporary use, 6. myth, 7. symbol, 8. art.

The Postmodern View of Landscape Appreciation

Before considering these eight items, however, it is useful to note one point of view, which, if correct, would seemingly make the whole question of a correct curriculum for appropriate landscape appreciation quite pointless. It might be argued that if, as Santayana suggests, the landscape is indeterminate and promiscuous, if it is such that its appreciation is dependent upon that which is vague and whimsical, upon reverie, fancy, and emotion, then it follows that anything and everything, and nothing in particular, should be included in the curriculum. When it comes to the aesthetic appreciation of landscapes, this point of view suggests, it is not a matter of appropriate or inappropriate appreciation, but simply a matter of "the more, the merrier." Without, I hope, doing too much injustice to all concerned parties, I call this point of view the postmodern view of landscape appreciation. I select this label for two reasons: first, because of the obvious and frequently made comparison between the landscape and a text and, second, because of one postmodern position on the reading of a text. This is the position that in reading a text, we rightly find not just that meaning its author intended, but any of various meanings that the text may in one way or another have acquired or that we may for one reason or another find in it. And, moreover, and this is the important point, none of these possible meanings has priority, no reading of a text is privileged.

On the postmodern view of landscape appreciation, whatever of Santayana's vague and whimsical reverie, fancy, and emotional response we may bring to the landscape is seemingly as good as any other, no reading of the landscape is privileged. On this view, it is perfectly fine, to take an example from Ronald Hepburn, that if "the outline of our cumulo-nimbus cloud resembles that of a basket of washing, . . . we [simply] amuse ourselves in dwelling upon this resemblance."[2]

In short, there is no appropriate appreciation of landscapes and thus no correct curriculum for landscape appreciation. Those who subscribe to the postmodern view of landscape appreciation might find support for their position not only in Santayana's remarks about the landscape as indeterminate and promiscuous, but also in some of his comments on aesthetic education. He says, for example: "Aesthetic education consists in training ourselves to see the maximum of beauty."[3] Indeed, looking for the *maximum* of beauty certainly sounds a lot like the aforementioned "the more the merrier" idea. And one might think that to obtain the *maximum* of beauty, that is, the richest form of appreciation, everything is relevant and nothing should be excluded. However, Santayana's comments on aesthetic education also contain the seeds of a refutation of the postmodern view. We must *train* ourselves to see, he says, the maximum of beauty. The implication is that seeing the maximum of beauty, attaining the richest appreciation, is a matter of training, of learning. Vague and whimsical reverie and fancy may give us an occasional thrill, a delight in this or that possible reading, or a chuckle at a puffy floating-by basket of washing. But ultimately it will give us only titillating chaos, not the richest possible appreciation of landscapes. For such appreciation we need training, and for training we need a correct curriculum, not just anything, everything, and nothing in particular.

Consequently, I leave the postmodern view, at least for now. In doing so, I suggest that insofar as we maintain the parallel between the landscape and a text, we should do so, at least initially, with the somewhat out-of-fashion, modernist notion of the reading of a text. On this view, at least some readings of a text are mistaken: misinterpretations that are simply read into it, rather than, as it were, read out of it. Likewise, I think some readings of the landscape are mistaken, that is, misinterpretations that are not a basis for appropriate appreciation. Thus, there is the possibility of mistaken, inappropriate aesthetic appreciation of landscapes. I assume this view of landscape appreciation for now and use it as the background assumption as we work through the above-noted eight topics, asking about the role of each, if any, in the correct curriculum for the appropriate aesthetic appreciation of landscapes. Thus, the question is: which topics should be included as proper parts of the curriculum and which are only a dimension of postmodern landscape appreciation?

Form and Content

With this background, I turn to the first of the eight suggested curriculum items, what I label form. By this term, I mean something like that which traditional formalist theoreticians, such as British art critic Clive Bell, refer to as significant form, that is, aesthetically moving combinations of lines, shapes, and colors. I think it is difficult to deny either that the appreciation of form in this sense is an important dimension of aesthetic appreciation or that it is relevant to the appreciation of landscapes. Even Bell, whose focus is almost exclusively on art, entertains the possibility of seeing the landscape as, in his words, "a pure formal combination of lines and colours"; for example, at one points he asks: "Who has not, once at least in his life, had a sudden vision of landscape as pure form? For once, instead of seeing it as fields and cottages, he has felt it as lines and colours."[4] Bell has in mind something like seeing a landscape as it might look in a Cezanne landscape painting. And he is correct in thinking that we frequently appreciate landscapes in this formal manner. It is a mode of appreciation imposed on the landscape not only by certain kinds of landscape painting, but also in a less subtle way by many popular presentations of landscapes, such as postcard images, in which dominant shapes, strong lines, and striking colors are emphasized. Such images facilitate a superficial yet appropriate formal appreciation of landscapes. Consequently, I conclude that the correct curriculum for teaching the appropriate aesthetic appreciation of landscapes must include those skills and that information necessary for formal appreciation.

Having granted this much, however, it is important to resist the additional step that many formalists have taken. This is to insist that the formal dimension is not only a fundamental dimension of aesthetic appreciation but also the only dimension. As is well known, Bell and other formalists are notorious for holding that formal appreciation exhausts aesthetic appreciation, that consideration of form is all that is involved in such appreciation and that, by contrast, any consideration of content is irrelevant. However, as is also well known, there are many problems with this kind of pure formalism.[5] Moreover, concerning landscapes in particular there is one crucial problem. The problem is that, on the one hand, landscapes, as noted by Santayana, are indeterminate and must be composed to be appreciated, but, on the other hand, formal elements in themselves typically do not provide adequate resources for composing a landscape. This is in part because by reference to themselves alone the formal elements of a landscape can hardly even be identified. The way in which they are identified is by reference to something other than themselves, typically by reference to content. For example, consider any formally impressive landscape, say, a forested mountain landscape with one major and two minor peaks, and ask yourself: How many shapes does it have? One? Three? Or about three hundred? How many lines does it have? The point is that in order to identify the shapes and the lines in a landscape, we make reference to content. If we say there is one basic shape, this is in part because one major thing, the major peak, is present. If we say three, it is because three things, the major peak and two minor ones, are taken as constituting its content. If we say about three hundred, it is because we are taking each identifiable tree as identifying a particular shape. These considerations demonstrate that the formal appreciation of a landscape in terms of shapes, lines, and colors necessitates the essential consideration of the content of that landscape. In short, in landscape appreciation we cannot appreciate form without considering content.

If formal appreciation requires us to also consider content, this takes us beyond pure formalism and beyond the first item of our suggested curriculum items. It shows that the correct curriculum must include content as well as form. However, it should be clear that all of the remaining seven candidates for the curriculum are in one sense or other content items. Thus, the question is: Which and how many of these are relevant? Consider the first item after form, which I label common knowledge. By this I mean the normal classifications and categorizations we employ in our common sense conceptualization of the world. It is in fact the kind of knowledge that pure formalists such as Bell seek to exclude from aesthetic appreciation. Bell, as noted, requires us to see the landscape in terms of shapes and colors and *not* in terms of fields and cottages. Ironically, however, if the above argument is correct, this is the exact knowledge required for formal appreciation of landscapes, for it is by reference to these common sense conceptualizations that we typically organize or, to use Santayana's term, compose a landscape. We compose, for example, the above-described mountain landscape by reference to that which we conceptualize by means of classifications such as mountain, peak, tree, and so forth. Thus, this basic kind of content is seemingly required for any aesthetic appreciation of landscapes whatsoever. It must be an essential part of the correct curriculum, although it hardly needs extensive treatment in teaching the curriculum, for it is the kind of knowledge we acquire in our language learning and in our socialization.

Science and Landscape Appreciation

The third candidate for the correct curriculum I label science, by which I mean the natural history of a landscape as it is elaborated by the natural sciences, especially geology, biology, and ecology. I discuss the role of scientific knowledge in the aesthetic appreciation of landscapes elsewhere, so I do not dwell on it here.[6] I only briefly note two arguments, which demonstrate that scientific knowledge of landscapes is as vital to their aesthetic appreciation as is common knowledge, and thus that it must have an equally central place in the correct curriculum. The first argument depends on the fact that in one important sense scientific knowledge is simply an extension of common knowledge. A scientific conceptualization of a landscape may be finer-grained and theoretically richer than a common-sense conceptualization, but it is not essentially different in kind. Compare two descriptions of a typical mountain landscape: first, a common-sense description of it as a series of rocky peaks jutting forth from a surrounding rolling valley; and, second, a scientific description of it as faulted igneous uplifts exposed by the erosion of surrounding sedimentary deposits. There is, of course, some of what might be called conceptual movement from the common-sense description to the scientific one. However, what is important here is that insofar as this movement makes any difference in appreciation of the landscape, it does not involve a change from aesthetic appreciation to something else. Rather, if there is a difference in appreciation, it is a movement from superficial to deeper aesthetic appreciation, that is, what Hepburn describes as "a passage . . . from easy beauty to difficult and more serious beauty," or, in other words, a movement away from the "basket-of-washing" appreciation of his clouds.[7] Thus, according to this line of argument, scientific knowledge deepens and enhances the appropriate aesthetic appreciation of landscapes that is initiated by our common knowledge.

The second argument for granting scientific knowledge an essential place in the correct curriculum involves a comparison with the aesthetic appreciation of art. The argument takes for granted that in the appropriate aesthetic appreciation of works of art, the knowledge that is provided by disciplines such as art history and art criticism is essential. Such knowledge is without doubt included in the curriculum for art appreciation. Moreover, the knowledge that these disciplines provide about art is knowledge about the nature of and the creation of works of art, in short, knowledge about the classification and categorization of works and about what might be called their "histories of production." And, this is the kind of knowledge that science provides about landscapes. For example, geology classifies and categorizes the elements of landscapes and tells the story of how they came to be—their histories of production, as it were. Thus, for the same reasons that art critical and art historical knowledge is given a prominent place in the curriculum for the aesthetic appreciation of art, scientific knowledge must be given a similar place in the curriculum for the aesthetic appreciation of landscapes. In light of this argument, and the previous one, I conclude that the essential reading list for the correct curriculum must include the works of natural historians, naturalists, and scientifically informed nature writers, individuals such as John Burroughs, John Muir, Aldo Leopold, Joseph Kurtch, Marston Bates, Sally Carrighar, Sigurd Olson, Loren Eiseley, Barry Lopez, Ann Zwinger, David Quammen.[8]

Historical and Contemporary Uses of Landscapes

We now have what might be thought of as the heart of the correct curriculum for the appropriate aesthetic appreciation of landscapes. It includes the first three items of the initial suggestions: form, common knowledge, and scientific knowledge. Does it follow that the remaining five items, history, contemporary use, myth, symbol, and art, are not essential in the correct curriculum? Does it follow that these should be involved only in postmodern appreciation? In fact, the comparison with art appreciation would seem to indicate this. Consider the next item, which I call history. By this I mean the historical use of a landscape rather than its natural history. The comparison with art appreciation seemingly suggests that the history of a particular landscape in this sense is indeed irrelevant. This is because the history of a particular work of art is usually thought to be irrelevant to its aesthetic appreciation. For example, for most standard works of art, historical facts such as that the work was first displayed in a certain place, was then shipped here and there, and is now at a particular gallery would not normally be considered relevant to its appropriate aesthetic appreciation. For instance, is knowing that *The Guernica* was displayed in New York City for many years before it was moved to Madrid significant for its appreciation? It seems to me that such information is not relevant. Or, that it is relevant only if we embrace the postmodern view that since no appreciation is privileged, anything that happens to interest us can be accepted as relevant.

However, I suggest that, on the issue of the relevance of landscape history to landscape appreciation, the comparison with art appreciation is somewhat misleading. There is an important disanalogy between landscapes and works of art that must be considered. It concerns the fact that typically a work of art is completed at a specific point in time. What happens to it before this point is what I called its "history of production" and, alternatively, what happens after the point of completion is its history. And typically while its history of production, like the natural history of a landscape, is clearly relevant to its aesthetic appreciation, its later history is not. By contrast, however, there is no specific point in time at which most landscapes are completed. For this reason their natural histories and their actual histories, their historical uses, are in a sense continuous, both constitute a single ongoing history of production. This is another sense in which landscapes can be said to be, using Santayana's terms, indeterminate and promiscuous: most landscapes are continually in the process of being made and remade. All that happens to them, their ongoing histories, continues to shape them.

The upshot is that for most landscapes knowledge of their ongoing histories is vital to their aesthetic appreciation. In fact, in many cases it is the most important key to such appreciation. Consequently, studies of the long term development of modern landscapes, such as, for example, W. G. Hoskins's seminal volume, *The Making of the English Landscape* and J. B. Jackson's classic studies of the American landscape, are absolutely necessary for the appropriate aesthetic appreciation of the landscapes in question. They, just as the works of the natural historians and naturalists noted above, must be essential reading in the correct curriculum.[9] Moreover, other less gradual and more dramatic changes in the history of a landscape, again because of how they shape a landscape, are equally a part of history of production and therefore equally aesthetically relevant. For example, consider two North American mountain landscapes: that of Devils Tower in Wyoming and that of Mount Rushmore in South Dakota. The former was set aside as the first United States National Monument in 1906. By this act it was removed from further development and change, and thus the act is in a negative sense extremely relevant to appreciating its present somewhat pristine state. Indeed, without this moment in Devils Tower's history, the tower today might be crowned with golden arches or sculpted into a great stone Mickey Mouse. On the other hand, Mount Rushmore, as is well known, was indeed sculpted, not into a stone mouse, but into likenesses of the heads of four United States presidents. Such a momentous event in a landscape's history is obviously relevant to its appropriate aesthetic appreciation. In a similar fashion, another mountain in South Dakota is presently in the process of being turned into a sculpture of the great Sioux leader, Crazy Horse. Without knowledge of this, it is impossible to appropriately appreciate the mountain's current state.

This brings us to the fifth candidate for inclusion in the correct curriculum, what I call the contemporary use of a landscape. Once we see past the misleading nature of the analogy with art and thus come to understand the way in which the fourth item, the actual history of a landscape, is relevant to its aesthetic appreciation, it should become clear that this fifth item is equally relevant. The contemporary use of a landscape is continuous with its actual history just as that history is continuous with its natural history. All three are a part of its ongoing history of production. However, there is a difference between the history of a landscape and its contemporary use that is worth noting, if only because the difference tends to obscure the sameness of the two. This is that, seemingly in part because of our closeness to it, we as appreciators of landscapes are much more apt to regard the contemporary use of a landscape and the making and remaking that it brings with it in a negative fashion. We frequently consider the contemporary remaking of landscapes to be *abuse* rather than simply *use* and look upon it with aesthetic dismay. This is certainly true of some current uses of many natural landscapes. Consider, for example, the remaking of landscapes brought about by strip mining or clear cutting. Few view the resultant new landscapes in an aesthetically positive way. This is also true of many recent changes that are visited upon some traditional human landscapes. There is, for example, great concern about the changes that modern agricultural techniques are bringing to traditional farming landscapes.[10]

However, what needs to be stressed concerning this issue is that even if we regard the contemporary making and remaking of a landscape in a negative manner, this fact does *not* make knowledge of this part of its history of production irrelevant to its aesthetic appreciation. Here another analogy with art is helpful. Consider Michelangelo's *Pietà*. In 1972 it was attacked by a vandal with a hammer. After the attack the sculpture was reconstructed and missing fragments were replaced with a mixture of ground marble and polyester resin. Most likely we regard these dramatic events in the contemporary history of this work in a negative manner. However, given the way in which *Pietà*'s destruction and subsequent reconstruction necessarily brought about changes in the object and its appearance, knowledge of this part of its contemporary history is absolutely essential to its appropriate aesthetic appreciation. Along the same lines, consider the recent remaking of Michelangelo's works of art on the ceiling of the Sistine Chapel. In this case the remaking was brought about by cleaning, and, however one regards the results, it must be admitted that knowledge of this cleaning is vital to the appropriate aesthetic appreciation of the works in their present state. In fact, in many of such cases the knowledge may not only be essential to appropriate appreciation, but may actually help to make more positive appreciation possible, when without such knowledge such appreciation may be difficult. For example, the bright new, nearly pastel works in the Sistine Chapel are much easier to positively appreciate in light of the knowledge that the new look is the result of restoration, rather than of, for instance, retouching or, worse, updating. Thus, I conclude that knowledge of the contemporary use of landscapes has an essential, and perhaps even somewhat special, place in the correct curriculum for their appropriate aesthetic appreciation.[11]

Myth, Symbol, and Art

I have now considered the first five candidates for a possible curriculum and found all five to be essential components of the correct curriculum for appropriate aesthetic appreciation of landscapes. This leaves the last three items, which I label myth, symbol, and art. By these labels I indicate what are also *uses* of landscapes, in particular, the uses of landscapes within the mythical, symbolic, and artistic creations of different peoples and cultures. However, these uses, unlike the previously considered more concrete physical uses of landscapes, do not seem to be directly involved in the making and remaking of landscapes. Thus, the issue is whether or not we have finally left the essential curriculum and come, with these three uses, to items that play a role only in postmodern landscape appreciation. The question is: Is knowledge of these three uses of the landscape thus unessential and therefore best omitted from the correct curriculum? Before addressing this question, it is useful to briefly illustrate each of these kinds of uses.

The use of landscapes in mythical and folk traditions is common to most cultures. For example, consider again the previously mentioned landscape of Devils Tower. In the traditions of some native American cultures, principally the Cheyenne and Kiowa, it is the landscape of *Mateo Tepee* or "Bear Lodge." One version of the mythological account of the formation of the tower goes as follows:

> Eight children were there at play, seven sisters and their brother. Suddenly the boy was struck dumb; he trembled and began to run upon his hands and feet. His fingers became claws, and his body was covered with fur. Directly there was a bear where the boy had been. The sisters were terrified; they ran, and the bear after them. They came to the stump of a great tree, and the tree spoke to them.

It bade them climb upon it, and as they did so it began to rise into the air. The bear came to kill them, but they were just beyond its reach. It reared against the tree and scored the bark all around with its claws. The seven sisters were borne into the sky, and they became the stars of the Big Dipper.[12]

Such mythical accounts are frequently closely related to what I term the symbolic uses of landscapes. For example, in part because of its place in this myth, the Devils Tower landscape is considered a sacred place by some native American cultures, symbolic of the creation of the earth and the sky. It is said that when *Mateo Tepee* rose from the earth, it was the "birth of time" and "the motion of the world was begun."[13] Other landscapes have comparable symbolic roles within different cultures. Mountains and similar formations seem to be particularly good bearers of such symbolic import. For instance, Mount Fujiyama, as is well known, has a special symbolic role within the culture of Japan. Likewise, what were called the Shining Mountains by the early explorers of North America, actually the eastern faces of the Rockies as they caught the morning sun, are still for many the symbol of the American West as the ever-beckoning land of opportunity. And, of course, a landscape feature such as Mount Rushmore has, for obvious reasons, powerful symbolic importance for many Americans. Such examples could be multiplied almost endlessly. Consider not just Mount Rushmore, Mount Fujiyama, and Devils Tower, but the Matterhorn, Pikes Peak, Mount Kilimanjaro, the Black Hills, Mount Edith Cavell, Mont Saint-Victoire, Ayers Rock, Half Dome, Mount Ararat, Ship Rock, and Mount Olympus. Each in its own way has a symbolic role for certain individuals, groups, or cultures.

This brings us to the last of the eight curriculum candidates, the use of landscapes in art. This use is often connected to the mythological and symbolic uses. For example, the very common use of images of Mount Fujiyama in Japanese art is closely linked to its symbolic role within Japanese culture, each continually reinforces the other. Other examples have somewhat less intimate cultural ties. And they also differ in yet other ways. For example, many uses, like those of Mount Fujiyama, involve mainly images of landscapes, while some involve the use of actual landscapes: On the one hand, there are, for instance, Cezanne's many studies of Mont Saint-Victoire, where the mountain is only a source of various images; on the other hand, there are the uses of landscapes in environmental works of art, for example, works such as Christo's *Running Fence* and *Valley Curtain,* where the actual landscape is for a limited time a part of the work.[14] Perhaps somewhat intermediate cases are the uses of actual landscapes in realistic photographic and cinemagraphic works of art. The photographic images of photographers such as Edward Weston and Ansel Adams are for many the classic images of the natural landscapes of western North America. Equally classic, although perhaps in a somewhat different sense, is the use of the landscape of Mount Rushmore by Alfred Hitchcock in his 1959 thriller *North by Northwest.* Also equally classic, and perhaps classic in the same sense, is the use of the Devils Tower landscape by Steven Spielberg in the immensely popular 1977 science fiction film *Close Encounters of the Third Kind,* in which Devils Tower is the fictional landing site for visitors from outer space.

Having illustrated the mythical, symbolic, and artistic uses of landscapes, I turn to the question of the relevance of these uses to the appropriate aesthetic appreciation of landscapes. Is knowledge of these uses an essential part of the correct curriculum for landscape appreciation? Indeed, does such knowledge have any place at all in such a curriculum? Initially, a negative answer to this question seems intuitive. After all, who would want to hold that in order to appropriately aesthetically appreciate, for example, the landscape of Devils Tower, we need to know about the Cheyenne and Kiowa creation myth of the formation of *Mateo Tepee,* let alone about Spielberg's story of humankind's first "third kind" close encounter with aliens from outer space.[15] Likewise, to suggest that to appropriately appreciate Mount Rushmore we must recall *North by Northwest* seems ludicrous, and perhaps even unpatriotic. Intuitively it seems plausible to abandon such information to the vague and whimsical reverie and fancy favored by the postmodern view. Indeed, these seem to be just the right kinds of associations for postmodern landscape appreciation.

Moreover, in addition to this intuition, there is a more substantial reason for skepticism about the place of knowledge of mythical, symbolic, and artistic uses in the correct curriculum. It is that these uses of landscapes are seemingly essentially different in kind from the other items previously considered. As noted, the first two, form and common knowledge, are at the very foundation of the aesthetic appreciation of landscapes, and the next three, natural history, history, and contemporary use, all involve matters that directly impact the nature of actual landscapes. They constitute the histories of production of landscapes. Consequently, these items are relevant to the appropriate aesthetic appreciation of landscapes at least in part because they explain the way that landscapes are and thus explain the way that they look to us. By contrast, the mythical, symbolic, and artistic uses of landscapes seemingly have nothing to do with the histories of production of landscapes. Landscapes are not made and remade by these uses. Unlike the natural histories and the historical and contemporary uses of landscapes, the mythical, symbolic, and artistic uses leave landscapes just as they find them. The landscape of Devils Tower was not altered by being called *Mateo Tepee* nor by fictionally hosting humankind's first big close encounter of the third kind. Mont Saint-Victoire was not changed by Cezanne, nor was Half Dome remade by Ansel Adams. And even Christo, after his works of art are completed, religiously restores the landscapes he has used to their original condition.

In light of this seemingly significant difference between these last three items and the preceding five, it is tempting to conclude that the three indeed have no essential place in the correct curriculum. Thus, concerning the mythical, symbolic, and artistic uses of landscapes, it is also tempting to accept the postmodern view of landscape appreciation. Recall that this view allows that we may read in the landscape any of various meanings that it may in one way or another have acquired or that we may for one reason or another find in it. And, moreover, none of these possible meanings has priority, no reading of the landscape is privileged. Thus, the mythical, symbolic, and artistic uses are relegated to the realm of vague and whimsical reverie and fancy. Just as we may, if we fancy to do so, see Hepburn's cumulus clouds as a basket of washing, we may read the landscape text of Devils Tower in light of the myth of *Mateo Tepee* and its great clawing bear or in light of whimsical tales of close encounters with childlike aliens, but there is absolutely nothing to choose between the two different readings, neither reading is privileged. And thus knowledge of neither belongs essentially in the correct curriculum for appropriate aesthetic appreciation.

The "Close Encounters Phenomenon"

There is, however, something wrong with the postmodern view even for the mythical, symbolic, and artistic uses of landscapes. The view does not appear to do justice to the seeming importance and vitality of such landscape uses. The difficulty is illuminated by what I call, after Spielberg's film, the "Close Encounters Phenomenon." It is that, even if we believe that knowledge of, for example, the use of Devils Tower in *Close Encounters of the Third Kind* is absolutely irrelevant to its appropriate aesthetic appreciation, we may find, if we have seen the film, that it is almost impossible to free ourselves from its images. For instance, I have a photograph of my family standing at the base of Devils Tower, and I find it almost impossible to look at it without imagining a large ominous-looking space ship emerging over the top of the tower! It is as if we become caught in a state similar to that of the main character in *Close Encounters,* a character played by Richard Dreyfuss, who, because of an alien encounter that "imprints" the image of the tower in him, cannot shake it from his mind. He finds himself possessed by the image: he sculpts it in his mashed potatoes, he makes a mud model of it in the middle of his living room. In a somewhat similar way, once we have had an "imprinting" encounter with the film, it is difficult to shake its images from our minds. And they color our appreciation of Devils Tower. I think this "Close Encounters Phenomenon" is quite common.[16] For example, having seen Hitchcock's *North by Northwest* only once and many years ago, I yet have difficulty seeing Mount Rushmore without imagining Cary Grant and Eva Marie Saint scampering in the moonlight among the faces of Theodore Roosevelt, Lincoln, and Jefferson. And I expect there are native Americans who imagine *Mateo Tepee* and its great clawing bear when they look at Devils Tower. Moreover, this phenomenon has not escaped the notice of artists. For example, even though Christo faithfully restores the landscape sites of his works to their original states, when he was asked, "whether he thought that the canyon at Rifle Gap remained unaffected by having hosted *Valley Curtain,* he replied: 'Perhaps not. Was Mont Saint-Victoire ever the same after Cezanne?'"[17]

The "Close Encounters Phenomenon" reminds us of the extent to which, to paraphrase Wittgenstein: Our pictures hold us captive. Its significance here is that, because many of our mythical, symbolic, and artistic images of landscapes do in this way hold us captive, these uses of landscapes are after all more like the other uses than they at first appear to be. It is true that such uses are not a part of the history of production of actual landscapes. They do not make and remake actual landscapes and by this means explain how such landscapes look to us. Nonetheless, they yet have explanatory power concerning the way that landscapes look, at least with respect to the way they look to those who are held captive by the relevant images. We might say that the mythical, symbolic, and artistic uses of landscapes make and remake not the actual landscapes themselves, but rather the landscape images of individuals, of groups, or of whole cultures. We might characterize them as making and remaking imaginary landscapes in the individual or in the collective mind. And thus knowledge of these uses does indeed explain the way landscapes look to certain individuals or to members of certain groups or cultures. Of course, the explanatory power of the knowledge of these uses of landscapes is somewhat limited in that it is relative to specific contexts. Nonetheless, knowledge of these mythical, symbolic, and artistic uses of landscapes is yet in this contextually relativized way relevant to the aesthetic appreciation of landscapes.

Landscape Pluralism and the Correct Curriculum

The "Close Encounters Phenomenon" suggests yet another way in which landscapes can be said to be, returning again to Santayana's words, indeterminate and promiscuous: They lend themselves to and allow themselves to be appreciated in terms of the different landscape images that various individuals and cultures bring to them. It also suggests that concerning this dimension of landscape appreciation, perhaps the postmodern view is not quite suitable after all. Rather, what might be called landscape pluralism seems more appropriate. Like the postmodern view, the pluralist view accepts the comparison between the landscape and a text and recognizes that we can read in a landscape many of various meanings that it may have acquired or that we may find in it. However, unlike postmodernism, landscape pluralism holds that for particular readers, groups of readers, or cultures, some of these possible meanings have priority and thus constitute privileged readings of the landscape. Which readings are privileged depends upon which imaginary landscapes of the mind hold sway for individuals, groups, or cultures, that is, upon which landscape images hold them captive. Consequently, the pluralist view gives a contextually constrained role in appropriate aesthetic appreciation to mythical, symbolic, and artistic uses of landscapes. These uses, by means of contributing to imaginary landscapes of the mind, form the basis for contextually privileged aesthetic appreciations of landscapes. However, the knowledge required for such appreciation will not contribute to appropriate aesthetic appreciation in the same way in which knowledge of the histories of production of actual landscapes contributes to such appreciation. The latter is essential to the appropriate aesthetic appreciation of landscapes by any appreciator whatsoever, while the former is significant only for certain individuals, groups, or cultures.[18]

In conclusion, in light of this pluralist view of landscape appreciation, I return to the question of the correct curriculum for the appropriate aesthetic appreciation of landscapes. As noted, matters concerning form and common knowledge, together with information about the histories of production of actual landscapes, are essential to the appropriate aesthetic appreciation of landscapes by any appreciators whatsoever, while knowledge of various mythical, symbolic, and artistic uses is significant only in certain contexts. This difference suggests a model for a correct curriculum that includes one central core curriculum together with a number of alternative supplementary curricula. On this model, the core curriculum would include only material concerning the first five of our original topics, that is, form, common knowledge, science, history, and contemporary use, while the alternative supplementary curricula would cover the last three, that is, myth, symbol, and art. In aesthetic education, the core curriculum would be the basic curriculum to be taught in every context, while different supplementary curricula world be relevant or not depending upon the context in question. Perhaps by an approach to aesthetic education that utilizes such a combination of curricula, we may not only instill appropriate aesthetic appreciation of landscapes but also realize Santayana's "maximum of beauty." If so, we move toward achieving what he characterizes as the "marriage of imagination with reality" and identifies as the ultimate aim of aesthetic education:

> Aesthetic education consists in training ourselves to see the maximum of beauty. To see it in the physical world, which must continually be about us, is a great progress toward that marriage of the imagination with reality which is the goal of contemplation.[19]

Notes

1. George Santayana, *The Sense of Beauty: Being the Outline of Aesthetic Theory* [1896] (New York: Collier, 1961), 99.

2. R. W. Hepburn, "Contemporary Aesthetics and the Neglect of Natural Beauty," in B. Williams and A. Montefiore (eds.), *British Analytical Philosophy* (New York: Routledge and Kegan Paul, 1966), 305.

3. Santayana, 100–01.

4. Clive Bell, *Art* [1913] (New York: Putnam's Sons, 1958), 45.

5. I discuss these problems in "On the Possibility of Quantifying Scenic Beauty," *Landscape Planning* 4 (1977):131–72, and in "Formal Qualities and the Natural Environment," *Journal of Aesthetic Education* 13 (1979):99–114.

6. See "Appreciation and the Natural Environment," *Journal of Aesthetics and Art Criticism* 37 (1979):267–76, "Nature, Aesthetic Judgment, and Objectivity," *Journal of Aesthetics and Art Criticism* 40 (1981):15–27; "Nature and Positive Aesthetics," *Environmental Ethics* 6 (1984):5–34; "Appreciating Art and Appreciating Nature," in S. Kemal and I. Gaskell (eds.), *Landscape, Natural Beauty, and the Arts* (Cambridge: Cambridge University Press, 1993), 199–227; "Nature, Aesthetic Appreciation, and Knowledge," *Journal of Aesthetics and Art Criticism* 53 (1995):393–400; and "Aesthetic Appreciation of Nature," in E. Craig (ed.), *Routledge Encyclopedia of Philosophy*, vol. 6 (London: Routledge, 1998), 731–35. The topic is also discussed in a number of the essays published in Arnold Berleant and Allen Carlson (eds.), *Special Issue: Environmental Aesthetics, Journal of Aesthetics and Art Criticism* 56 (1998).

7. "Contemporary Aesthetics," 305. Also see Hepburn's "Trivial and Serious in Aesthetic Appreciation of Nature," in Kemal and Gaskell, *Landscape*, 65–80.

8. The works of the individuals listed are so extensive and so well known that it is neither practical nor necessary to reference them here. However, the following three collections provide a sample of the writings of most of these individuals, along with numerous others of equal note: William Beebe (ed.), *The Book of Naturalists: An Anthology of the Best Natural History* [1944] (Princeton: Princeton University Press, 1988); Daniel Halpern (ed.), *On Nature: Nature, Landscape, and Natural History* (San Francisco: North Point Press, 1987); Stephen Trimble (ed.), *Words from the Land: Encounters with Natural History Writing* (Salt Lake City: Gibbs M. Smith, 1988). It is worth pointing out that the Beebe volume is historically oriented, while the other two feature mainly contemporary work. The Halpern has a very useful annotated booklist compiled by the advisory editors as well as an excellent bibliography. Also of interest, in that they are the contributions of working naturalists, are the short pieces gathered together in John K. Terres (ed.), *Discovery: Great Moments in the Lives of Outstanding Naturalists* (New York: J. B. Lippincott, 1961). These four collections feature material reflecting primarily biological and ecological knowledge; for a selection of writings focusing more on geological information, see Frank H. T. Rhodes and Richard O. Stone (eds.), *Language of the Earth* (New York: Pergamon Press, 1981).

9. W. G. Hoskins, *The Making of the English Landscape* (London: Hodder & Stoughton, 1955); J. B. Jackson, E. H. Zube (ed.), *Landscapes: Selected Writings of J. B. Jackson* (Amherst: University of Massachusetts Press, 1970); *The Necessity for Ruins and Other Topics* (Amherst: University of Massachusetts Press, 1980); *Discovering the Vernacular Landscape* (New Haven: Yale University Press, 1984), and *A Sense of Place, A Sense of Time* (New Haven: Yale University Press, 1994). In addition to Hoskins and Jackson, there are, of course, many other individuals, most notably cultural geographers, whose writings

illuminate the landscapes that we have created. Many of them appear in the pages of the journal that Jackson founded and edited for many years, *Landscape,* and more recently in the more academic *Landscape Journal.* The following two collections provide an earlier as well as a more recent sample of this kind of material: D. W. Meinig (ed.), *The Interpretation of Ordinary Landscapes: Geographical Essays* (New York: Oxford University Press, 1979) and Michael P. Conzen (ed.), *The Making of the American Landscape* (London: Harper Collins Academic, 1990). The latter has a valuable bibliography. My own favorite landscape guidebook, which features what I think is a near-perfect blend of natural and cultural history is May Theilgaard Watts' classic work, *Reading the Landscape* [1957] (New York: Collier Macmillan, 1975).

10. I discuss these issues in "On Appreciating Agricultural Landscapes," *Journal of Aesthetics and Art Criticism* 43 (1985):301–12.

11. I argue for similar conclusions in "On Appreciating Agricultural Landscapes," ibid, "Reconsidering the Aesthetics of Architecture," *Journal of Aesthetic Education* 20 (1986): 21–27, and "Existence, Location, and Function: The Appreciation of Architecture," in M. Mitias (ed.), *Philosophy and Architecture* (Amsterdam: Rodopi, 1994), 141–64.

12. N. Scott Momaday, quoting his grandmother, in *The Way to Rainy Mountain* (Albuquerque: University of New Mexico Press, 1969), quoted in United States Department of the Interior, *Devils Tower* (Washington, DC: Government Printing Office, 1991), 1.

13. Ibid.

14. I discuss related issues in "Interactions between Art and Nature: Environmental Art," in *The Reasons of Art: L'Art a ses raisons,* P. McCormick (ed.) (Ottawa: University of Ottawa Press, 1985) and "Is Environmental Art an Aesthetic Affront to Nature?," *Canadian Journal of Philosophy* 16 (1986):635–50. For an introduction to environmental art, see Alan Sonfist's excellent collection, *Art in the Land: A Critical Anthology of Environmental Art* (New York: Dutton, 1983).

15. The intuition here is nicely exemplified in the Devils Tower guidebook in the National Parks "The Story behind the Scenery" series. It notes, in a somewhat normative tone, that although since its "cameo role" in *Close Encounters* the tower "has been host to millions of curious moviegoers," they "soon leave memories of the film behind to capture the geological, historical, and natural stories of the Devils Tower National Monument." Moreover, "today the 450,000 yearly visitors are in awe of the Tower for its own dramatic presense and not as the setting for an imaginary spaceship landing." See Stephen L. Norton, *Devils Tower: The Story behind the Scenery* (Las Vegas: KC Publications, 1991), 1, 20.

16. For example, the Devils Tower "The Story behind the Scenery" guidebook reports that after *Close Encounters* "the monument's attendance rates skyrocketed. For quite some time, the most frequent question became, 'Now, where did the spaceship land?'" Ibid.

17. This remark is reported in Donald Crawford, "Nature and Art: Some Dialectical Relationships," *Journal of Aesthetics and Art Criticism* 42 (1983), 56.

18. I develop a somewhat similar line of thought concerning mythological descriptions of landscapes in "Landscape and Literature," in *Aesthetics and the Environment: The Appreciation of Nature, Art and Architecture* (London: Routledge, 2000). However, I do not apply the same line to artistic, in particular, literary, descriptions of landscapes.

19. Santayana, 100–01. Different versions of this chapter were presented at The "Natturumal" (Nature's Voices) Conference, Reykjavik, Iceland, September 1998; The American

Society for Aesthetics, Rocky Mountain Div., Santa Fe, NM, July 1995; The American Society for Aesthetics, Pacific Div., Pacific Grove, CA, April 1995; The Canadian Society for the Study of European Ideas, Calgary, Alberta, June 1994; and The First International Conference on Environmental Aesthetics, Koli, Finland, June 1994. I thank those present for valuable suggestions, and I especially thank Yrjo Sepanmaa, in discussions with whom the basic idea of the chapter emerged.

CHAPTER 7

Wim Wenders's Everyday Aesthetics

Andrew Light

> *I don't ever want to make another film in which a car or a petrol station or a television set or a phone booth aren't allowed to appear.*
> —Wim Wenders

AN INQUIRY INTO the aesthetics of everyday life tempts a normatively social as well as a more purely aesthetic form of inquiry. For if we can argue that the world around us is beautiful or not, then we beg the question of whether we want to live in a world configured so that it preserves and respects that beauty, or else goes on indifferent to it. In this chapter I explore this intuition with respect to the representation of an aesthetics of the everyday, with strong social (even moral) overtones, in the work of the German filmmaker Wim Wenders.[1] In particular I will look at Wenders's portrayal of our relationship to built space in his 1973 film *Alice in the Cities*. My intention here is not so much to examine this film (or Wenders's broader body of work) as an aesthetic object in itself, but to argue that Wenders's work reflects a broader view of how we should aesthetically understand, and consequently value, certain kinds of spaces encountered in everyday life.

Rather than analyzing this film by itself, I frame this discussion in the context of a relevant debate currently under way in philosophy of technology, a subfield of philosophy that ought to be able to say something about the social, and perhaps aesthetic dimensions of everyday material life. In particular I look at the debate between Albert Borgmann and Andrew Feenberg on the possibility of technological reform for the purpose of enriching everyday life and consequently mitigating the pernicious effects of some modern technologies on social interaction. So, in addition to the general issue of what Wenders's *Alice* tells us about the normative dimensions of an everyday aesthetic, it will also be interesting to see if thinking through Wenders's films helps us to better envision the kinds of transformations called for by theorists like Feenberg and Borgmann. Hopefully, situating the film in this philosophical debate will help us to better understand its potential for understanding the aesthetics of everyday life while also demonstrating that some films can contribute to ongoing philosophical debates in their own right.

Of course, the tendencies in Wenders's work to provide us with novel ways of thinking through our relationship to built space is not the exclusive focus of his films. But there is enough there to "startle us," as Stanley Cavell would say, to see the important philosophical content of the films on these questions.[2] What becomes of these images, again following Cavell, is the raw material of film criticism, and in this case I would say, substantive philosophical inquiry.

Thick and Thin Spaces

Much contemporary work in philosophy of technology concerns arguments that different kinds of technology create different forms of social relations. Certainly one of the best examples of such a theory can be found in Albert Borgmann's distinction between devices and things. Borgmann's distinction expresses the intuitive difference between context-filled and contextless artifacts and the different social relationships they can engender. The richer sorts of technologies are called "focal things," (or just "things"). Our active engagement with these things are called "focal practices."

Things, Borgmann argues, are inseparable from the context in which they are embedded. To stand in some relation to a thing is to engage in the social relations that it helps to make up. The benefits of a thing cannot be reduced to only one identifiable commodity.[3] The social relations created by the wood stove in the frontier North American prairie house is Borgmann's paradigmatic example of the complex effects of focal things on human relationships. Each person fulfills a special function in relation to the stove with some gathering the wood, others stoking the stove, and others cooking.[4] The stove is in this sense a medium for family life in at least three ways: it provides temporal regularity for the household, marks the different seasons, and serves as a locus for familial responsibility, and in that respect, individual identity.

We can also acquire skill in relation to things, as in the case of the wheelwright or blacksmith. Skill in relation to a thing "molds the person and gives the person character."[5] The skill we get in relation to things helps to shape our identity. Our engagement with the world through focal things potentially enriches our engagement with others as it thickens our own identity.

A conceptual universe away, for Borgmann, is the "device." Here is the foreground of modern mass technologies for which the world of things is the rapidly receding and contrasting background.

A device such as a central heating plant procures mere warmth and disburdens us of all other elements. These are taken over by the machinery of the device. The machinery makes no demands on our skill, strength, or attention, and it is less demanding the less it makes its presence felt.[6]

As an artifact that needs no particular context, devices do not connect us to particular places, relationships, or forms of agency. We can enjoy devices almost anywhere, anytime, with anyone. Since we do not need to engage with devices in the same way that we do with focal things, they do not require the skills we would have needed to use their counterpart focal things. As a consequence, however, we lose whatever identity we had through our connection with focal things. This in turn diminishes the quality of any social relations that may have been influenced by our identification with specific focal practices. It is because of this focus on the pernicious effects of devices on our social relationships that Borgmann calls his theory the "device paradigm."

But how does Borgmann's ontology of technology help us to understand more complex technical systems and relationships? Can the claims of the theory be extended to conglomerations of artifacts—for example, everyday social spaces, both public and private, such as cities and suburbs?

In principle the theory should be extendable to discussions of space. The first reason is that one common method of making a normative argument for evaluating social spaces is to evaluate their component parts. This is a defensible assumption provided that an important rider is attached: while such a theory may offer a necessary component of a full description of a space, it probably won't be a sufficient description in most cases. I am not arguing that cities, for example, are solely reducible to their parts. Several writers have adequately pointed out that a full description of a city must include other elements. But an analysis of cities as collections of things and devices is at least an important part of a full account of the character of that space.[7] If a space is dominated by one type of artifact, and we have a good theory of the normative implications of that artifact type, then a legitimate claim can be made that the normative assessment of the artifact type can be extended as an important part of the description of that space.[8]

For Borgmann, following the device paradigm, we can therefore say that there are both *thick* everyday spaces (constituted by focal things) and *thin* spaces (constituted by devices). We might then argue that the world of the suburb, dominated at first glance by its devices of convenience is a thin space, and older, more densely-populated cities, even with all of their problems, are thick spaces. But such a simple dichotomy will not work. While it is certainly true that material spaces can be dominated by one primary artifactual type, or one mode of experience, scale can sometimes add to complexity. We can expect to find thick and thin (or thing-like and device-like) spaces of many types and many combinations. The trick, following Borgmann, would be to unearth the terrain of complexity of a space under the weight of the device paradigm, and then to carefully discern the things and devices in each space.

Borgmann's theory is concerned with how technologies affect human identities and human relationships. By extension, whatever can be understood about the dominant artifacts of a space should help us to assess the probable social effects of that space. So by providing a theory for how artifacts socially influence us, Borgmann has already provided us with a way to account for spatially influenced identities and relationships. The preferred normative content of social space given the device paradigm should be clear: thick spaces that give us a sense of *place*. This is the second reason the device paradigm ought to be easily extended to questions of space. Borgmann's theory is in essence a social aesthetic of place and how artifacts shape our everyday sense of place. We are better off, on Borgmann's account, when we attach ourselves to a specific location for specific reasons. One might say that our view of the world is thus aesthetically enriched by such interaction. Borgmann's is not a theory of how isolated individuals relate to artifacts, but how artifacts shape us in relation to others to form places, or, thick spaces.[9]

But as Borgmann's view is not explicitly aesthetic, we need a further comparison to bolster this interpretation. Philosophical reflection on this nexus of artifacts, spaces, and places—on the intuition that an investigation of one of these areas entails (or perhaps requires) an investigation of the others—is central to what Henri Lefebvre was working toward in his *Critique of Everyday Life*.[10] Though too complex to go into here, Lefebvre's target is an "unearthing of the human world that lies buried" beneath the commodofied world.[11] Or, following the device paradigm, an investigation of the possibilities of thing inspired relationships in thick spaces despite the abundance of devices. Lefebvre's thesis here stands in striking contrast to other European critics of the first half of the twentieth century who had degraded the everyday. For Lukács the everyday is *Alltäglichkeit*, or, "trivial life," the world of objects that drearily stands in contrast to "authentic life" found in works of art. But following Lefebvre, one can argue that there is an aesthetic to be found in the everyday and it can be contrasted not with the arts as institutions but with an overly commodified and deviced life.[12] Both the fine arts and the aesthetics of the everyday stand against the homogeneity of thin spaces and deskilled practices. Indeed, Lefebvre contrasts the everyday with "the modern," where modernity marks out certain pernicious forms of technology.[13] We can therefore also describe a serious reflection on spaces and artifacts, following Lefebvre and perhaps Borgmann, as an investigation into the aesthetics of everyday life.[14]

But before going further, let us contrast Borgmann's approach to technology, with its everyday aesthetic implications for the understanding of space and place, with a different view advocated by Andrew Feenberg. Feenberg's focus is on the potential for modern commercial technologies designed for passive use and consumption to contribute to social injustice. One of his central claims however is that public involvement, either in the design process or at the point of consumption, can result in what he calls a "subversive rationalization" of those technologies. Successful subversions occur when the social relations embedded in the design process are overcome in an act of "democratic technological change."[15] Feenberg's examples include the subversion of the Minitel videotext system in France from a passive information technology to an interactive network connecting thousands of people for purposes never anticipated by its creators. In this example, the French government sponsored the production and distribution of information retrieval units in private households primarily for the purpose of supporting government services. For example, train schedules and tickets could be called up and purchased over this primitive electronic mail system. But eventually users learned to "hack" the Minitel and subverted the social role of the design of the machine for a variety of purposes.[16] The transformed videotext service was used both to clandestinely arrange for sexual liaisons and to organize protests against government policies.

Feenberg's argument assumes a description of technological design that is socially relative. Political intents can be built into designs, and designs can have unintended political consequences. Artifacts and technical systems need not necessarily exert social control, but because they often do a more critical theory of technology than Borgmann's is needed to give an account of the peculiarities of different forms of design. We might, however, ask after the breadth of the processes described by Feenberg's notion of subversive rationalization. Is this process limited only to artifacts or can it be extended to more complex systems and everyday built spaces as well?

Feenberg identifies his subversion thesis as a conscious political strategy. But such strategies are surely not the only way to resist the potentially pernicious effects of a technological environment. Following the suggestion of the aesthetic implications at work in Borgmann's device paradigm, we might presume that artistic representations of technology, space, and everyday life which stand against dominant forms of social control could also serve the process of subversive rationalization.

But this conclusion leaves us with a bit of a tension. While Borgmann's device paradigm might in the end be useful for examining the everyday aesthetics of artifacts and spaces, it is not sufficient to explain the transformative potential in some technology that theorists like Feenberg envision. Borgmann has given us a way of describing different kinds of social relations mediated by different kinds of technology, but he has not given us an argument for how we can transform the relations (aesthetic or otherwise) produced by one form of technology to those embodied by another.[17] How do we thicken spaces and hence improve the social relationships they affect?

Because of problems like this Feenberg finds substantive theories such as Borgmann's inherently conservative.[18] Such theories, he argues, tend to embrace a romantic notion of what we have lost, or of the importance of a sense of place that is not helpful when faced with the problem of transforming the world of mass-commodity devices. Is there instead a way to give particular devices, or systems of devices, thing-like qualities, or at least expand and open up what we take to be the world of focal things? I think there is. But an account of such transformations ought to do something Feenberg's argument does not—it ought to begin with Borgmann's assumptions that there really are different sorts of technology, and hence spaces, which have different social effects. In what remains of this chapter I will argue that Wim Wenders's films provide an example of an everyday aesthetic that encompasses an account of spatial and technological subversion while also clearly marking out different types of artifacts and spaces. It therefore combines the virtues of both Feenberg's and Borgmann's theories.

In Wenders's work we find an interesting description both of the transformative potential of particular technologies, and new social relations possible within built spaces. Mass commodity devices are subverted in these films to serve the interests of focal practices and thick spaces. New social relations can be created, or at least, aesthetically represented, where we do not ordinarily see such potential.

A World on the Road

Many of Wenders's films are driven in part by a desire to reappropriate something that has been corrupted: first, our appreciation of everyday material culture and second, our sense of place in an environment of increasingly sterile and characterless built spaces.[19] These two tasks are not distinct for Wenders as a film-maker—he embraces Béla Balázs's idea that film as a medium is supposed to "show things as they are" and specifically, "*rescue the existence of things.*"[20] Film-making itself is sometimes a heroic act because it halts "the gradual destruction of the world of appearances." "The camera is a weapon against the tragedy of things, against their disappearing."[21] This explains the quotation that opened this chapter. Wenders was expressing his frustration over his own production of *The Scarlet Letter*. There, because of the need for representing a kind of historical authenticity, Wenders wasn't allowed to show the things and built spaces in the vicinity of the production site.[22] Wenders's films ought to be a good candidate for an analysis of the everyday aesthetics of built space if only because he is so concerned with representing and holding onto the world of focal things.[23] Wenders's films are inextricably linked to some place, not just as a description of the landscape but as an occasion to call attention to the materiality of the space itself. Wenders, Lefebvre, and Borgmann all argue that the everydayness of space should be preserved against the erosion of its thick materiality by a commodified culture.[24]

Let us examine one of Wenders's films, *Alice in the Cities,* with an eye first toward its commentary on the aesthetics of built space and briefly second, toward its appeal to the potential to preserve the focal quality of film itself.[25]

The First Road Trip

Alice is bracketed by two road trips, the first in the United States and the second in Germany. The first trip is an exposition of the banality of the world of devices as located in American suburban and, increasingly, urban space. Our protagonist, Philip Winter, is first seen under an unidentified pier, taking pictures with a Polaroid camera, comparing the view with its photographic representation.[26] Slowly, the film provides some sense of location, but only vaguely. A water tower advertising the place as "surf city" puts us on a coast somewhere in the United States. Spanish moss on trees along the highway make the Southeastern United States a likely candidate for the opening sequences.

Eventually, we learn that Philip is a German journalist on assignment to write an article about America. The specific topic is never mentioned consistent with the sense that his travels lack focus. Philip is only collecting images by taking pictures, images that, he says, in some of the first lines of the film, "never really show what you've actually seen." But since Philip is never able to accurately express what the images do not reflect, it is unclear if any *thing* (in Borgmann's sense) is really being seen at all, or any place ever encountered.

The opening sequence captures the banality of American highway culture, an endless stream of monotonous sameness for which there is only one overriding relationship: commodities and consumers. Philip drives through this commodified wasteland with increasing frustration. He starts talking to himself in a mixture of English and German, gets frustrated with the babble of commercial radio, and shows signs of coming apart. One outburst goes like this:'

"To shoot pictures." (English)
"Mow down anything you can't stand." (German)
"Channel 6. WTVR!" (English)
(pause)
"Talking to yourself is more of a listening than talking." (German)[27]

The theme of searchers getting frustrated out on the road is a common one in Wenders's films. Robert Philip Kolker and Peter Beicken argue that the common road theme in the films is indicative of Wenders's fascination with searching. But unlike John Ford's *Searchers* (a film and a director much admired by Wenders),

Wenders's characters are not clearly looking for anything. Kolker and Beicken claim that Wenders's male characters "rarely gain insight into the traumatizing conditions and the hidden forces that drive them." They search without reason and what they ever find is not altogether clear.[28]

But in this case I think Philip has found something. Paradoxically what he has found is the aesthetic impoverishment of suburban spaces, or perhaps more accurately, the spaces between cities. Later in the film Philip returns to New York City (where we eventually learn he had launched his trip). In trying to explain his journey to a German friend he lets us know what he has found on the road:

> Soon as you leave New York everything looks the same. It seems impossible to imagine things being different. I completely lost my bearings. All I could imagine was things going on and on. Sometimes on the road, I was sure I would turn back next morning. But still I went on and on and listened to that sickening radio. And in the evening in the motel, looking just like the previous one, I watched that inhuman television. I almost took leave of my senses.

Even if it is true, following Kolker and Beicken, that Philip (as a standard Wenderian searcher) is only interested in more movement without clear reason, one of the consequences of his travel is a discovery of the banality of thin space.

We can clearly ascribe Borgmann's description of the device paradigm to the world on the road created in the opening sequences of the film. But if this was all we could get from this story, it wouldn't be very interesting in the context of the previously mentioned philosophical discussion. There are many texts from which we could draw images that correspond to Borgmann's picture of the world as constituted by devices. And hence, many places from which we could make the argument that the device paradigm can be applied fairly straightforwardly to discussions of the aesthetics of everyday space.[29] But the remarkable element of this film is that even with the banality of the road, there is something out there that Philip also maintains could have been retrieved as thick space.

New York

In *Alice* the first indication that Philip might have found something significant on his trip comes out during a conversation with his New York editor once he returns from his seemingly aimless wanderings. In this scene, consistent with Kolker and Beicken's interpretation, Philip seems genuinely confused with what he has come across in his travels. Confronted with the editor, angry that no story has been produced in all this time on the road, Philip shows him his many pictures. These instant images, flawed on Philip's own account, are evidence that he has seen *something*. Philip maintains that the pictures are crucial to the story he is writing, but he cannot offer any explanation as to their significance. In fact, we never really find out the relationship between the photographs and the article in progress. We can conclude however (from the opening shots of the film) that their narrative significance rests on their inability to represent whatever it is that Philip thought he saw on the road.

At least Philip's disappointment with the Polaroids is understandable. Instant photographs are a poor excuse for photographs. The images are bad, insofar as they embody a cheap flat copy of the world. But if suburban built space really is as thin as Borgmann's device paradigm suggests, ought not such an image suffice? For Philip it seems that the answer is no. The image is flawed because it does not reproduce the world as he at first perceives it. In the opening sequences Philip seems genuinely disappointed with the pictures, remember, not simply because of their poor quality, but because they don't show what he has seen and found worth noting.[30]

There is other evidence in the film which also suggests that the quality of the images is not the source of Philip's malaise. From at least one other perspective we have reason to believe that Philip's need for representation is a symptom of a deeper problem. The type of representation really doesn't matter; the problem is Philip. We get this view from Philip's aforementioned New York friend. In answer to Philip's suggestion that he almost "took leave of his senses" on the road, she replies, "But you lost them a long time ago. No need to travel across America for that." Philip's identity, she claims, is empty, perhaps as empty as the open road. So empty at least, that he needs external confirmation of his experiences to verify them. His need to take pictures on the road is ground in his peculiar solipsism. This she claims is the point of the photographs. They provide needed proof that Philip really exists: "Your stories and your experiences are handled by you as if you were the only one to experience things. That's why you keep taking those photos," she says, "further proof that it was *really you* who saw something."[31]

Even if this is true, the first point raised by the New York friend still needs answering: Why does Philip have to travel across the United States as evidence of his rootlessness? Why can't he simply wander around New York City taking unsatisfying pictures?[32] One answer is that since the pictures are thematically connected to the wanderings, it is helpful for them to be viewed together. But this answer seems too simple. The film takes pains to show us particular spaces on Philip's trip, spaces that we may intuitively find as flat and thin as Philip does his Polaroids. While it is certainly true that Philip does not need to travel across America to learn that he had lost his identity, it may very well be the case that we needed to see him do this in order to infer another possible cause of his problems.

Philip's friend clearly sees his solipsism as a sickness, a sickness bound up in his stories and photographs. But it is plausible to interpret a significant part of Philip's problem to the disjunction between what he sees and the produced image rather than from the mere fact that he takes these pictures. It isn't the case that

Philip takes pictures of just anything, he carefully selects the images of spaces and things that he finds meaningful. But the attempt to preserve them as thick spots on a thin field of view falters. Following Borgmann, the importance of thick built space is its grounding effect for our identification with a place. If this is true then the claim by Philip's friend that he has lost his identity may be spatially diagnosed: Philip has no sense of identity because he has no sense of place. He has no place because there is no space that grounds his identity. At the very least, the searches compound his identity problems when the spaces he passes through suffocate him in their homogeneity. Such spaces will not provide an identity that could pull him out of his solipsism. The New York friend is partly wrong in her diagnosis of Philip's sickness. Philip's need to represent his experience with photographs is not itself the problem. The cause of his malaise is his thin relationship to any kind of spatial representation that in turn is caused by his susceptibility to the identity problems associated with thin space.

The general worry in the film then can be argued as follows: aesthetically thin spaces help produce thin personal identities. Though Philip may think he sees something on the road, something that perhaps may enrich his identity, the surrounding device-like environment corrupts his access to thicker spatial relationships. If there are thick spaces in the world that can help his identity he needs some better way of gaining access to them, some more secure way of holding onto their meaning. But more importantly, the narrative appears to suggest that there is a particular harm that results from a banal built landscape: thin spaces produce a thin self incapable of meaningful human contact.

Working on the assumption that for Philip, and for many of us, built space has implications on the health of our identities, then it is in part through the access to new spaces that we may enrich our identities. On the question of how to gain access to new spaces, the film moves closer to Feenberg than to Borgmann. Philip is not just moved to better surroundings to cure him of his solipsism. He does not realize the aesthetic cause of his problems and then embrace thicker spaces as the solution. Though he does decide to return to Germany after getting back to New York, there is no clear indication that he thinks this change will really improve his state. Instead, following the established connection in the film between spaces and their produced image, Philip will be provided with a new way of seeing the world, which will help him to hold onto the thickness of some places. This move will be closer to Feenberg's idea of subversion. From here on Philip will see essentially the same world (and the film will use noticeable aural and visual cues to signify the capacity of European spaces to be as thin as American), though it will be seen in a new way. A new lens will emerge that helps Philip to see built space differently, subvert the homogeneity of thin space by bringing out the thickness that it masks, and most importantly, help him to learn to secure the thickness of those spaces to his identity.

Introducing Alice

The new lens is provided by another human. A child, Alice, who Philip meets in New York at an airline ticket agency where she is trying to get back home to Germany with her mother. Alice becomes the new medium which provides Philip with fresh descriptions of the world, even a world on the road. The embodiment of the new lens in another person seems appropriate, as it represents the shift from one of the newest forms of representation, the Polaroid camera, to perhaps the oldest—the descriptions we get of things through the eyes of other people.

Like Lewis Carroll's protagonist, this Alice finds herself in a wonderland, but here, a wonderland of cities. When Philip first sees her he watches for some time as she plays in a revolving door, perhaps reminding us of how things and spaces can be transformed for alternative purposes other than those reasons for which they are designed. The city is alive with possibility for Alice, as perhaps it could be for Philip. But it is Alice who must remind him of the pleasures of the thick cityscape. Philip becomes engaged with the city space with her. In a wonderful scene he pretends to blow out the lights on the Empire State Building from Alice's hotel room window. He later takes her to the top of the building and surveying the cityscape, has no need to try to capture it in Polaroids.

Still, the picture of this transformation of perspective for Philip is not so simple. It is not the case that Philip is simply drawn into Alice's perspective, and it is certainly not the case that once her perspective is introduced the film is transformed into a merry Disney-esque precocious tyke movie. Philip must be drawn into this new way of seeing, and into this thicker world, slowly and with difficulty. After an initial fascination with Alice, a break comes when, following an excursion to the city, Philip returns her to her hotel room and discovers that he will have to take her to Europe alone. Alice's mother will follow and meet them later.

The strain of suddenly being left alone with Alice becomes wearing. This new responsibility, though ultimately transformative for Philip, breaks any easy association connecting the way Alice sees things with the ability of Philip to recognize thick spaces in the world. In the airport, getting ready to fly home (via Amsterdam because of a ground-crew strike in Germany) he finds her absorbed in a coin-operated television and fascinated by the plastic wrapping on a premade sandwich. But everything cannot be renewed for him simply by seeing it through her eyes. The film's message about finding thick space cannot simply be reduced to an appeal that we should all think more like children. Even with these awkward moments, there are still times in this tense part of the film worth noting. Alice finds a Polaroid image of the sky taken from the plane window lovely *because* it is blank. But it is not the picture that is lovely, it is the amazing sky, noticed for a moment rather than simply passed through without recognition. But Philip resists such an aesthetic view for now. The numbness of pointless travel returns to him with the long flight to Europe. He appears to have nothing waiting for him there and he is burdened with a child, increasingly restless to be reunited with her mother.

The Second Road Trip

After Philip and Alice arrive in Amsterdam, Alice's mother fails to meet them at the airport as planned. After many tense scenes, the second road trip of the film begins. In desperation to find someone who can take responsibility for Alice, Philip agrees to try to find her grandmother who the girl believes is in the German city of Wuppertal.

The trip to Wuppertal begins with a sense of definite direction and purpose. This is not an aimless trip in search of a vague sense of a country, or of an identity, but a search for a particular thing—Grandma's house. All of the predictable metaphors of such a journey at times come into play. Still, any interesting new way of seeing the world that could be gained along the way is subsumed at first in the broader goal of disburdening Philip of responsibility for Alice. After checking into a hotel in Wuppertal the search begins, first by tram and then by car. Wenders uses repetitive, rather haunting, guitar music to signal the return of the monotony of the road. This monotony soon appears to effect Alice as it had Philip before. The fascination with the cityscape that Alice had for New York evaporates in Wuppertal.

After driving around the city for two days looking for the house, Alice reveals during a rest break at the hotel cafe that Grandma actually does not live in Wuppertal. This small city, so different from the aimless, nameless suburbia of the first road trip, has now also become subsumed into thin material space. Importantly, the reason is not for lack of something about the place. It is quite a lovely little city, with narrow streets and old buildings which seem to be ideal as the sort of spaces that Wenders must appreciate. But the significance of any space cannot only reside in its structural qualities but also must rest in part in the role one has in it. Like Borgmann's wood stove, the significance of the city is not only in the potential connection we may have with it, but also in the attachment we actually have with the thing. Like a wood stove in a museum, Wuppertal is interesting, but ultimately not actually connected to Alice. After this revelation any interesting meaning to this search has been lost and the closing road trip seems to be as pointless as the one that opened the film. The search for Grandma's house is as elusive now as the search for America. With the refrain from Canned Heat's "I'm On the Road Again" playing from the cafe jukebox, and the prospect of another frustrating journey ahead, a now penniless Philip takes Alice to the local police station and leaves her there.

A crucial turning point in the film comes next. After leaving the police station, Philip goes to a Chuck Berry concert. The concert revives him. Arguably it represents a rich reengagement with public spaces for him, and a participation in a technological practice which makes up that space. Live music, unlike the monotonous radio stations encountered on the road, can be a focal practice. Unlike listening to prerecorded music, live music is embedded in the context of the site of its performance and the interaction of the audience is part of the performance. Here, clearly for Philip, a new thinglike relationship with the world is stimulated through his participation in the concert space.

This everyday experience of attending the concert is enough to reawaken Philip to the thick aesthetic world of things, both artifactual and spatial. Lefebvre points out in his *Critique* that medieval festivals were both separate from and undeniably a part of everyday life. Similarly, the concert provides a pause and occasion to reflect upon the aesthetics of the everyday by highlighting a space for a moment. This experience may later thicken one's interaction with other everyday spaces. The camera moves in the scene between Philip and Berry, lingering on both as they are caught in moments of total absorption. By the end of the scene, even though there has been no dialogue, and no overlaid sound track or voice over has indicated a shift in the narrative, we know that a big change has occurred. The everyday aesthetic of the event has subverted the monotony of the experience of Wuppertal, and has provided a place in which the events of the road trip for Philip, and the film for the viewer, could be reconsidered.

Upon returning to the town, Philip finds Alice again, and rejuvenated, resumes the search. At a rest stop, Alice now remembers that Grandma's house is somewhere in the Ruhr and that she has a picture of it. This simple photograph, on which the continuation of the second road trip is ultimately based, is the key to a reading of the film that completes the narrative's social and aesthetic message about space. It also provides an opening for the filmmaker's argument about the technological practice of the medium of film.

Like Philip's pictures on the road in America, the picture of the house is an unimpressive image. Yet this picture is imbued with a meaning that Philip's Polaroids never had. Philip, through Alice, has a connection to this photograph because it stands for an end to the search. But now the end seems much more exciting. While the picture's significance could be reduced to its direct representational value, it is more than that. It is a reminder that searches need not be monotonous and pointless, and that identity can be figured concretely in space. The sense of movement in this part of the trip changes.[33] Though it is a difficult search—there is only a picture to go on and not even a name of a town—it continues for a definitive reason. Even the return of the lonely guitar music on the driving sequences here feels different. The act of searching, of traveling through space has been legitimated, and the music is more soothing than strange.[34]

Now we see too that the renewed journey is a road trip in a sense that the earlier part of the search for Grandma's house was not. This is not a mindless, endless drive around a city with which a tenuous connection is growing thinner, but a definite engagement with the open road between places. Philip, through Alice, feels the difference and the two of them appear to enjoy the trip—comically they stop at a roadside rest area and perform the recommended calisthenics. Alice's role resumes as the lens through which the world is seen new. Philip is now able to latch onto thick spaces in this engaged search and Alice helps him to retrieve the everyday aesthetic of the artifacts that compose those spaces. The two go to a drugstore automatic photo booth for pictures, and later in the film even stop for a swim.[35] There is enjoyment and proof of a growing connection between the two searchers. Philip also knows what the picture of Grandma's house means. There is no confusion as to what role it plays, as there was with his earlier photographs. It is not an image of space thought to be thick, whose meaning is lost by the time the image emerges. This is an image of something with prefigured meaning, a place that helps form the identity of a person to whom he is now intimately attached. Through Alice, Philip now has a thick relationship to a spatial representation.

Finally, with the aid of the picture the house is found. But just when we think the searching is over, we discover that Alice's grandmother is not there. She has long since moved away and the present occupants do not know where she went. At this point we might expect the film to return to themes of monotony and failed expectations. We might expect this last journey to become as banal as the opening journey of the film. But it does not. Even though the ostensible point of the trip, a journey to Grandma's house, has been irretrievably lost, the larger emphasis on traveling through space for a reason is regained.

The importance of the discovery of the house without Grandma should not be lost on us. If the point of the film was simply a romantic return to a pre-artifactual home (the sort of thing Feenberg worries is the goal of Borgmann's work), Grandma would have been there ready to welcome Alice home. But if the point of the narrative is more that physical space can have meaning and that identity can be thickly sustained in an aesthetically thin world, it is enough that Philip and Alice find the house and that the search ultimately enriches them. This is what happens, and to give away a bit of the ending now, the two never make it home in the film. They will continue searching as before, but now with a different sense of the possibilities of experiencing space.

Another point about this scene is crucial: when Philip sees Grandma's house it is ultimately because the picture was an accurate representation of a thing actually in the world. This is not a picture taken by a solipsist only as an attempt to convince himself of the existence of the outside world. This is a picture of a thing, a place, that has a connection to its observers and is important. The house, regardless of its present occupant, is a place embedded with meaning. Here the narrative manages to subvert the flatness of the photographs that had been held up earlier in the film as an example of the flatness of technical reproduction when faced with spatial banality. This experience makes it clear to Philip that the outside world really does exist and that its flatness is not caused by the camera. If mechanical reproduction destroys the "aura" of images, as Walter Benjamin claims, then perhaps Philip has discovered the lesson that artifactual and built space are not susceptible to poor reproduction simply because they were only aesthetically thin spaces in the first place.[36]

The rootedness of this picture replaces the ambiguity of all the previous photos, as the thickness of this place replaces the thinness of the previously encountered spaces. Importantly though, the key again is Alice. Without her connection to this place the thinness of space would have remained with him unresolved. Alice is the lens through which the picture and the place are recognized for their importance.[37]

Film as Technology

As we see Philip looking in amazement at the picture and the house in front of him, we can begin to see a new issue raised by the film. This is also an act of subversion, though now directed at the device-like qualities of image-making in general rather than at aesthetic or social considerations of space. This issue, though connected to the investigation of the narrative now in progress, is important enough for us to consider on its own before returning to the end of the film. It may be the most direct point raised by the filmmaker about the relationship between the arts and technology and further make the case for the importance of this film in understanding everyday aesthetics.

Much of the first wave of film theory focused on the technological aspects of film pointing out how its reproductive capacities both blessed and cursed this art form as compared with other media.[38] More recently, some Marxist-inspired critical theorists have argued that in Hollywood, for example, the techniques of film have all but destroyed the positive aesthetic qualities of the art.[39] If Hollywood has had a spillover effect to the medium as a whole, as many contemporary theorists worry, then Wenders's work represents a unique challenge to that form of technological hegemony.

To understand how this claim works, we will have to rethink the point of *Alice* as how *we* see things, rather than how Philip does. The reproduced images that we are most closely inspecting are not the Polaroids, or the picture of Grandma's house, but the film itself. Benjamin says that, "The audience's identification with the actor is really an identification with the camera."[40] In this film we are first asked to acknowledge the device-like qualities of the Polaroid's images, which in the beginning are the primary form of representation and understanding of the world for Philip. To take Benjamin literally, it is not too much of a stretch to also suggest that we are drawn into a consideration here of the kind of technology film has become as well. If we are critical viewers then once invited to consider the fate of one form of image reproduction, it makes sense to open up the question of others, particularly those we are engaged with at the moment.

Wenders's images are carefully constructed. It is clear from the beginning that we are watching an artistic text, something other than a standard Hollywood road movie. But the medium of film is unfortunately more associated with the worst banalities of device culture than with the subtle and rich social commentary typical of the New German Cinema. Movies often bear no relation to particular places, agents, or communities and often "disburden" us of the complexities of important events in our lives. The social role of film is often thought to be the escape it provides from everyday worry, rather than the engagement with the everyday it can provide. There is also little skill associated with watching mainstream Hollywood cinema; we are in fact encouraged not to be critical viewers, but simply to enjoy the images.

But at least with most of Wenders's films this is not the case. On all of Borgmann's criteria we relate to these films as a focal practice. First, the texts are rich with meaning, the context is specialized, and when we watch them we are drawn into a relationship with the issues they raise. Second, these films are not escapes from everyday life, they are attempts to formulate an everyday aesthetic in which the audience has an identifiable social role. Our identity in the film process is to be an active viewer, and as such our character is in part molded by our willful participation in the film. If Philip discovers the richness of things with Alice, we also make this same discovery with *Alice,* both about the world and about the possibilities of the medium of film. Finally, we are asked to acquire a viewing skill rather than only to passively consume the film's "entertainment value." Wenders makes us work through his films; they are not easy to watch. If most audiences do not have an ability to critically view this work, the films' social potential will be lost. Once we lose our ability to engage with film as critical viewers, challenging films will lose one of their most important components—an audience. If there is anything to the intuition that films are made to be seen, that they are produced in order to communicate a message to an audience, the lack of receivers for that message is a threat to the institution of film-making. But Wenders hopes to reverse this by making films like *Alice,* which sharpens our skills and our identities as viewers.[41]

But if Wenders's work is a presentation of films as a focal practice, then it is also a subversion (following Feenberg) of first, the Hollywood system, and second, the effects of video and television on the art of film making. As mentioned above, many critical theorists now claim that most films serve an ideology of homogenous mass cultural consumption.[42] Wenders (and other independent film-makers) have subverted that rationality by breaking out of the mainstream, producing films that are critical of the culture they often depict. Wenders films are clearly reactions to the artistic restrictions of the Hollywood system. An argument could be made that this system encourages just the sort of indifference to the subtleties of technology and built space that Wenders resists.

Against the effects of the Hollywood system Wenders has been very vocal. At Cannes in 1982 he set up a 16mm camera in a hotel room to film the reactions of several independent and commercial film directors on a question concerning just this subject. The film-makers were asked to enter the room, sit in front of the camera and answer the following question:

> Increasingly, films are looking as though they had been made for television, as regards their lighting, framing and rhythm. It looks as though a television aesthetic has supplanted film aesthetic. Many new films no longer refer to any reality outside the cinema—only to experiences contained in other films—as though 'life' itself no longer furnished material for stories. Fewer films get made. The trend is towards increasingly expensive super-productions at the expense of the 'little' film. And a lot of films are immediately available on video cassettes. That market is expanding rapidly. Many people prefer to watch films at home. So my question is: Is cinema becoming a dead language, an art which is already in the process of decline?[43]

This question amply demonstrates Wenders's concern. Notice specifically that part of his worry about the effects of television and large Hollywood productions is conjoined with a concern that film has become entirely self-referential in content. When Wenders suggests that "'life'" has dropped out of cinema I think it is fair to say that the concern is over the loss of an everyday aesthetic in film. To make films without passing on such an aesthetic to the viewer would not be very effective if the point of film is to create a viewing audience that resists the homogenizing trends of TV and Hollywood.[44] So, as Philip sees the picture of Grandma's house as something that has important representational value at last, we are directed to see this film in particular as having subversive potential against what Wenders sees as the mass cultural destroyers of the film art and hence of an everyday aesthetic.[45]

Conclusions

Now, let us return to the narrative and combine these different aspects of *Alice*. Where are we left with Philip and Alice? How is their journey finally resolved? After not finding Grandma at Grandma's house, Philip at first decides to take Alice to his parents who live nearby. Later, he learns that her mother has at last returned to Germany and the two travelers now continue at their leisure to reunite Alice with her family. The road itself, and the journey, and the aesthetic engagement with the world of thick spaces has been retrieved and focused. Philip and Alice continue more relaxed than they have been for the entire film.

But the film's message in the end is not an overly simplified claim that the thick space—city or suburb—is defined only by its subjective value. Something deeper is at work here. By the end Philip has learned that the banality of contemporary built space must be subverted in order to retrieve thick spaces from a thin landscape. He doesn't learn this lesson in these terms, but as a character he is transformed by exactly these sorts of processes. The film ends with a new journey by train, through a landscape in which we can imagine Philip is finally able to see more *things*. As the train journey begins we see Philip reading a magazine article about John Ford, possibly pointing out one last time that the film has shown that searching, movement through space, is still possible without being tainted by the malaise of homogenous space. We learn that Philip has decided to go to Munich and Alice asks him what he will do there. "I'll finish off this story," he replies. His identity as a writer, a chronicler of everyday aesthetics of sorts, has finally been restored. But this restoration was not accomplished by a simple move from thin to thick spaces, it was an act of subversion of aesthetically thin spaces, device relationships, and their effects on identity.

The final shot shows Alice and Philip opening the window of their train compartment and sticking their heads out for a better look at the landscape rolling by. We too are given a better look as the shot slowly pans back to a perspective above the train down on the travelers as they move forward. The search music fades back in and we know that the experience of moving through space for the searchers will continue better than before. They are not necessarily going home, or magically resolving their problems. But they are also not suffering as they had before in their misdirected movement from disconnected place to place. In this last shot the film dramatically brings to life movement forward through a landscape using a completely different shot not used in the film before. But not just the physical landscape is recovered, also the dying terrain (or as Wenders put it in the Cannes question, the "dead language") of film is restored. The last shot shows what a striking role film can play in reviving an everyday aesthetic if it is only employed for that reason.

For Wenders the journey of the film is his own, matching the subversion of space with a subversion of the film medium. Following Lefebvre, Wenders has unearthed the human beneath the world of Borgmann's device paradigm using Feenberg's subversive rationality. The film shows how the differences between the two philosophers of technology may in part be resolved. The film at least succeeds in challenging our sophisticated intellectual intuitions about the hopeless banality of built space, and the role of film in a subversion of the pernicious effects of that banality. Wenders has demonstrated by example how an everyday aesthetic may be preserved against the thinning out of everyday life.

Acknowledgments

My thanks to Allen Carlson, Ed Dimendberg, Dorit Naaman, Albert Borgmann, Andrew Feenberg, Murray Baumgarten, and Patrick Maynard for helpful comments on this chapter.

Notes

1. The opening quote for this chapter is from *The Logic of Images,* tr. Michael Hofmann (London: Faber and Faber, 1991), 8. My thanks to Camille Watts for giving me this wonderful book long before I knew I was interested in writing this chapter.
2. See Stanley Cavell, *Themes Out of School* (San Francisco: North Point Press, 1984).
3. Borgmann acknowledges that he is using "commodity" in a specialized sense here. He only means by this expression a way of answering the question "What is a device for?" He does not mean to associate this sense of a commodity with the economic term, which would of course consider artifacts entirely as abstractions. Certainly, though, we would have hoped he could have found a less confusing term.
4. Borgmann, *Technology and the Character of Contemporary Life* (University of Chicago Press, 1984), 42. For more background on Borgmann's views and critical discussions of them, see Eric Higgs, Andrew Light, and David Strong (eds.), *Technology and the Good Life?* (Chicago: University of Chicago Press, 2000).
5. Borgmann, *Technology,* 42.
6. Ibid.
7. See for example Kevin Lynch, *The Image of the City* (Cambridge, Mass.: Technology Press, 1960) and Michal de Certau, *The Practice of Everyday Life* (Berkeley: University of California Press, 1984).
8. Given the intuitive plausibility of this sort of argument, it is no surprise that many philosophers of technology have also been theoreticians of social space, in particular, cities and suburbs. Diverse theorists such as Murray Bookchin, John McDermott, and especially Lewis Mumford, not only have written on both topics, but also often used the same theoretical base for their criticism of certain types of artifacts and specific types of spaces. See for example Murray Bookchin, "Toward a Liberatory Technology," in *Post-Scarcity Anarchism* (Montreal: Black Rose Books, 1986), and *Urbanization without Cities* (Montreal: Black Rose Books, 1992); John McDermott, "The Aesthetic Drama of the Ordinary" and "Glass Without Feet: Dimensions of Urban Aesthetics," in *Streams of Experience* (University of Massachusetts Press, 1986); and Lewis Mumford, *Technics and Civilization* (New York: Harcourt, Brace, 1934), and *The Culture of Cities* (New York: Harcourt, Brace, 1938).
9. Let me preempt one possible misreading of this claim. I am not arguing that an extension of Borgmann's account would result in a critique of thin spaces interpreted as meaning sparsely populated. If thick spaces are inhabited by focal things, or at least share the relationships Borgmann wishes us to have with focal things, then thin spaces are those made up by devices, inhabited by devices, or share the relationships we associate with devices. A device-generated space need not be sparsely populated. A typical

thin space might be an overpass crowded with the same gas stations, fast food restaurants, and chain motels that are found all along North American highways. There is nothing distinct about these areas as places, and their virtue (to their owners) is that such franchises can be found anywhere and have devoted consumer followings. A thick space in contrast could be either a multifaceted, wonderfully crowded urban area, or a simple "mom and pop" store in the country that is marked by it distinct connection to its surroundings.

10. Henri Lefebvre, *Critique of Everyday Life: Volume I,* tr. John Moore (London: Verso, 1992).

11. See Michel Trebitsch's preface to the *Critique,* xxiv.

12. Ibid., xvii. Lefebvre puts it somewhat extravagantly: "In so far as a science of man exists, it finds its material in the 'trivial,' the everyday." Lefebvre, 133.

13. See Lefebvre's *Everyday Life in the Modern World* (London: Penguin Books, 1971).

14. Not surprisingly, Borgmann has made an attempt to extend the device paradigm to spaces, particularly cities. Borgmann argues that cities need to be preserved as bastions of what I am calling thick spaces and that their "energetically chaotic qualities" need to be preserved. See Borgmann, *Crossing the Postmodern Divide* (Chicago: University of Chicago Press, 1992), especially chapter five. I have some reservations about this application of the device paradigm because Borgmann introduces a wholly new distinction to talk about spaces and artifacts in this book—conglomerations of artifacts are either "real" or "hyperreal." I have questioned this change in Borgmann's argument in part because I think that the real-hyperreal distinction does not do any work that the device paradigm does not; instead, the old distinction should have been applied more straightforwardly. I am also worried that the effect of this shift may open up the possibility of a wholesale critique of city space using Borgmann's new distinction. See Andrew Light, "Three Questions on Hyperreality," *Research in Philosophy and Technology* 15 (1995), 211–22.

15. See Andrew Feenberg, *Alternative Modernity: The Technical Turn in Philosophy and Social Theory* (Berkeley: University of California Press, 1995), 3. For more on this argument also see Feenberg, *Critical Theory of Technology* (Oxford: Oxford University Press, 1992), as well as his "Subversive Rationalization: Technology, Power and Democracy," *Inquiry,* 35 (1992): 301–22, and *Questioning Technology* (London: Routledge, 1999).

16. See Feenberg, *Alternative Modernity,* chap. 7.

17. The reason for this gap in Borgmann's account is simply due to the fact that his argument is not structured so that such a transformative view is needed. It is not the case that Borgmann does not have a theory of social transformation. His claims are coherent without the sort of argument made by Feenberg. My argument is simply that Borgmann's and Feenberg's views would do better to incorporate part of the structure of each other's accounts.

18. Feenberg, *Critical Theory of Technology,* chap. 1.

19. These themes are familiar for anyone who has followed Wenders's career and can be picked up in a variety of his films—*Kings of the Road, The State of Things, Wings of Desire,* and others.

20. Wenders, *The Logic of Images,* 1, my emphasis. I am not suggesting that Wenders (or Balázs) is using "things" in Borgmann's philosophically substantive sense. There is however a striking resemblance between the two uses.

21. Ibid., 2.
22. Wenders mentions, for example, a two-story saloon that couldn't be changed to fit the historical requirements of the shots: "We would eat lunch in that saloon, sitting at long tables, but such genuine and arresting images of ourselves in the saloon (which we never shot) weren't allowed to appear in a film from which reality had to be strictly excluded, cut away like a bit of bad apple." Ibid., 8.
23. Of course I realize the problems with basing any substantive claim on the intentions of the artist. Nothing, however, hangs on the correlation I have identified here to the substance of my argument about the film's narrative.
24. Wenders would admit his focus on such themes is primarily true of only some of his films, specifically what he calls the "A" films—those that are in black and white that originate in his own ideas and impressions (rather than from someone else's script): "In these films, I saw my task as bringing in as much as possible of what (already) existed." Ibid., 56. Ed Dimendberg reminded me that Wenders is a great admirer of Siegfried Kracauer's *Theory of Film: The Redemption of Physical Reality* (Oxford: Oxford University Press, 1960), which is an explicitly Benjaminian theory of film. On that evidence we have a reason to think seriously about the A films as locations of a thick account of space, technology, and place.
25. While I hope it is clear that *Alice* demonstrates the potential of Wenders's films to sever as a commentary on the philosophical issue previously discussed, I realize that it is not the most accessible film in Wenders's filmography. The film has been out of print for over ten years and is not available in many video rental stores. But the themes covered in the film that I find of interest are common in much of Wenders's work. In a series of footnotes I have pointed out some common themes in this piece with other films that may be more readily available.
26. Wenders himself once did exactly this, getting a free camera from the Polaroid company to use in a trip across the United States.
27. Readers of Susan Sontag may see some similarities between the play on pictures and shooting here and the themes of *On Photography* (New York: Farrar, Straus, and Giroux, 1977). A complete argument for the connection between Wenders and Sontag still awaits treatment.
28. Robert Philip Kolker and Peter Beicken, *The Films of Wim Wenders* (Cambridge: Cambridge University Press, 1993), p. 36. This is the first significant book-length introduction to Wenders in English. Other titles in French and German include: Michel Boujut, *Wim Wenders* (Paris: Edilig, 1986); Uwe Küntzel, *Wim Wenders: Ein Filmbuch* (Freiburg: Dreisam, 1989); and, Reinhold Rauh, *Wim Wenders und seine Filme* (Munich: Heyene, 1990). Also, several books on the New German Cinema in English contain significant sections on Wenders: Thomas Elsaesser, *New German Cinema: A History* (New Brunswick, N.J.: Rutgers University Press, 1989); James Franklin, *New German Cinema: From Oberhausen to Hamburg* (Boston: Twayne, 1983); John Sandford, *The New German Cinema* (New York: Da Capo, 1980).
29. For theoretical examples, see McDermott, "Glass Without Feet"; Murray Bookchin, *The Limits of the City* (New York: Harper, 1974); and Patrick Ashton, "Urbanization and the Dynamics of Suburban Development Under Capitalism," in *Marxism and the Metropolis,* ed. William Tabb and Larry Sawyers (Oxford: Oxford University Press, 1984).

30. Interestingly enough, the picture that we first see him complain about is of an old petrol station that we know Wenders himself would find of interest as one of those things whose existence must be "rescued."

31. Kolker and Beicken would take these scenes as evidence for their claim that photographic images in Wenders's films are signs of angst and rootlessness. The artifact of the camera and of the produced image is directly connected to the aimless wanderings of the male characters: "The images made by the Polaroid camera or the five-and-dime photo booth become, for Wenders's characters, signs of their insecurity and a mark of their creator's interest in the problems of representing individual experience" (*The Films of Wim Wenders,* 42). But I will reject such a narrow interpretation of the photographs in this film. The role of image-making in identity problems shows up more directly in other Wenders's films. It is particularly evident in *Until the End of the World,* which warns us of the potentially hazardous connections between image production and self-identity. In this film several characters get addicted to watching the technically produced representations of their own dreams.

32. In fact there is one scene in New York where a cab driver shows signs of the same malaise suffered by Philip, evidently caused by driving around the city all day.

33. Again, contra Kolker and Beicker's interpretation of Wenders's searches as movement without reason, here a search is undertaken for a definite place in space.

34. The purposeful searching of this part of the film also does not fit well with Kolker and Beicker's claim that Wenders's films, in their search mode, "attempt to establish a transnational space, unstable and full of longing for someplace else" (*The Films of Wim Wenders,* 36). In *Alice* the second search, after Wuppertal, is not simply for any place, but a particular place imbued with a definite meaning. There is a longing for someplace else, but it isn't just any place.

35. There is no angst in the photo booth scene as Kolker and Beicken would assume (see note 31), and no staring at pictures wondering what happened to their images. The experience is clearly a happy one.

36. Walter Benjamin, "The Work of Art in the Age of Mechanical Reproduction," reprinted in *Film Theory and Criticism,* ed. Gerald Mast, Marshall Cohen, and Leo Braudy (Oxford: Oxford University Press, 1992), 669.

37. The way in which this particular image reminds Philip of the existence of thick spaces, and hence, of identities connected to places, also again answers Kolker and Beicken's earlier cited claim that photographs in Wenders's work are signs of a character's insecurity.

38. See Benjamin, "Work of Art."

39. See for example Doug Kellner and Michael Ryan, *Camera Politica: The Politics and Ideology of Contemporary Hollywood Film* (Bloomington: Indiana University Press, 1990).

40. Benjamin, "Work of Art," 672.

41. This theme of the deadening of the audience, and consequently of the social sphere of films and film-making shows up in several ways in *Kings of the Road.* There a film projector repairman travels through Germany and, among other themes, we discover with him the corruption and loss of local cinema in part caused by the disappearance of critical viewers. In one scene he attends a pornographic movie and notices that the image is marred by something obstructing the projector's lens. No one else in the theater seems to

notice anything. The repairman walks up to the projection booth to complain and finds that the projectionist has hung a small mirror in front of the camera's lens so that it projects a reverse image onto the back wall of the projection booth. When the repairman walks in the projectionist is masturbating to the image on the wall, which is the source of the obstruction of the image on the screen. One may interpret this scene to fit nicely into my analysis here: participation in the film is reduced to the most unreflective level of enjoyment and in such an atmosphere the quality of the image becomes relatively unimportant in the delivery of the needed stimulation.

42. See Kellner and Ryan, *Camera Politics.*

43. Wenders, *The Logic of Images,* 24.

44. Other, more recent films of Wenders also speak to this worry about the relationship between film and TV, or video. In his documentary, *A Notebook on Cities and Clothes,* Wenders experiments by shooting different portions of the film with a video camera, and others with an old film camera. He talks about the differences between the two and experiments with interviews that depict the subject on film alongside a delayed representation of the subject on a video screen. This is a hard film which requires a lot of skill on the part of the viewer, but it is clear by the end that there is at least an issue concerning the difference between the two mediums that must eventually be addressed by a critical audience.

45. I find telling Wenders's remark that, "Every film is also a documentary of itself and the way it was made" (*The Logic of Images,* 8).

PART III

Finding the Everyday Aesthetic

CHAPTER 8

Sport Viewed Aesthetically, and Even as Art?

Wolfgang Welsch

Introduction

The Status of Contemporary Sport: Mere Aestheticization, or Art?

There is no doubt that contemporary sport shows a highly aesthetic constitution—it can even be taken as a paradigm example of today's aestheticization.[1] But perhaps one could go further and not only connect sport with aesthetics but even consider it to be art.

Intuitively, it seems clear that sport isn't art. Although most people would agree with the idea that contemporary sport is highly aesthetic, very few—if any—would say that sport is art. But when I started examining the arguments for sport's exclusion from the sphere of art I found myself—to my surprise—in ongoing trouble. The conventional arguments turned out to be insufficient. Step by step they could be overcome by better counterarguments. The following considerations are a report on, and the result of, these reflections.

My hunch is that the modern transformations of the concept of art in particular allow sport to be viewed as art, and no longer allow this to be denied. So, in the foreground, the following reflections are about sport, while in the background they pertain to the concept of art.

Phenomenal and Conceptual Transformations— the Possibility and Admissability of Novel Categorizations

Of course, if the structure and concept of sport, of the aesthetic, of art were invariant, then sport could not be viewed as art—except mistakenly. But then it could not even be considered as aesthetic. For traditionally—and for understandable reasons—it was not. It was considered to be more of an ethical enterprise, with the ethical being understood as being opposed to the aesthetic. So sport's shift to the aesthetic already demonstrates that we are not dealing with invariant structures here. Hence a further shift of sport to the artistic is not impossible in principle. Such an occurence, however, would presuppose phenomenal as well as conceptual changes—with respect both to sport's constitution and the concept of art.

In the course of history it has often been the case that something originally not labeled as art later came to be considered as such and is in the meantime quite naturally viewed in this way. Artifacts—of occidental or other cultures—that were designed for ritual purposes were later designated as art. When you attend an auction of Indian art at Sotheby's none of these precious objects were originally meant to be art and yet they are quite naturally considered as such today. The concept of art is a flexible—and voracious—one.

So in order to answer fairly the question as to whether sport can be viewed as art, we have to take into account the flexibility of the concepts involved and to analyze whether phenomenal and conceptual changes might justify this claim. In the following I will try to argue for this claim. A last remark beforehand: in my analysis I will focus on high-level sport and take it as a phenomenon incorporating both the athletes' and the spectators' point of view.

Sport's Shift from Ethics to Aesthetics

Ethics as Constituting the Traditional Framework of Sport

Let me start by considering sport's contemporary shift from the ethical to the aesthetic. In earlier times, sport was praised as demonstrating and realizing the domination of the body by the mind and will. Sport was a kind of profane triumph of the metaphysical conception. Man was to be governed by mind and, to do this, had to subjugate the body's weakness and desires. Sport was to discipline the body and to make it fit to support the mind and its ends. In this sense Hegel praised the Greek Olympic games as being demonstrations of freedom in transforming the body into an "organ of the spirit."[2] In modern times, sport was praised because of its benefits for self-control or for heightened productivity. The ideological formula read "Sport builds character." But already in 1971 a sport study found no evidence at all for this claim and recommended "If you want to build character, try something else."[3] Today, faced by athletes such as the basketball player Dennis Rodman—who, significantly enough, published a book titled *Bad As I Wanna Be*—nobody can believe in sport's affinity with ethics anymore.[4]

Shift to Aesthetics

Well-known developments. Instead, sport has developed striking new affinities with aesthetics. This is obvious from the new style of sport clothing (some athletes, like Carl Lewis, have in the meantime even become professional fashion designers), the increased attention to the aesthetic element in performance (even the alteration of rules today is often motivated by aesthetic considerations) to the spectators' aesthetic delight—sport having become a show for the amusement of the entertainment society.

From the subjugation to the celebration of the body. The most revealing point, however, is the new relationship to the body. Previously, so long as the mind was to be the commanding master and the body the obedient slave, the triumph of an iron will over the body was praised; today nobody would employ this rhetoric any more. Sport, on the contrary, has turned into a celebration of the body.

Not only do we admire the female and male athletes' perfect bodies, the athletes themselves tend to exhibit them. After Linford Christie's victories, didn't we always wait for the moment when he lowered his running suit to the waist, revealing his impressive shoulder, chest, and stomach muscles? This dotted the "i" of his victory. And who could fail to have admired Merlene Ottey's grace and beauty—and therefore have regretted that she never won an Olympic gold medal? (But Gail Devers isn't bad either.)

But what is perhaps more important is the following: aesthetic perfection is not incidental to sporting success, but intrinsic to it. What is decisive for the sporting success is perfect performance. And it is this feature, above all, which is aesthetically appreciated in sport. We admire the elegance of a high-jumper clearing the bar or a runner's power toward the finish—and this is why we enjoy looking at these bodies during, as well as after, the event, in order, say, to understand better their achievements or to be surprised that the runner shows so little sign of exertion after having crossed the finish line. In this sense we, as spectators, are right to focus on the body and athletes are right in seeking perfection of their body and in demonstrating this both when performing and when exhibiting it. In sport the aesthetic and the functional go hand in hand.

Parallels with the original project of aesthetics. The new emphasis on the body and sport's shift from the ethical to the aesthetic seems to me to be of great interest—also with respect to the professional aestheticians' reflections. For aesthetics, when first established as a philosophical discipline by Baumgarten, strove for an emancipation of the body and the senses. Of course, this intention was inscribed within an epistemological perspective: it was to improve our sensory capacity for cognition. But under this epistemological cover aesthetics obviously tended to free the body and the senses from old metaphysical constraints. And Baumgarten himself became increasingly aware of (or was increasingly prepared to point out) the far-reaching consequences of his project, which indeed aimed at a radical cultural change, with the body and the senses becoming just as important as intellect and reason.

However, the times, it seems, were not prepared for this. The subsequent transformation of aesthetics into a philosophy of the arts is an indication of this. It reversed the critical impulse of aesthetics, fell back on the metaphysical pattern, and once again declared our sensory capacities to be an organ of the spirit—this time drawing on purported evidence from the arts. Aesthetics became an enterprise of cultural discipline again, which instead of bringing to bear the rights of our sensory capacity, turned against sensory experience and widely made the "war against matter" its (declared or concealed) maxim.[5]

So what is occurring today in sport's emphasis on the body in a way reinstates the original—and subsequently lost—intention of aesthetics. Another attempt at the emancipation of the body is being made. Contemporary sport is, with respect to the body, clearly an emancipatory rather than a disciplinary enterprise. Foucault's perspective on modernity's disciplinary strategies might apply to modern sport, but it no longer does so to postmodern sport.

The erotic element. Today's uncovering of the erotic element in sport, in contrast to its traditional oppression, is another case in point. According to the traditional disciplinary model, sport was associated with ascesis.[6] As sport was to serve to keep bodily desires in check, its inherent erotic connotations were to be kept quiet too. Today they are allowed to come to the fore. Contemporary sport is one of the spheres where the intrinsic relationship between the aesthetic and the erotic is allowed to manifest itself.

Sport and health. A further example of sport's shift from an ethical to an aesthetic perspective is health. For a long time sport was said to enhance health. This was understood as an ethical aim because a healthy body would, on a metaphysical view, ideally serve our spiritual tasks and would, on a modern view, serve the fulfilment of our working duties and thus match the new ethics of economic efficiency.

But the gap between this ideology that connects sport with health and what's actually happening is more than obvious. Modern high performance sport is an enterprise that systematically produces young invalids. Take Marc Girardelli as an example, who with five overall World Cup wins was the most successful skier ever. In the course of his career he underwent knee surgery fourteen times. When he got up in the morning he had to exercise for half an hour in order to be able to walk in a straight line. Already at the height of his success he was officially acknowledged as a 30 percent invalid. Today no high-ranking decathlete can realistically hope ever to be completely free of injury when going into a competition and the injury rate of soccer players is known to everyone. High performance sport and health simply don't go together.[7]

But now, it seems, I'm in trouble. Doesn't this tendency to produce invalids contradict my thesis that today's sport is an emancipation and celebration of the body? Doesn't sport rather ignore and destroy the body?

Today's athletes are adopting a different attitude.[8] They refuse to disregard the body. Mika Myllylä, the Finnish world champion in the 50 km cross-country race in 1997, Olympic champion in the 30 km in 1998, and world champion in the 10, 30 and 50 km in 1999, is a telling example. He practices a new type of training, rejecting the usual scientific training and coaching where a precise plan is established that one then has to follow, no matter how the body feels. He avoids this old-fashioned type of training that is still shaped by the ideology of mastering the body. Myllylä relies instead on his own knowledge and feelings. When he trains he listens to his body and tries to find out what it wants and needs. And he enjoys this new type of training. He even insists that for him "the greatest enjoyment comes from training, not from winning."[9] With this method he manages not to be exposed to injuries and to be extremely successful at the same time. This novel type of training respects the body and does away with the old ideology of mastering the body, which in most cases ended up in the Girardelli-trap. Many athletes see Myllylä's (and others') way as a promising model of future training.

The point is very important. Sport is changing one of its basic features. While some people say that in today's sport everything is getting worse, in fact one of sport's most threatening problems is solved. The new body-focus of sport engenders a new care for the body. So in various aspects—from its aesthetic appearance and appreciation through to its emphasis on the body in performance, self-presentation, and training—contemporary sport has largely turned aesthetic.[10]

Modern Changes in the Concept of Art Allowing Sport to Be Viewed as Art

But this move to aesthetics represents only the uncontroversial part of my essay. What, however, is highly disputed is that for this reason—or others—sport could be viewed as art.[11] So let me turn to this controversial claim for which—to my own, initial surprise—I am now going to argue.

As I said before, the legitimacy—and even the plausibility—of this further-reaching claim depends, first of all, on the concept of art one has. My main point is that during the twentieth century the concept of art has undergone transformations that open up new chances of sport's being viewed as art. I will discuss four aspects. Later, in the third section of this essay, I will have to explain how contemporary sport actually makes use of these new opportunities.

Art, Instead of Defining the Aesthetic, Has Become an Instance of the Aesthetic

First, a reversal of the relationship between the artistic and the aesthetic is to be observed. Formerly, the artistic provided the basic definition of the aesthetic. The realm of the aesthetic was certainly broader than that of art, but the concept of art was meant to provide the core concept of the aesthetic. In recent times, however, things have changed. Now art is considered as just one province of the aesthetic—certainly still a particularly important one, but nonetheless just one. While art has lost its privileged definitional status for the aesthetic, this has rather been assumed by *aisthesis*.[12] So the definition of the aesthetic is no longer to be taken from art, rather art's definition is to be established within the framework of the aesthetic: preferably, for instance, conceiving of art as an intensification of the aesthetic.

An obvious consequence of this change is that now everything that is emphatically aesthetic has better chances of counting as art than before. For this reason sport, being a novel and obvious instance of the aesthetic, might well enter the predicational sphere of art.

Modern Art as Striving for Interpenetrations with Life

Many of modern art's variants strive to transcend the art sphere, to achieve interconnections with the sphere of life. The poles of this tendency are marked by attempts to draw elements of the everyday into the artwork (say through collage or montage) on the one hand, or by trying to dissolve the artwork within life on the other hand (think of the Living Theatre or of the claim that good art and design should be unnoticeable and invisible).[13]

Regrettably enough, modern art's striving for connections with the lifeworld often suffers from utter misunderstanding. After Joseph Beuys, during and after the *documenta VII*, planted seven thousand oaks in Kassel and its surroundings, his devoted followers today undertake to preserve every one of these oaks and produce extensive documentation of what they indeed see as a very innovative artwork, but which they treat as an absolutely traditional one. What was meant to transform art into life and nature is—in a complete misunderstanding of Beuys's intention by these devotees—being fetched back into the realm of art. Understandably enough, it is above all the art market that still wants art to be a clear-cut concept; this serves to distinguish art and to make it a marketable product. But the marriage between art and market is tenable only at the cost of an ongoing disregard of modern art's own initiatives. Unfortunately, many theoreticians also follow the art market's demands rather than art's impulses; they eagerly try to establish a clear-cut concept of art—whose only purpose today seems to consist in serving the market.[14]

Wherever the art-world definition of art remains binding, of course, nothing other than the items distributed by the art market has a chance of counting as art. Redistributions between art and sport then simply cannot occur. But if art's impulse to be transformed into life—which is one of the strongest impulses of modern art—is taken seriously, then aesthetic forms beyond the realm of art could be seen as corresponding to art's own initiative, and in this sense be appreciated as instances of a fulfilment of art's intention, as a novel kind of art that modern art's impulse gave birth to.

This is a second line that might allow us to consider contemporary sport as a major new candidate for 'art.'

The Tendency Towards a Fraying of the Arts

A third aspect is modern arts' tendency to merge into one another. Adorno has described this as the fraying of the arts.[15] "The borders between the artistic genres are flowing into one another, more precisely, their demarcation lines are fraying."[16] "It is as if the artistic genres, by negating their firmly outlined forms, were gnawing away at the concept of art itself."[17] Adorno interprets this fraying of the arts as a consequence of their attempt to escape their autonomy-centered ideological constitution, an attempt that he calls "the vital element of all actually modern art."[18]

This tendency to neutralize the borders of art—among its genres in the first place, but also between art and the everyday—is, of course, another reason why an entry of nonart into the realm of art becomes possible in principle.

From Highbrow to Lowbrow—The Advancement of Art and Aesthetics Toward the Popular

The increasing insecurity about the borders of art leads to a fourth point: the revaluation of popular art. The distinction between high and low is increasingly being rejected—by art as well as by its aesthetic reflection. Pop Art was the decisive event in the field of arts, and, with respect to aesthetics, I'd like to remind you of Richard Shusterman's "defense of popular art" and his demonstration "that works of popular art do in fact display the aesthetic values its critics reserve exclusively for high art."[19]

This opening of the concept of art toward the popular clears a further path for the inclusion of sport, this highly popular aesthetic phenomenon, among the arts. In this second section, I have pointed out four reasons why possibilities arise through the development of the modern concept of art itself for sport to access the notion of art. When, for something to be art, its aesthetic character is more important than a specifically artistic one; when art itself strives for transformation into phenomena of the everyday; when art tends to blur its borders; when, finally, the popular is increasingly being recognized as art—then sport becomes a good new candidate for being viewed as art.

Sport as Art

Now let me turn to the decisive question: does sport actually make use of these possibilities? Does it fulfill at least some—and perhaps enough—of art's criteria to be considered art? From now on I will go through the common objections to sport's potential art status step by step in order to examine critically and refute them.

Does Sport—by Aiming for Victory—Lack Art's Requisite Character as an End in Itself?

One basic objection says that even if contemporary sport exhibits the four shifts mentioned, it nevertheless cannot be art because it runs counter to two other basic conditions of art: its symbolic status and its being an end in itself.

This objection is based on the assumption that sport is merely a profane activity aiming at victory. Hence sport falls short of symbolic meaning as well as of being an end in itself.

Let me discuss the various errors inherent in this apparently plausible line of thought.

The symbolic status of sport as well as art. Sport is as distant from ordinary life as is art. When Othello smothers Desdemona, this is a symbolic act, the actress will survive. Likewise sport's relationship to life is at most symbolic. Many sports originated from types of aggressive action in ordinary life, but being practiced as sport, this remains only as a symbolic background to them. In sport the struggle is "raised to the level of imagination."[20] Or as Santayana put it: "Sport is a liberal form of war stripped from its compulsions and malignity."[21]

This is why sport, viewed (and sometimes ironically assessed) from life's perspective of necessity, often appears absurd: Why do marathon runners enslave themselves so? Why do sporting marksmen compete with such embitterment when all they're shooting is useless clay pigeons and not real pigeons that one could roast afterward? Isn't it simply idiotic to constantly drive in a circle at high speed (as Niki Lauda said when retiring from Formula One sport)?

The following point also makes evident the difference between sport or art on the one hand and life on the other hand. If Othello were to carry on smothering someone in normal life, after having left the stage, he would be arrested, as would a linebacker who continued hurling all his weight into bruising tackles away from the football field and into the streets. Sport as well as theater take place in particular spaces, separate from the everyday world. What the stage is to theater, the playing field, boxing ring, or the race track are to sport. Art as well as sport are, compared to life, symbolic activities in terms of their structure.

Sport's oeuvre: the performance. But another difference still seems to remain: sport is said to be about winning, while art is about the creation of an artwork.

But let's be careful when talking about a 'work'. Of course, in painting, works are produced that have an independent existence after the act of painting. Not so, however, in theater, dance or music—in the performing arts. Nor in sport: when the competition is over, garbage may remain but no work of art.

Yet there is a different type of work implied in those artistic as well as in sporting performances: the performance itself. That painting produces a work in the sense of an object might make the status of painting even dubious instead, for in doing this it does not (as it does in other respects) raise itself beyond the level of a craft to the higher level of art,[22] whereas the performing arts and sport do. This even makes them comparable to those activities which, ever since Aristotle, have been considered to be our highest ones, precisely for the reason that their proper work is imminent to the process and not something achieved at the end and remaining as a result, an outcome, a product, a work-entity. Aristotle pointed out the difference between activities producing a work and those that constitute ends in themselves. The acts of seeing, reflecting, or thinking have their end in themselves, not beyond, they are fulfilled in themselves.[23] They are distinguished by the imminence of the work—which is nothing but the process itself—in the process. Here we are concerned with activities that are exemplary as ends in themselves.

Sport, just as the performing arts, is of this type. The sporting performance has, above all, its end in itself. In principle it does not serve outer purposes.[24] Of course, all self-purposive activities can have outer effects too: thinking can make you a lonely person, musical performance can make you famous, and sport can make you rich. But it would be wrong to declare these secondary effects the primary thing and, so doing, to overlook these activities' inner character as an end in themselves, whose excellence is the condition for these outer effects being able to take place.

Bearing this in mind we might be in a position to disprove the objection that sport is about winning whereas the arts are not. If 'winning' means that one tries to do what one does as well as one ever can, then this is common to all these phenomena—to sport as well as to art. If 'winning' implicitly connotates 'money-making,' then again this can apply to both of them. The main point, however, is that in sport the aim of winning cannot be reached *directly* but only *through the sporting performance*. It is the superiority of one's sporting performance that leads to victory. So the proper work of the athlete is in any case his or her performance, which then may result in a win.[25] In this, it seems to me, sport and art are completely alike.[26]

And, interestingly enough, many athletes today emphasize the value of performance more than that of winning. Even when they have lost, they can be very happy with their excellent performance. They did their best, and this is satisfying—though it was not enough to win. Sport is more about the best possible performance than about winning. And some athletes go even further. For them pure performance—that of training, which is exempt from competition and victory—brings the greatest enjoyment. As Mika Myllylä said: "Winning brings a feeling of success, it is a reward for a job well done, but the greatest enjoyment comes from training. Competition is not the main thing."[27]

Sporting Performance: Determined Too Much by Its Rules to Be Counted as Art?

Another objection against sport's potential art status runs as follows: sport lacks creativity, because it simply runs through fixed schemes within a strict set of rules. Art on the contrary problematizes and transcends rules.

This is true. Art—and modern art in particular—does not simply follow a given set of rules but questions and changes the status of art and develops new paradigms, each of which may establish a peculiar set of rules for art's existence and meaning and for the artwork's construction as well as reception. This characteristic of art, its not being led by rules, was already expressed by the traditional formula of *Je ne sais quoi* and clearly comes to the fore through the modern prominence of reflective judgment. Sport, on the contrary, presupposes definitely established rules. As soon as ambiguities arise here—when, for instance, a hammer thrower suddenly wears ankle weights—the rules are added to. Art creates its rules, sport follows rules.

Sport does not exhaust itself in following rules. But does this mean that sporting performance does not contain an artlike potential at all? By no means. The performance is regulated, but not *determined* in every aspect by the respective rules. Great memorable competitions are such because something happened that went beyond the mere fulfillment of rules. If following the rules were everything, all competitions would have to be more or less the same. In actual competition and performance something more enters in: the event and occurrence, drama and contingency, good or bad luck, success or failure, surprise and excitement. These elements make the sporting event a particular and possibly unique one.[28]

Taking a closer look at these surplus elements we will be able to discover the main reason for sport's artistic character.

Fascination with the event. Let us consider first the obvious parallel with the performing arts. While with painting or poetry what I said before holds (they establish rather than follow rules), theater or music constitute a different case: the actors or players are bound by the preestablished structure of the written play or the piece of music. Yet what makes their performance remarkable is not the rule-governed reproduction of the script or the composition, but the additional element of their performance, one that displays all kinds of personal skills, individual interpretation, and openness to the event they create (while creating it). None of this is straightforwardly determined by the given script or composition. It is these surplus elements that we appreciate and remember most. And while true for the performing arts, this is equally true for sport.[29]

What we appreciate is what transcends the sphere of mere rule-fulfillment. Or rather what supervenes while the rules are being followed: the events' unforeseeable dynamics. Ideally, the rules provide good conditions for an event of this kind. Indeed they are designed and often adjusted in order to allow for the ultimately unforeseeable dynamics of the event. They are boundary conditions for possibly great sporting events. Take soccer as an example. During the last World Cup the rules for the match between Brazil and the Netherlands were certainly the same as for the match between Iran and Germany—but what an enormous difference there was between the unforgettable soccer evening in the first case and the pitiful prodding around in the second! The rules don't make the game. The performance does, it creates the miserable or great event. Just as in the performing arts.

Sport's Semantics: Drama without Script

But another objection still awaits an answer. What is the sporting event about? Does it carry with it any relevant meaning?

It was often said that while art expresses ideas, feelings, states of mind, and therefore has a meaning, sport expresses nothing and therefore has no 'meaning'[30] Sport may, in its event character, be similar to theater, but while a play is about human conflicts or the drama of the *condition humaine,* sport is about running or throwing or performing sophisticated movements like the Gienger salto.

This assessment, however, is profoundly mistaken. It is based on a confusion about meaning and aboutness, assuming that only what is explicitly about something can be meaningful. The script of theater is about something, hence theater is meaningful, while sport lacks a script, hence it is meaningless—this is the line of reasoning here. Yet this misses the point insofar as artistic meaning is not necessarily and exclusively constituted by aboutness, but—even in its essence—by the artistic event itself. And this applies equally to sport. Considering the potential meaningfulness of sport one does not have to look for a script—there is indeed none—but for the typicality of the event.

Sport can display all the dramatic traits of human existence. In this lies its symbolic dimension. Think of a 10,000m race. You can witness the tactical battle between the opponents, the leading group's break away, the leader's coming unstuck or the tragedy of a Sonya O'Sullivan, the risk of taking the outer lane on the last curve, the dramatic closing spurt, and the luck of a runner who is suddenly able to break through on the inner lane as it becomes free and wins. Or think of the unforgettable moment when, for the first time, in a 400m race a runner tried to win Olympic Gold by thrusting himself over the finish line.

The crucial point is that *all this is created uniquely by the performance and the event itself*—it does not follow from the implementation of a script. When we witness something dramatic, this—in the case of sport—is due to nothing but the event itself. The actual occurrence cannot be anticipated, the athletes' performance is creative in the highest sense. There was no script. Sport is drama without a script. It creates its own drama.[31]

In this respect sport appears more artistic still than many of the arts—more so, for example, than all the performing arts as these are based on a script, choreography, or a composition. In sport, however, the drama is due to the event alone. The freedom and event character of sport's production of meaning is eminently artistic.

Sporting events act out most basic features of the human condition, and the way they do this is marvellously self-creative. In so doing sport is sport semantically intense and intrinsically artistic. In this respect I see every reason to view sport as art.[32]

Identification: The Spectators' Fascination with Sport

My analysis focuses on the event and the spectacle of sport. The spectators, in my view, are an integral part of the event. But why do we admire athletic performances at all? Shouldn't we be envious instead—because we, the nonathletes, will never achieve this kind of perfection? How can the contemporary fascination with sport be explained?[33]

One essential point is that we take the athletes' performance to be not totally beyond our scope. We even take it to be ours in a way. There is a feeling of *mea res agitur*—like in theater, where when we see kings or people of excellence, we don't think they are of an ontologically different kind, but rather take them to be fellow human beings whose destiny confronts us with human potentials that are in principle relevant to our being and lives too. Athletes are perceived as human beings— even if we consider them to be somehow superhuman. It would be quite different if we were to see beings from a different planet. Sport is not science fiction. It's real and human. Something connected with human character is going on.

The athletes demonstrate a potential of the *human body as such* that is certainly factually unattainable for most of us, but is not in principle beyond, so to speak, the idea of our body. The athletes realize an outstanding potentiality of our kind of body. They are performing for us and instead of us. As they are actors of the human being, we can and do identify with them.

Nothing is simply beyond us—neither the bodies nor the activities nor the emotions—everything is familiar to a certain extent. It's a fellow human being who is performing, suffering, and winning or losing out there.[34] This makes the sporting event a shared event and the drama one that we too experience. From this it follows that the structure of sport comprises both athletes and spectators.[35] We are fascinated by the realization of an ideal potentiality of the human being, one factually unavailable to us but actualized in the sporting event; in this sense we experience the event as being representative for us and enjoy and participate in the drama displayed.

Celebration of Contingency

Contingency is another main point in sport's dramatic character and appreciation. Sport is not only the celebration of physical perfection, but also of contingency. This element may be difficult to describe—partly because contingency has
never received adequate attention in our culture, which has tried instead to ignore
or overcome contingency, so that adequate concepts are lacking—yet contingency
is one of the most evident and appreciated aspects in sporting events.

A competition can take the course one expected. The superior athlete wins,
perhaps even achieves a new world record, and this too may have been expected
and supported—in long-distance runs, for example, by hiring "pacemakers." So
the time attained was great—but not the event, because nothing unpredictable
happened. It just confirmed expectations, did not create a dynamics of its own,
and no contingency came in. Despite being a record-breaking run, *as an event* it
was pretty dull.

How different if something unpredictable happens—if there is a real fight, if
the result is uncertain during a race, if, finally, a new star is born; or when, in a
Formula One race, the outcome is permanently incalculable—a slight lapse in
attention, or a competitor's crazy driving when being overtaken, or sudden rain
showers, can change everything. In such cases the event creates its own course,
and contingency is permanently in play. And we appreciate such a pure event,
with the permanent emergence of possibilities and its self-organizational character more than a predictable result.

Or take soccer as an example. Certainly, the skill and perfection of outstanding players' actions is part of its fascination. But we also expect the whole game to
be exciting and—if we're lucky—can be fascinated by the way the players react at
every moment to the course and experience the game has provided so far. Things
are most fascinating when it's permanently touch and go, with both the game as a
whole and almost every single action. Whether a 50m dream pass is in fact this, or
a failure, can depend on 10 centimeters or a player's outstanding reaction. What
can bring one team the decisive goal might also open up an excellent counter-
chance for its opponents. And when the pass is made, you have no precise idea
what it will result in. Success and failure here lie unbelievably close to one another.
Soccer, to me, seems to be so fascinating because it is subject in the most intense
way to contingency. It is a celebration of contingency. (And it's probably for this
reason that many scholars and intellectuals like it—it demonstrates to them the
insuperability of what in their professional work they try to outdo: contingency.)

But doesn't precisely this prominence of contingency hinder the declaration
that sport be art? Isn't art a paradigmatic attempt to overcome contingency, with
one of the first criteria of an accomplished artwork being that you cannot change
an iota without destroying its perfection and extraordinary effect? Well, traditionally this opinion was held. Modern art, however, is (in some schools at least) char-

acterized by a turn to contingency. Think of Marcel Duchamp who introduced contingency in many ways into art and, when his "Great Glass" (which he had declared "definitively unfinished") was broken during transportation, called this "the happy completion of the piece" and made the cracks prominent elements of its final rearrangement.[36] Or think of John Cage, with whom the emancipation of musical contingency took place—with respect to sounds as well as to notation. The welcoming of contingency is part of modern art's aforementioned struggle against its traditional constitution.

Therefore the celebration of contingency that takes place in sport certainly cannot be an argument against sport's potentially having an artistic status.

Intermediate Summary

To wrap things up: I have gone through several constituents of the modern concept of art and discussed various traits of contemporary sport. Some of the new conceptual elements of art (the prominence of the aesthetic, art's striving for connections with the everyday world, the fraying of art forms, and the reevaluation of popular art) proved favorable from the start for viewing sport as art; and the elements that at first glance denied such admission (symbolic status and selfpurposiveness, meaningfulness, striving for necessity instead of contingency), turned out on closer inspection to be either quite fulfillable by sport, or elements of a concept of art that has been surpassed by the development of art itself.

Perhaps sport does lack some traits constitutive to some kinds of art—but so do other kinds of art too. Painting and sculpture produce object-like works, the performing arts don't. Their type of work is different. And so is sport's. And if there are some traits of arts that sport lacks altogether this too does not necessarily mean that sport cannot be art. For the concept of art is a complex and open one. Nothing must, in order to be art, fulfill *all* the aspects that can be responsible for calling *something* art. A series of traits—differing partly from one genre to the next—is sufficient.[37] And sport meets a variety of those traits—and obviously important ones at that.[38] Therefore it seems highly plausible to me to view today's sport as art.

Contemporary Sport: A Postmodern Art for Everyone

Finally, sport has a big advantage over what is usually considered art: it is understandable and enjoyable for practically everyone. To be fascinated with sport you don't need a diploma—whereas for the enjoyment of modern, difficult art you apparently do. Of course, even in the case of sport some knowlege is required: you need to know, or to find out, the rules, and the more you are acquainted with a type of sport the more you will be able to enjoy the competition.[39] Modern art, however, is—despite the protestations of our art pedagogians—hardly accessible to everyone.

Whereas sport—for obvious reasons—is popular, art is—for equally good reasons—elitist. Many artists are aware of this and suffer from not having the support of the crowd, they share Paul Klee's complaint that "no people carries us."[40] From the other side, Arnold Gehlen gave the corresponding diagnosis: "We have all learnt to live alongside today's art."[41] But most of us have learnt to live with sport and to enjoy it.

Contemporary sport—in contrast to modern art—matches the *sensus communis*. It is art for everyone. It probably is *the* popular art of today. It is certainly the most social art form. The huge increase of public interest in sport is an indication of this.[42] Where art, by becoming difficult and a matter for experts, has turned away from common taste, sport fills the gap. It offers the extraordinary and yet understandable event. And with sport things are so obvious. In the case of sport you don't have to ask yourself critically whether what you enjoy is indeed art and whether your pleasure is legitimate or just mistaken because in fact you are a philistine who usually mistakes kitsch for art.

Sport as a Neglected Topic of Aesthetics

My interest here is not to promote sport. Rather, I would like to point out its artlike traits in order to show what a valuable topic it could be for aesthetics. Sport is usually neglected by the discipline; one just sees sport's aesthetic traits and judges these to be simply obvious and not an interesting matter. The pleasure in sport is considered to be lowbrow or mass pleasure—one not worthy of positive consideration by aesthetics. But by neglecting the artlike character of sport we also fail to understand why it is so fascinating for a large public. In fact, the very fascination with sport derives from aspects that, in a different form, we are used to experiencing and admiring in the arts. Recognition of this is what I would like to promote. In sport, elementary aspects of the human condition are at stake and are acted out—in a very direct and at the same time symbolically intense manner.

Art-Art Versus Sport-Art

With all this I am of course not saying that sport *replaces* art, or that it could or should do so. I am arguing only that it fulfills functions of art for a broader audience no longer reached by art.

And I'd like to suggest complementarity. Art, in my view, should remain difficult, elitist, and experimental. In other words: it should not succumb to popular taste. I don't see its future prosperity in competing with the abundant satisfactions that the demands of an entertainment and amusement society experience through current design, everyday aestheticization—and postmodern sport. Where art chooses to take this direction, it is at a disadvantage anyway and, more importantly, falls short of its genuine task. Unyielding art on the one side and arts of entertainment on the other side could be useful and appreciable in a complementary way. A distribution and differentiation of this kind would, in my view, constitute not the worst outcome of the modern transformation of the artistic.

Or, to be more outspoken on this point: after all the efforts of modern art to escape its golden cage of autonomy, to turn to life and to acknowledge and make us appreciate the aesthetic outside of art—a tendency that obviously furthers aestheticization of the everyday and that provides strong arguments for my assessment of sport as art—it might be time to reinforce the distinction between art in the proper sense and aestheticization of the everyday.[43] Avant garde art, revolting against art's autonomy and aesthetically sacramenting the everyday, has done its job. Its victory is obvious and has no need of any further proof. Art could return to its different task once again—one closer to its older aims, with the opposition to current aestheticization now being one of its constituents.[44] Sport best fills in for the everyday longings of art. But it cannot substitute for Schönberg, Pollock, or Godard. Art's exception is to occur in a different way from sport's.[45]

Conclusion

Ultimately my intention was not to decide the question as to whether sport *is* art or not. This would, in my view, be phrasing the question too essentialistically. What I tried instead was to offer some reasons why—in today's conditions of art as well as of sport—many people find it highly plausible to call sport an art.

My hunch is that all objections against this are out of step with the modern understanding of art as brought forward by art itself. When, toward the end, I suggested complementarity between art and sport, I did not mean to question sport's status as art. Sport is *one* kind of art. Art (in the usual sense) is another one. That is all.

Notes

1. Cf. my "Aestheticization Processes: Phenomena, Distinctions and Prospects," in *Undoing Aesthetics* (London: Sage, 1997), 1–32.
2. Georg Wilhelm Friedrich Hegel, "Vorlesungen über die Philosophie der Geschichte," in *Werke* (Frankfurt/Main: Suhrkamp, 1986), vol. 12, 298.
3. Bruce C. Ogive and Thomas A. Tutko, "Sport: If You Want to Build Character, Try Something Else," *Psychology Today*, October 1971, 61–63.
4. Dennis Rodman (with Tim Keown), *Bad As I Wanna Be* (New York: Delacorte Press, 1996).
5. So Schiller, for instance, in his conception of what he paradoxically named an "aesthetic culture" (Friedrich Schiller, *On the Aesthetic Education of Man in a Series of Letters*, tr. R. Snell, Bristol: Thoemmes 1994, here 23rd Letter, 112), called sensory experience a "dreadful foe" that is to be "fought" against; he praised the mechanical and fine artist for not hesitating "to do . . . violence" to matter (ibid., 4th Letter, 32); and declared "the real artistic secret of the master" to consist in "his *annihilating the material by means of the form*" (ibid., 22nd Letter, 106). Similarly, Hegel was to allow the sensory aspects in the

work of art to appear only "as surface and *semblance* of the sensory" (Georg Wilhelm Friedrich Hegel, *Ästhetik,* ed. Friedrich Bassenge, 2 vols. [Frankfurt/Main: Europäische Verlagsanstalt n.d.], vol. 1, 48), art bringing forth "from the sensory side, intentionally, only a shadow world of shapes, tones and intuitions" (ibid., 49).

6. We should not forget, however, that the English term 'sport'—in contrast, say, to the old Greek term 'gymnastics'—originally had a hedonistic meaning. The word 'sport' originated in the mid fourteenth century and, until the end of the seventeenth century, designated 'pleasant pastime', 'entertainment', 'amusement', 'recreation', 'diversion', 'taking one's own pleasure' (*The New Shorter Oxford English Dictionary on Historical Principles,* ed. Lesley Brown, Oxford: Clarendon Press, 1993, vol. 2, 2999). In the late sixteenth century, it even had the particular sense of 'lovemaking', designating sexual intercourse viewed as a game (ibid.). In Shakespeare's *Othello,* for example, Iago says when vilifying Desdemona that "the blood is made dull with the act of sport" (II,1,230). "Venus sport" was a common expression at that time. Only later did the concept of sport shift from pleasure to discipline. Nietzsche was, in this respect too, an exception when he called "sexual love . . . a kind of sport" (Friedrich Nietzsche, *Nachgelassene Fragmente. Herbst 1885 bis Anfang 1889,* in *Nietzsche, Sämtliche Werke. Kritische Studienausgabe in 15 Bänden,* ed. Giorgio Colli and Mazzino Montinari (Munich: Deutscher Taschenbuch Verlag, 1980), vol. 12, 482 [autumn 1887].

7. Already in 1928/29, Bertolt Brecht had stated: "Great sport begins long after it has ceased to be healthy" (Bertolt Brecht, "Die Krise des Sportes", in *Werke,* vol. 21 (Berlin and Weimar: Aufbau-Verlag; Frankfurt/Main: Suhrkamp, 1992), 222–24, here 223.

8. In fact, the old claim that high performance sport would improve health has—while this ideology dominated—always been mistaken. When a weightlifter's heart increased in size through permanent overexertion, this caused him lifelong problems, and many weightlifters died significantly prematurely of heart attacks. The former antibody ideology of sport simply hid this contradiction. As the body was to be dominated for "higher" goals, its repulsion was just not to be taken seriously.

9. Source: http://www.slu.fi/hiihtoliitto/myllyla.html.

10. A valuable case study of sport's aesthetic status is Hans Ulrich Gumbrecht, "Die Schönheit des Mannschaftssports: American Football—im Stadion und im Fernsehen," in *Medien—Welten—Wirklichkeiten,* ed. Gianni Vattimo and Wolfgang Welsch (Munich: Fink, 1998), 201–28. Compare also Gunter Gebauer and Gerd Hortleder, "Die Epoche des Showsports," in *Sport—Eros—Tod,* ed. Gerd Hortleder and Gunter Gebauer (Frankfurt/Main: Suhrkamp, 1986), 60–87.

11. There was already discussion of whether or not sport is art in the 1970s and 1980s. It was triggered by Pierre Frayssinet's investigation *Le Sport parmi les Beaux-Arts* (Paris 1968) and was continued above all in the English-speaking world, with authors such as L.A. Reid (1970), P. Ziff (1974), J. Kupfer (1975), David Best (1979, 1980, 1985), S.K. Wertz (1984), and Christopher Cordner (1988) participating. The answer given was for the most part negative: in spite of numerous obvious parallels sport should not ultimately be seen as art. I do not want to go into these arguments in detail, but to note that obviously for sensitive minds a tendency toward sport's potential art status was already taking shape, which in the meantime has made its breakthrough. It is just that the reaction then

was predominantly academically cautious and conceptually conservative—although many arguments (for instance those of Roberts and Cordner against Best) might have suggested a different outcome (cf. David Best, "The Aesthetic in Sport," *British Journal of Aesthetics*, vol. 14, no. 3, summer 1974, 197–221, reprinted in *Philosophic Inquiry in Sport*, ed. William J. Morgan and Klaus V. Meier [Champaign, Ill.: Human Kinetics, 1995], 2d ed., 377–389; David Best, "Sport is Not Art," *Journal of the Philosophy of Sport*, 12 (1985):25–40; Terence J. Roberts, "Sport, Art, and Particularity: The Best Equivocation," in *Philosophic Inquiry in Sport*, 415–24; Christopher Cordner, "Differences Between Sport and Art", in ibid., 425–36).

12. I have developed this in more detail in "Aesthetics Beyond Aesthetics: For a New Form to the Discipline" and in "Aestheticization Processes: Phenomena, Distinctions and Prospects," in *Undoing Aesthetics*, 78–102 and 1–32, respectively.

13. Cf. *Design ist unsichtbar*, ed. Helmuth Gsöllpointner, Angela Hareiter, and Laurids Ortner (Vienna: Löcker, 1981). Remember in this context also the old Schillerean project of art's transformation into the "art of living" ("Lebenskunst," Schiller, *On the Aesthetic Education of Man in a Series of Letters*, 15th Letter, 80) and Nietzsche's polemics "*against the art of artworks*": this "so-called actual art, *that of artworks*," he said, is "merely an *appendix*," not "the actual"; one should not, as the artworld thinks, fit out a bad life with artworks, but deploy artistic energy directly for the improvement of life (Friedrich Nietzsche, *Menschliches, Allzumenschliches. Ein Buch Für freie Geister. Zweiter Band*, in Nietzsche, *Sämtliche Werke*, vol. 2, 453 f. [1 174]). According to Nietzsche, artworks are legitimate only when also serving an art of life.

14. And if a theory is ever proposed that effectively questions the concept of art, then this theory can—paradoxically—be highly esteemed among art market people while its content is not taken at all seriously by them. Arthur Danto's indiscernibility thesis would, taken literally, be disastrous for the art market—it states that there is simply no such thing as an 'artwork', hence one cannot sell any. The only artworks, according to Danto, consist of interpretations (as developed by critics and philosophers, and by Arthur Danto in the first place)—so at least books can still be sold.

15. Theodor W. Adorno, "Die Kunst und die Künste," in Adorno, *Ohne Leitbild: Parva Aesthetica* (Frankfurt/Main: Suhrkamp, 1967), 168–92. Cf. also Arthur Danto's more recent description of "contemporary artistic practice": "It is a practice in which painters no longer hesitate to situate their paintings by means of devices which belong to altogether different media—sculpture, video, film, installation, and the like" (Arthur C. Danto, *After the End of Art: Contemporary Art and the Pale of History;* Princeton: Princeton University Press, 1997, XII).

16. Adorno, "Die Kunst und die Künste," 168.

17. Ibid., 189.

18. Ibid., 191.

19. Richard Shusterman, *Pragmatist Aesthetics: Living Beauty, Rethinking Art* (Oxford: Blackwell, 1992), 171 f. and 200. Shusterman points out in particular "that popular art has those formal qualities thought to distinguish high art as aesthetic: unity and complexity, intertextuality and open-textured polysemy, experimentation and foregrounded attention to medium" (ibid., 200).

20. Cordner, "Differences Between Sport and Art," 432.

21. Ibid.

22. Hence in the past arts like painting and sculpture were pursued under the heading "artes mechanicae," that is alongside, for instance, agriculture, ironmongery and weaving. Indeed—precisely because what mattered to them was the resultant product and not the process—they were not counted as "artes liberales." This original classification can still be seen in the reliefs of the Florentine Campanile (representations from around 1340 and 1437–39): architecture, sculpture, and painting figure amid the mechanical arts—below the liberal arts which are represented above them.

23. Cf. Aristotle, *Metaphysics*, IX 6, 1048 b 18–36.

24. Sport's character as an end in itself is often rendered by emphasizing its play characteristic.

25. A similar structure is typical for mountain climbing. The popular formula "the way is the goal" gives a good account of this. Sure, you want to get to the summit. But don't forget that you also have to get back down afterward. The satisfaction arises from having done all this well—not just from having reached the top. Ultimately all the challenges of the route including the altitude of the summit are an integral part of the process of the climber's successful performance.

26. The common objection to contemporary high level sport (in particular to basketball, soccer, and other highly paid sports) that the athletes only run after money is much too simple. Excellent performance is the indispensable condition for whatever may follow from it: a series of wins, earning immense amounts of money, or being overexerted by permanently being the best. This applies to sport as well as to art. The prospect of additional earnings may make tenors sing more often—but if the level of their performance drops, so too does their reward.

27. Source: http://www.slu.fi/hiihtoliitto/myllyla.html.

28. And this is all the more remarkable the more memorable the event is. To a certain extent, however, it is to be found in every event.

29. Note also that in the late sixteenth hundred 'sport' could signify 'theatrical performance', 'show', 'play' (Brown, *New Shorter Oxford English Dictionary*).

30. This view, advocated for instance by David Best ("The Aesthetic in Sport") is criticized by Christopher Cordner ("Differences Between Sport and Art"). Best claims that while "any art form, properly so-called, must at least *allow for* the possibility of the expression of a conception of life issues, such as contemporary moral, social and political problems," the sporting performer does not "have the possibility of expressing through his particular medium his view of life situations" (386). To this Cordner objects that while "the representational arts seem to do so . . . the situation is different with the nonrepresentational arts." Hence it would be better to say that "works of art manifest or enact or realize life-values" and are in themselves "most deeply meaningful or value-laden" (429). In view of this, however, "sports quite clearly can have meaning in a very similar way" (430).

31. This might, however, provoke another objection against sport's potential status as art. One might say that art requires repeatability, hence sport can, because of the uniqueness of the sporting event, not be art. But again modern art does away with the argument, for it no longer subscribes to a general repeatability thesis. Happenings were and performances often are single events. Afterward one can witness them only through photos or videotapes—just as in the case of sporting events.

32. It appears notable that Hegel linked the origin of Greek art with Greek sport: "The Greeks first made beautiful forms of themselves before they expressed such objectively in marble and in paintings. The harmless competition in *games,* in which each shows what he is, is very old" (Hegel, *Vorlesungen über die Philosophie der Geschichte,* 297). Hegel is of the opinion that Greek sport preceded and prepared the way for Greek art.

33. That there is such fascination is obvious: today more than sixty percent of the population in Western countries watch sport on a regular basis; the last soccer World Cup was attended by almost three million and watched on TV by thirty-seven million the world over. I have attempted an explanation in more detail in the paper "Just what is it that makes today's sport so appealing?" (Stanford University, Athletic Department, Colloquium "If You Want to Build Character Try Something Else: Ethics and Sports in 1997 and Beyond," 16 May 1997).

34. It's not only the athlete's body that is within our comprehension as physical beings, but the activities he performs are also largely familiar to us. This is obviously the case with cycling, soccer, basketball, swimming, skating, car racing, and the like—most of us have at least at some time in our lives tried the respective activity or one similar to it, no matter how modest the level. And indirectly it is the case even if we haven't much experience with these kinds of sport, or none at all as perhaps with fencing or pole vault or the javelin. We are at least to some extent familiar with the motoric patterns relevant to these activities from our daily physical experience, and if we aren't, as in the case of pole vault, we can still—by a sort of physical empathy—imagine and even feel what's going on there. We always have at least some initial access to the *pattern* of activity, and this is enough to get in touch with it, whereas, on the other hand, it reinforces the distance between our own capacities and the outstanding event we are watching and are fascinated by. The same holds for the emotional processes we witness and that are often so dramatic. We understand what concentration before the start is, or what it means during a long-distance race to hold a good position waiting for one's chance, and finally, when the second-placed runner attacks and takes the lead toward the end of the last curve, our heart starts beating with his. Or during a tennis match we not only admire the wonderful shots but also have some perception of the players' mental ups and downs and might be able to predict just by watching the body language of a player before and during his serve whether or not it will be good.

35. Cf. Cordner's remark: " . . . it is arguable that our concept of sport, perhaps unlike that of our ancestors, is in part a concept of that which is to be seen and evaluated from a spectator's point of view" (Cordner, "Differences Between Sport and Art", 426).

36. I am referring to the original piece, today located in the Philadelphia Museum of Art. There are, in the meantime, some break-free reproductions around in various museums. In my view they reflect the art world's resistance to the step made by Duchamp. One still prefers the illusion of necessity over the acceptance of contingency. Consider also that the break lines of the original piece not only correspond to the mechanical features of the work (marvellously so from the left to the middle in the lower part) but add a new semantic layer to the work; it now displays the breakdown of the mechanical attitude (and this as a consequence of a mechanical event itself) rather than the sophisticated usage of this attitude. We now witness the vulnerability and the overcoming of this ideal (which, decades later, took place in the cultural area in general).

37. With this, I am of course relying on Wittgenstein's concept of "family resemblances" that in my view constitutes one of the biggest breakthroughs in conceptual matters.

38. Additionally, the question of kitsch might serve as a test case. In the realm of the arts kitsch is typically possible. So are there instances of kitsch in sport? My hunch is that above all the sports that directly strive to be aesthetic are in danger of producing events which for an educated sensibility come close to kitsch. Take ribbon gymnastics as an example. The playfulness, which stems not from bodily exertion but from interplay with a fancy toy, borders—to say the least—on kitsch. Or imagine a skier who only tried to ski beautifully and not efficiently: some might admire him, others would certainly recognize and despise this as kitsch. What was so marvellous with Ingemar Stenmark was that in his case aesthetic appeal and efficiency resulted from the same movements; further developments, in slalom for example, however hindered such congruence: once you were allowed to ski over instead of around the slalom posts (as has been the case since the introduction of flexible poles), your descent can still be impressive in its efficiency but no longer for its beauty. If my guess is somehow correct, then—interestingly enough and seemingly paradoxically—the apparently 'aesthetic' sports would largely be exposed to the kitsch trap, whereas the 'purposive' ones would be good candidates for 'art'.

39. And, of course, there are degrees of competence in viewing sport; not every spectator is a good spectator.

40. Paul Klee, *Das bildnerische Denken*, ed. Jörg Spiller, 3d ed. (Basel: Schwabe, 1971), 95.

41. Arnold Gehlen, *Zeit-Bilder*, 2d ed. (Frankfurt/Main: Athenäum, 1965), 221.

42. Already in 1928 John Dewey noted "that the spread of sports and games is one of the characteristic features of existing social life" (John Dewey, "What Are the Russian Schools Doing?", in *John Dewey: The Later Works, 1925–1953*, vol. 3: 1927–1928, [Carbondale and Edwardsville: Southern Illinois University Press 1984], 224–32, here 225). In 1931 he commented with respect to newspapers: "Politics may appear on the first page and on the editorial page of newspapers, but the sport pages occupy more space, and the average reader turns to these pages with an eagerness which contrasts with the languid way in which he reads the political news and skips the editorials" (John Dewey, "Is There Hope for Politics?" in *John Dewey: The Later Works, 1925–1953*, vol. 6: 1931–1932 [Carbondale and Edwardsville: Southern Illinois University Press 1985], 182–89, here 182).

43. Cf. my criticism—on aesthetic grounds—of many phenomena of aestheticization in "Aestheticization Processes: Phenomena, Distinctions and Prospects" (*Undoing Aesthetics*, 1–32). My formula for those failures is that hyperaestheticization breaks into anaestheticization (cf. also my "Ästhetik und Anästhetik," in *Ästhetisches Denken* [Stuttgart: Reclam, 1990; 5th ed. 1998], 9–40).

44. Cf., as a case study on this, my "Contemporary Art in Public Space: A Feast for the Eyes or an Annoyance?" in *Undoing Aesthetics*, 118–22.

45. Likewise Adorno's remark that "art that runs away from illusion, seeking refuge in play, actually ends up in a class with sports" (T. W. Adorno, *Aesthetic theory*, tr. C. Lenhardt [New York: Routledge & Kegan Paul, 1984], 148) did not mean to ignore modern art's contributions to an aesthetic revaluation of the everyday but to emphasize that, notwithstanding all this, the proper task of art should not be lost.

CHAPTER 9

The Aesthetics of Weather

Yuriko Saito

Introduction

IN THE MODERN Western aesthetic practice, an aesthetic object is typically identified as a work of art. The experience of art does constitute a very significant and prominent aspect of the aesthetic life for many of us. We also invest a lot of time and energy not only to creating some works of art ourselves but also to developing and improving our artistic literacy through formalized disciplines and institutionalized practices such as art history, music theory, literary criticism, as well as philosophical aesthetics. But our experience of art, facilitated by these discourses, tends to stand out from our everyday life. We go to an art museum to enjoy paintings, set aside time to immerse ourselves in a novel, and listen to a symphony at a concert.

It may appear then that our aesthetic experience is limited to these specific occasions which are isolated from our everyday life. However, the absence of formal and systematic analysis does not imply a lack of aesthetic experience in our daily lives. On the contrary, though perhaps rarely recognized nor articulated, our everyday life apart from our experience of art is brimming with all kinds of aesthetic experiences. Such aesthetic experiences are universally shared, unlike art appreciation, which is limited to those cultures with institutionalized artworld and, even within that culture, only to those who have some access to and knowledge about the artworld.

Some recent thinkers have pointed out that identifying aesthetic experience with art appreciation is rather peculiar to the modern Western aesthetics. Arnold Berleant, a philosopher, for example, in developing his environmental aesthetics, points out that "the custom of selecting an art object and isolating it from its surrounding . . . has been . . . most pronounced since the eighteenth century, with its aesthetic of disinterestedness. Yet it is at variance with the ubiquity of the aesthetic recognized at other times in the West and commonly in non-Western cultures."[1] Another philosopher, Jerome Stolnitz, in his discussion of the notion of disinterestedness, remarks how this concept was originally proposed by the eighteenth-century British aestheticians, founders of modern Western aesthetics, as a way of defining aesthetic experience in general, including nonart objects, but "this catholicity in the denotation of 'aesthetic object' . . . has gone strangely unremarked."[2]

With regard to other cultural practices, philosophers Melvin Rader and Bertram Jessup call attention to the fact that the majority of non-Western cultures lack the equivalent notions of art, artist, and artworld, though their aesthetic life is as rich as ours. The Balinese, for example, is said to have a saying: "We have no art, we do everything the best way we can."[3] Victor Papanek, himself a designer, praises the Inuit people as the world's best designers because, as in the case of the Balinese, everybody is an artist in the sense "a man should do all things properly."[4] Finally, the aestheticism regarding everyday objects, phenomena, and activities in the traditional Japanese culture has been a subject of many writings.[5]

In light of these observations, I believe that our modern Western aesthetics, with its almost exclusive emphasis on art appreciation is rather limiting. In the following discussion, I would like to examine this inadequacy of art-centered aesthetics. I do so with a conviction I share with Berleant:

> humans along with all other things inhabit a single intraconnected realm, and . . . we must realize that our ultimate freedom lies not in diminishing or denying certain regions of our world in order to favor others but in acknowledging and understanding them all. This does not confer equal value on all. It admits rather that all activities, processes, and participants that together constitute nature have an equal claim to be taken seriously.[6]

I choose weather as my subject matter for investigating the everyday aesthetics because of its many dissimilarities from art. First, weather is not "an object" in the sense of a spatially or temporally enclosed entity independent of us; it is rather that which surrounds and interacts with our whole body. Second, weather affects us through many senses, not just through vision or hearing. Third, weather is intimately bound up with our various practical interests, unlike art objects that are usually regarded exclusively with aesthetic interests. Fourth, weather is not stationary; it is constantly changing. Finally, and perhaps most importantly, weather has been, is, and will be, experienced by every human being (unless one lives one's entire life within a temperature-controlled, windowless dwelling) regardless of the geographical and cultural contexts and despite one's familiarity with the artworld.

Frameless Character of Weather as an Aesthetic Object

Let's first examine a quintessential aesthetic object, say a painting in a museum, as a way of comparison. A painting is an object clearly framed and demarcated from the rest of space. By conventional agreement, we almost automatically ignore or suspend from our experience the relationship between the painted canvas and the surrounding wall paper, the smell of the fresh paint, the contrast between the front and back of the painted canvas, the way in which the painted canvas looks if we look at it obliquely or upside down, *even if* these are within our experiencial field and *even if* their inclusion in our experience may make it more exciting or intriguing.[7]

Similar restrictions apply to other art objects as well. For example, a symphony is to be appreciated through *its* sound only, disregarding the traffic noise outside the symphony hall, the coughing of the audience, and the feeling of discomfort caused by extra-strong air conditioning and awkward seat, as well as the smell of the new carpeting. In the theater, the boundary is also conventionally determined so that we know that what happens before the curtain rises, during the intermission, and after the curtain closes, is not part of the performance.[8]

We *can* choose to, and sometimes indeed do, experience weather in a similar way, as when we look outside from a window, focus only on the visual appeal of the cumulus cloud, or concentrate on the sound of raindrops hitting the roof. Sometimes the phenomenon itself encourages us to experience it as if it were an art object. For example, a quick, passing rainstorm can be likened to a dramatic theatrical piece, beginning with an approaching dark cloud, followed by raindrops falling one by one, gradually increasing in volume and speed, climaxing with pouring rain as if a bucket were overturned, and ending with a gradual diminuendo of rain, finally giving way to bright sunshine.

However, accounting for the aesthetic value of weather by modeling it after art, I believe, is problematic. For one, regarding and experiencing weather as a "wanna-be" art will most likely render it falling short of the artistic values, such as internal cohesion and expressive power, of a landscape painting or a piano etude. A quick glance at the history of the perceived relationship between art and nature indicates that, even in representational art or in a cultural practice respectful of nature's beauty, art is often regarded as an improvement over untouched, raw nature.[9]

Of course the above concern is begging the question by presupposing at the outset that weather as an aesthetic object is not always inferior to art. But further reflections, I think, will lend credence to this claim. First, let's examine why our experience of art is guided by so many restrictions enumerated above. The initial response is that they result from the conventional agreements, though they are for the most part tacitly adhered to rather than explicitly articulated. But why these conventional agreements?

With all the controversies surrounding the objectivity of aesthetic judgment concerning art, there is no denying that art is designed and intended to convey some message, be it a story, vision, idea, feeling, or sensuous experience, to the recipient, regardless of whether it actually succeeds in doing so and regardless of whether the recipients will share identical responses. Some kind of (or at least an attempt at) communication underlies the creation and experience of art. As such, a minimal requirement must exist to ensure that the experience created by the art object will be relatively comparable from a person to a person. Such commonality of experience will be impossible if there is no conventional guideline as to what is and what is not a part of the art object as well as concerning how to experience the object. I could of course enjoy the relationship between the painted surface and the surrounding wallpaper, or the contrast between what happens on the theater stage and what happens in the lobby during the intermission. But such a deviation from the conventional agreement will put me at a disadvantage in regards to experiencing the artwork as it was intended and as it is shared by other people. I will miss the opportunity for joining in the common experience.

In the case of weather, however, although there is something satisfactory and special about being able to share the same feeling and experience regarding a particular phenomenon, there is no comparable, compelling reason to set the common stage for our aesthetic appreciation. Indeed, it seems to me that the experience of weather, as it affects our entire being and is bound up so integrally with our daily life, is very personal and intimate, varying in content and degree from person to person, situation to situation. Unlike art, there does not seem to be an overriding concern for inducing similar experience, perhaps partly because there is no maker or communicator behind the phenomenon. Viewed this way, the framed character of art turns out to be not so much a requirement for aesthetic experiences as a requirement for inducing a common aesthetic experience.

Thus, art and weather are different kinds of aesthetic objects and as such require different ways of appreciating. Even among art objects of the same medium, different kinds of objects require different ways of experiencing and appreciating, what Paul Ziff, an aesthetician, terms "aspection": "relevant actions . . . that prove worthwhile in connection with the particular work." For example, "I survey a Tintoretto, while I scan an H. Bosch. Thus I step back to look at the Tintoretto, up to look at the Bosch," because "a different act of aspection is performed in connection with works belonging to different schools of art, which is why the classification of style is of the essence."[10] If different sorts of aspection are expected of different sorts of art objects, it seems reasonable to suppose that different kinds of objects (such as art versus meteorological phenomena) require different kinds of aspection.

And indeed it is my contention that experiencing weather as if it were a landscape painting or a piece of music will be to miss the point of appreciating weather *as weather*. To experience weather as weather seems to me that we experience not just its visual or sound qualities, but the way in which it envelops and affects our whole being, as well as our interaction with it. The experience of a hot, summer sun is not limited to the look of a round yellow disk against the cloudless sky; it includes the oppressive heat and humidity, a momentary relief from occasional wind felt on our skin, and the feeling of parched lips and dry mouth. Furthermore, it is not clear whether we ever experience weather conditions in isolation from other environmental factors. Indeed it is not even clear what it means to appreciate sunny weather by itself. Our experience of a dog day of the summer consists not only of those factors mentioned above but also the shiny glittering sunlight dancing on the lake surface, clearly delineated shadow of myself and other objects against the dry, white, sunlit surface, and the smell of freshly mown grass accompanied by the droning sound of a lawn mower.[11] Our experience of a fierce autumn wind is not simply the feeling of wind against our body; the way in which fallen leaves swirl around, the dynamic swaying of the tree branches, the rustling sound they make, the slightly musty smell coming from half-decaying leaves accumulated on the ground, and the rapid movement of the clouds all contribute toward our experience of this windy weather. Thus, in terms of both the range of objects and qualities comprising the aesthetic experience and the senses affected, weather as an aesthetic object is not something neatly confined into a package.

Another important difference between art and weather as an aesthetic object is the way in which we relate to the object or phenomenon. With a typical case of art appreciation, we are a beholder, spectator, listener of the object without participation or involvement. We are distanced from the object, both literally and metaphorically. Indeed most of the conventional agreements and institutional settings for art facilitate such distancing and disengagement from the object. We are not supposed to touch paintings and sculpture, and we are supposed to remain silent and sit still during a classical music concert or a theater performance. These conventional agreements determine the proper stance we should take toward the object that would induce the optimal experience.

The appreciation of weather, however, engages our whole body most directly and literally.[12] We sometimes experience raindrops falling on our heads as we skip and jump over puddles while "singin' in the rain," all the while taking note of the gray sky, water rings around raindrops falling on the puddles, and the splashing sound my jumping into puddles causes. This physical activity creates a very different experience of rain compared to the way in which I experience it under a hanging roof of a Zen temple, looking out to its attached rock garden, attending to the way in which the surface of each rock glistens with wetness, and noting the elegant movement of raindrops as they dance downward along the linked chain hanging from the gutter, appropriately called "rain chains." One experience exudes vibrant and cheerful energy, while the other expresses gentle melancholy and quiet peacefulness.

Consider also our experience of snow. How many ways there are to engage ourselves in appreciating snow! Of course we can remain rather spectator-like and admire the snowscape. But how many of us have not experienced the fun of playing in and with the snow? As the noted seventeenth-century Japanese haiku master Basho exclaims:

> now then, let's go out
> to enjoy the snow . . . until
> I slip and fall!

> will you start a fire?
> I'll show you something nice:
> a giant snowball[13]

Even the act of urination does not escape the (male!?) aesthetic attention of another eighteenth-century haiku master, Issa:

> Pissing through my doorway
> I make a clean hole
> in the snow.[14]

Unlike in the case of art, then, there is no one privileged stance we should take to "properly" appreciate a particular weather condition. Some experience may be more intense, pleasant, or satisfactory than others, but each individual way in which we experience weather conditions gives rise to its own character and ambience.[15] A storm can be experienced in a boat tossed around in the middle of the ocean, on the beach while looking at gigantic waves, or in the middle of woods and even from a treetop, as John Muir did.[16] Our experience of weather is thus thoroughly intertwined with and entrenched in our particular circumstances and activities, affecting and being affected by where we are and what we do.

Weather and Everyday Concerns

One may point to this thorough integration of weather with our entire being as a detriment to our aesthetic appreciation of it. That is, weather affects us in our daily life in so many ways and these practical impacts on us detract from its status as an object of aesthetic appreciation. Although art objects can be regarded for various practical purposes, such as yielding information about the culture or the artist, being useful for therapeutic purposes, or providing a background for special events, our appreciation of art as art is primarily aesthetic. However, weather directly affects our well-being in a number of ways: it determines bodily comfort, the possibility of outdoor activities and events; it makes or breaks many people's (such as farmers' and fishermen's) livelihoods; and it sometimes threatens our very existence (as when a hurricane, tornado, or blizzard occurs). These very practical concerns with and interests in weather conditions make us less sensitive and receptive to their aesthetic aspects. Such is the claim maintained by many, though not all, thinkers who subscribe to the theory of aesthetic formalism or the theory of disinterestedness or distancing. To put it simply, these views share the notion that the aesthetic appreciation of anything has to do with its sensuous surface, (such as color, line, shape, texture, and sound) without regard to their various practical significance (such as utility, or scientific, historical, or economical significance).

For example, Mark Twain seems to be presenting such a view in his description of the protagonist's experience of the Mississippi River before and after he learns how to navigate the riverboat. After he learned how to read the book of the river written in meteorological and riparian languages, what to the untutored eyes were "all manner of pretty pictures . . . painted by the sun and shaded by the clouds" or "the glories and the charms which the moon and the sun and the twilight wrought upon the river's face" became "the grimmest and most dead-earnest of reading-matter," so that the sunset scene will simply imply that "we are going to have wind to-morrow." "All the grace, the beauty, the poetry had gone out of the majestic river," and "the romance and the beauty were all gone from the river," describes Twain.[17]

In a similar vein, Jerome Stolnitz claims that a meteorologist's interest is incompatible with appreciating a cloud aesthetically and that the aesthetic appreciation of the cloud has to do merely with its looks. "A meteorologist is concerned, not with the visual appearance of a striking cloud formation, but with the causes which led to it . . . the aesthetic attitude 'isolates' the object and focuses upon it— the 'look' of the rocks, the sound of the ocean, the colors in the painting."[18]

However, while there is no denying that the tourist's appreciation of the sunset over the Mississippi and the layman's appreciation of the look of clouds are aesthetic appreciations, what is misleading in these claims is that these are the only aesthetic appreciation possible with respect to each phenomenon. That is, to maintain that the aesthetic appreciation must refer to the sensuous surface of the object/phenomenon does not necessarily imply that other considerations, such as practical and scientific, always nullify, interfere with, or detract from our appreciation of the sensuous surface. We cannot derive a generalized aesthetic theory from some particular cases described by Twain and Stolnitz.

On the contrary, there are a number of cases where various conceptual considerations modify, transform, or enhance our experience of the sensuous surface. For example, consider our experience of cumulus cloud. As Ronald Hepburn, a philosopher, reminds us, we can "realize the inner turbulence of the cloud, the winds sweeping up within and around it, determining its structure and visible form."[19] The violent motion of air within the cloud is expressed by the powerful, striking sensuous surface of the cloud. The appreciation of this expressive quality of the cloud (of turbulence and power), instead of being the appreciation of simply some fact about the object, can also be aptly characterized as an aesthetic appreciation of the cloud.

By now the classic description of the fog at sea by the psychologist Edward Bullough in his theory of "psychical distance" also provides a good example of how a practical aspect of a natural object can be an important ingredient in our aesthetic experience. While he claims that the aesthetic appreciation of the fog is possible only with our "distanced" attitude, he does not claim that we must ignore its practical aspect (i.e., danger) in our aesthetic experience. The aesthetic experience of the fog at sea is no doubt constituted by its perceptual qualities such as its "opaqueness as of transparent milk, blurring the outline of things and distorting their shapes into weird grotesqueness." However, the source of our intense experience rather lies in "the uncanny mingling of repose and terror" brought about by the seemingly peaceful appearance of the phenomenon "hypocritically denying as it were any suggestion of danger" and that "contrast(s) sharply with the blind and distempered anxiety of its other aspects." Distancing, which Bullough claims is necessary for the emergence of this kind of aesthetic experience, is not abstracting from our awareness and ignoring the imminent sense of danger and terror; distancing rather has to do with viewing and regarding this phenomenon (seemingly calm and peaceful but really a sign of danger) with the "unconcern of a mere spectator."[20]

This fog example is also instructive for another reason. That is, this experience is intensely personal in the sense it is circumstance- and person-dependent. That is, in this experience of the fog at sea where we are concerned about our safety, the experience will include, and in turn be transformed by, the appreciation of the juxtaposition of calm repose and terror. A similar experience will most likely be shared by those of us flying on an airplane or driving a car. However, our aesthetic experience of the fog will take on an entirely different character if we are, for example, walking along the beach, or looking at the blurred outline of a distant mountain. The experience here will enhance the sense of quietude and solitariness without any notion of anxiety or uneasiness. Unlike our typical experience of an art object where we are encouraged to put aside or transcend any personal concern at the moment, the aesthetic appreciation of weather can be modified or intensified by integrating our very personal, practical concern with the phenomena.[21]

However, one may point out that many times the effect of weather looms so large in our daily living that it is often difficult to take an aesthetic interest in it, particularly if the weather condition affects us negatively. We don't like rain on our parade; snow causes a massive headache, from school cancellations to treacherous driving conditions; and relentless summer sun and heat with no rain spells trouble for our lawn and shrubs, not to mention a disaster for farmers. Most of us have to deal with the inconveniences and problems caused by these weather conditions and our overwhelmingly negative reaction to these weather conditions get in the way of any possible aesthetic experience.

While it is universally true that our everyday life is sometimes negatively affected by various weather conditions, it is not clear whether it is also universally the case that such negative effects of weather always get in the way of people's aesthetic experience of it. Let me take the Japanese aesthetic tradition as one example to show how weather conditions, with their sometimes inconvenient and negative effects on our practical life, can be a very prominent aspect of people's aesthetic life.

One way in which the Japanese aesthetic tradition celebrates various weather conditions, with all their discomfort and inconveniences, is to observe and appreciate the way in which a particular season, month, or occasion is epitomized by a weather condition characteristic of each. A quick survey of Japanese literature will reveal that its subject matters are dominated by the beauty of each season and month, most notably characterized by weather condition. The association of weather and season is most explicitly formulated in the designation of *kigo,* season word, which must be included in a haiku, a 5-7-5 syllable verse established during the seventeenth century which remains a popular literary form, often gracing the front page of major newspapers today. Though not exclusively consisting of terms describing or related to weather conditions, there is no denying that *kigo* is dominated by weather conditions, sometimes making subtle distinctions between different kinds of wind, rain, or mist.

But by far the oldest and most prominent literary work featuring the aesthetic character of various seasons, months, and occasions is *The Pillow Book,* essays and anecdotes written by an eleventh-century court lady, Sei Shonagon. Behind her appreciation of various events, seasons, and times of the day lies her general observation that "each month has its own particular charm, and the entire year is a delight."[22] The character of winter, for example, according to her, is best expressed by early morning: "beautiful indeed when snow has fallen during the night, but splendid too when the ground is white with frost; or even when there is no snow or frost, but it is simply very cold and the attendants hurry from room to room stirring up the fires and bringing charcoal, *how well this fits the season's mood!*" Indeed, the colder the better for winter's mood, as "in the First Month when I go to a temple for a retreat I like the weather to be extremely cold; there should be snow on the ground, and everything should be frozen." March Third, the occasion for the Festival of Young Herbs, is best characterized by "the sun, shining bright and calm in the spring sky." The Kamo Festival in April is best enjoyed if "in the daytime there is no mist to hide the sky and, glancing up, one is overcome by its beauty," while the Iris Festival on May Fifth should be "cloudy." The Star Festival on July Seventh "should also be cloudy; but in the evening it should clear, so that the moon shines brightly in the sky and one can see the outline of the stars." This clear moon is particularly appreciated when "it is so stifling hot . . . that even at night one keeps all the doors and lattices open." But July also welcomes a storm that gives a relief to this stifling heat "when there are fierce winds and heavy shower, it is quite cool and one does not bother to carry a fan. On such days, I find it is pleasant to take a nap, having covered myself with some clothing that gives off a faint smell of perspiration." As for the Moon Festival on September Ninth, "there should be a drizzle from early dawn. Then there will be heavy dew on the chrysanthemums, while the floss silk that covers them will be wet through and drenched also with the precious scent of blossoms."[23]

Many centuries later, we see in many haiku the same sensibility toward those objects, phenomena, and activities expressive of each season. Summer is characterized by heat, with all the accompanying discomfort:

heat waves shimmer
on the shoulders of my
paper robe

in a cowshed
mosquito buzz sounds dusky . . .
lingering summer heat

dead grass—
imperceptibly, heat waves
one or two inches high[24]

Winter is epitomized by the bone-chilling cold of its wind, rain, or snow:

first winter shower—
the monkey also seems to want
a small raincoat

a wintry gust—
cheeks painfully swollen,
the face of a man[25]

In all these examples, what is appreciated is not simply some aspects of various weather conditions but more importantly the way in which the essence of each season, month, or occasion is expressed by a certain weather condition. The object of appreciation is the summer-like ambience created by hot, humid air relieved briefly by a passing shower, or the winterly atmosphere conveyed by the biting cold morning air accompanying the sound made by stepping onto the frost-ridden ground. These experiences, which may not necessarily be pleasant in and by themselves, can nevertheless be appreciated aesthetically for defining the quintessential character of the respective season. As Sei Shonagon succinctly declares, "summer is best when it is extremely hot, winter is best when it is excruciatingly bitter cold."[26] Trying to find cool relief or trying to bundle up to keep warm, even if not always a pleasant experience, is nonetheless a part of our experience of each season, and it makes us become more aware of and sensitive to the characteristic of each season.[27]

Another way in which the traditional Japanese aesthetic sensibility celebrated positive aesthetic values of weather, regardless of its accompanying discomfort and inconveniences, is to transform the otherwise negative values into something positive through aestheticization. Again, as in other examples in Japanese aesthetics, the Japanese sensibility not only accepts experiences of frustration, disappointment, and inconvenience, but also elevates them through various means of aestheticization. For example, inconveniences caused by rain can heighten its poetic significance:

> spring rain—
> down along a wasps' nest, water
> leaking through the roof

> whereabout is
> Kasashima? this rainy month,
> this muddy road[28]

Similarly, snow, with its cold wetness that causes various practical problems, is appreciated not only by its expression of winteriness but also for the way in which it intensifies the feeling of desolation and loneliness.

> Each person I meet
> I ask the way to an inn—
> but no one replies.
> Hats against driven snow
> go down the path at a slant.
> (Shinkei, fifteenth century)

> Even when snowfall began
> this morning
> I longed for a visitor from the capital.
> Desolate mountain village at dusk

buried in snow.
(Priest Jakuren, twelfth century)

Thinking that
Perhaps today you might come and visit,
I gaze at the garden—
Trackless snow.
(Empress Guno Daibu Toshinari, twelfth century)[29]

The appeal of snow here is partly due to its power to heighten the already felt
loneliness experienced by one living in an isolated village or one awaiting the
lover's visit. The sense of melancholy or resignation becomes an object of aesthetic
contemplation through the contribution of snow.

Inaccessibility, such as caused by snow, is not limited to physical space; it can
also be a perceptual obstacle. Unlike under a clear sky, where everything will be seen
clearly and in its entirety, falling snow, mist, and passing clouds render a landscape
obscure, the moon indistinct, and other objects hidden. In these cases, too, the
Japanese sensibility cherishes, rather than laments, an obscured or concealed view
because it is considered more appealing and enticing than a clear, exposed view.

In a well-known passage, Yoshida Kenko, a fourteenth-century retired Buddhist monk, illustrates this aesthetic penchant for obscurity and implication by
the example of the moon. According to him, "to long for the moon while looking
on the rain, to lower the blinds and be unaware of the passing of the spring—
these are even more deeply moving."[30] The moon obscured or hidden by the mist
or cloud is more pleasing than the exposed moon, because the former stimulates
the imagination and increases excitement through anticipation, longing, or remi-
niscence. This judgment was shared by his contemporary thinkers and critics who
uniformly contend that "the moon is not pleasing unless partly obscured by a
cloud."[31] It was also inherited by haiku poets centuries later, as indicated by the
following two haiku by Basho:

clouds now and then
give rest to people
viewing the moon

in the misty rain
Mount Fuji is veiled all day—
how intriguing![32]

Such appreciation of weather conditions that normally affect us negatively,
either by causing discomfort and inconvenience or by blocking the maximum

view of things we want to see, results from a kind of dialectic movement. At first, we may be troubled or disappointed by the negative effects these weather conditions exert on our daily life because of our wish for comfort, convenience, safety, and a certain kind of aesthetic experience facilitated by the optimal view. What is unique about the Japanese aesthetic appreciation is the way in which our initially negative response becomes transformed into a positive experience through aestheticizing what otherwise is an unpleasant, inconvenient, or not optimally satisfactory situation. This aesthetic resolution adds pathos and poignancy to the experience that would be absent if one were to simply appreciate the snow-clad landscape or half-hidden moon without any wish or expectation of viewing them unconcealed.

But due to some weather conditions' power to threaten our safety and even existence, there is a limitation to our capacity to aestheticize weather conditions with negative effects on us. As Edmund Burke and Immanuel Kant remind us in their discussion of the sublime, those objects and phenomena that can overpower us can be appreciated positively *only when* we are, or regard ourselves to be, in safety. Things like "clouds piled up in the sky, moving with lightning flashes and thunder peals" or "hurricanes with their track of devastation," according to Kant, can be "the more attractive, the more fearful it is, *provided only that we are in security.*"[33] Without such provision, all we experience will be fear, terror, and pain, which do not allow us enough composure or "distance" to have a positive experience. Depending both upon our particular situation and capacity and upon the danger of a specific weather condition, there must be a point at which an attempt at aestheticization becomes impossible.

In this regard, it is noteworthy that, with all the predominance of weather conditions in Japanese literature, there is a conspicuous lack of description of the sublime attributed to weather. For example, the well-known reference to autumnal typhoon, both in *The Pillow Book* and in *The Tale of Genji* by Lady Murasaki Shikibu written during the first decade of the eleventh century, describes the after-effect of this violent storm, but not the storm itself.[34] It is also noteworthy that a Japanese David Thoreau, Kamo no Chomei (1153–1216), whose *An Account of My Hut* is well known for its sensitive description of natural beauty that he found in his mountain retirement life, gives a wholly negative account of a hurricane by emphasizing only its destructive power.[35]

Impermanence of Weather

The last feature that distinguishes weather from many other typical aesthetic objects such as artworks is its transient characteristic. Although there is variation among different climates, it is generally rare for the exact same weather condition to continue. The change is particularly prominent in temperate climates with distinct seasons. Cold, snowy weather gives way to warm spring, which gives way to hot, humid summer, which changes into the crisp cold air of autumn, sometimes with visits from hurricanes or typhoons in-between. Even within a short period of time such as one day, most of us in the temperate climate are familiar with the weather change, sometimes catching us off-guard because we dressed too heavily for a sudden hot spell, or we did not prepare ourselves for an unexpected shower. Furthermore, some weather condition is characterized by its very ephemerality, such as wind, rain, or snow.

A typical aesthetic object such as a work of art is expected to exist almost indefinitely with little change. As the saying goes: *Ars longa, vita brevis*. Indeed we go out of our way to ensure its permanence by preserving it under a specific condition in an art museum and to erase any mark of aging, wear, and tear by restoration work.[36] Even for those art objects that do not exist in space, such as music and literature, we expect some sort of unchanging continuity, despite changing interpretations and performing practices. In general, then, while our perception and interpretation of the art object may change with time, we expect that the object of our aesthetic experience stays relatively the same. Not so with weather; it exemplifies the exact opposite by constantly changing its condition. Such mutability and evanescence may appear to lessen weather's status as an aesthetic object.[37] On the contrary, however, transience and impermanence can be an intense source of aesthetic appreciation.

For one, transience and changeability can provide positive aesthetic experience by relieving fatigue factor. Constant movement, surprising change, or eventual extinction can stimulate our imagination and facilitate a pleasurable experience. Such is the consideration behind Joseph Addison's account of one of our pleasures of the imagination that he calls "the novel" or "the uncommon." According to him, "we are . . . so often conversant with one set of objects and tired out with so many repeated shows of the same things that whatever is new or uncommon contributes a little to vary human life and to divert our minds, for a while, with the strangeness of its appearance." His examples for "the new" include perpetually shifting and moving objects, such as "rivers, jetteaus, or falls of water," in addition to monsters, imperfections of nature, and spring landscapes.[38]

A similar consideration is at work behind Yoshida Kenko's claim that "if man were never to fade away like the dews of Adashino, never to vanish like the smoke over Toribeyama, but lingered on forever in the world, how things would lose their power to move us! The most precious thing in life is its uncertainty."[39] But the Japanese aesthetic appreciation of transience and impermanence, such as exemplified by weather conditions, is supported by a further, existential concern. It is noteworthy that the weather conditions most frequently cited for their aesthetic appeal in Japanese tradition are rain, clouds, fog, snow, wind, and mist. Consider the following figures. Of roughly one hundred poems celebrating weather conditions in the first court-sanctioned anthology of poems, *Kokinshu* (Collection of Ancient and Modern Poems completed in 905), one poem specifically refers to sunlight; the rest deal with wind, snow, mist, clouds, fog, and frost (in order of frequency). And in a subsequent court-sanctioned anthology, *Shinkokinshu* (New Collection of Ancient and Modern Poems completed in 1205), out of approximately 350 poems referring to weather, only two poems mention sunlight while the rest sing in praise of wind, rain, clouds, snow, mist, fog, hail, and frost (in order of frequency). In contrast to sunny weather, these weather conditions are generally passing phenomena. They also symbolize impermanence and evanescence because of their perishability. Snow melts away, rain dries, and fog lifts, without leaving any trace of their existence. Furthermore, the constant movement of falling snow, rain, and wind suggests changeability.

Though accompanied by a tinge of sadness, in traditional Japanese aesthetics qualities such as transience and evanescence were celebrated aesthetic values; similarly, transience and perishability symbolized by nature provide a justification for the human condition. While transience, the universal human condition, generally gives rise to pessimism, the Japanese traditionally sought solace in finding the same condition in nature. Focusing on more permanent objects in nature would make us become more aware of and sorry for our own evanescence. In contrast, recognizing and appreciating the impermanent, evanescent aspects of nature would gently assure us that nothing that exists can escape this condition of transience. Phenomena such as rain, snow, dew, and wind eloquently express transience and impermanence, making us become aware that humans and nature exist ultimately by the same principle. Aestheticizing the impermanence in nature then leads us toward an acceptance and sympathetic appreciation of our own transience.

> The wind of spring
>   Scatters the cherry flowers,
> Here in this fleeting world of ours.
> (Priest Saigyo, twelfth century)

> Like dew they fall, these tears of mine,
>   And vanish like the dew;
> Ah, my good days at Naniwa
>   Were nought but dreams within dreams, too.
> (parting poem of Toyotomi Hideyoshi, 1598)[40]

Indeed the Japanese tradition provides an artistic genre that elevates this notion of transience to its supreme aesthetic height: the tea ceremony. The art of tea ceremony, among others, lies in the awareness and appreciation that each occasion, constituted by various factors such as the season, weather condition, the time of the day, a particular group of guests as well as the host's preparation, happens only once, never to be repeated. This awareness is referred to as *ichigo ichie* (one time, one meeting) and lends intensity and poignancy to each event. Among various factors, weather, snow in particular, lends singularity to the occasion. Existing records show that many impromptu tea ceremonies were held when snow fell, and, as indicated by the specific instructions left by Sen no Rikyu, a sixteenth-century tea master, thorough care was taken to honor and celebrate this phenomenon by fussing over what to do with the snow on the stepping stones in the garden, the snow piled in the water basin, and the light from lanterns in the garden.[41]

Thus, in the Japanese aesthetic tradition, transience and impermanence not only do not detract from the aesthetic value of an object/phenomenon but rather constitute the very core of its aesthetic value. It is interesting to note that contemporary Western art genre termed land art or earth art derives part of its aesthetic appeal from its transient nature, particularly fresh and effective in the context of the traditional Western obsession with permanence in its handling of art objects. Because of its very nature of being situated outside, those earth art objects are subject to changing weather conditions all the time. Some earth art objects in fact capitalize on the changing nature of weather condition as their main appeal. Walter de Maria's *Lightning Field,* Nancy Holt's *Sun Tunnel,* James Turrell's *Roden Crater,* and many outdoor pieces and snowball creations by Andy Goldsworthy come to our mind.[42] Regarding his various snowball pieces, Goldsworthy remarks: "A snowball made in a day when the snow was good, fresh, not thawing, sunny and calm has to differ from one made in the wind, rain and dark with wet thawing snow. Each snowball is an expression of the time it was made."[43] The temporality of the snowball is also recorded by his photographic documentation of its melting process. Aesthetically appreciating weather, therefore, encourages us to be sensitive to the temporal aspect of this phenomenon, which in fact is the dimension shared by everything existent, including our own existence.

Concluding Remarks

In the above discussion I tried to show the ways in which we can celebrate the positive aesthetic value of all kinds of weather, including those that affect us negatively in our management of daily affairs. I conclude my discussion on weather by suggesting further that such maximization of aesthetic appreciation of weather is beneficial to us not only from the purely aesthetic viewpoint (by enriching the content of our everyday aesthetic experience) but also from a much broader persepctive. Weather, even among natural objects and phenomena, is one of the last frontiers of human cultivation, manipulation, and control. That is, we humans still have not figured out a way to control and manipulate, let alone pre-cisely predict, the weather, while we can change the course of a river, cure a dis-ease, or even clone animals. In this hi-tech age of manipulating most aspects of nature at our will, weather serves as a reminder that not everything around us is subject to our control. Rather than lamenting or feeling frustrated with our impotence before the force of nature, being able to aesthetically appreciate those that are beyond our power of control, I think, is particularly important today. It suggests to us that accepting and submitting ourselves to a natural force that can-not be tamed by humans does not necessarily have to be a disappointing or frus-trating experience; it can be a source of aesthetic pleasure, if we learn to humble ourselves to gratefully receive and celebrate the positive aspects of its gift to us.[44]

Acknowledgment

This chapter is an outgrowth of the sessions dealing with the aesthetics of snow in which I participated (American Society for Aesthetics, 1990; The International Congress of Geographers, 1992; The Kyoto Conference on Japan Studies, 1994), as well as the courses on the aesthetic appreciation of nature, the aesthetics of the everyday, and the traditional Japanese aesthetics, that I regularly teach at the Rhode Island School of Design. I particularly want to thank Barbara Sandrisser and Jo Ellen Jacobs for their insights on the aesthetics of snow that they shared in our three sessions together.

Notes

1. Arnold Berleant, *The Aesthetics of Environment* (Philadelphia: Temple University Press, 1992), 157.
2. Jerome Stolnitz, "Of the Origins of 'Aesthetic Disinterestedness'," originally published in *The Journal of Aesthetics and Art Criticism* (Winter 1961), included in *Aesthetics: A Crit-ical Anthology*, ed. George Dickie and R. J. Sclafani (New York: St. Martin's, 1977), 624, emphasis added.
3. Melvin Rader and Bertram Jessup, *Art and Human Values* (Englewood Cliffs, N.J.: Pren-tice-Hall, 1976), 116.
4. Victor Papanek, *The Green Imperative: Natural Design for the Real World* (New York: Thames and Hudson, 1995), 233. The whole chapter titled "The Best Designers in the World?" (223–34) is devoted to this discussion.
5. To list only a few sources: Donald Keene, "Japanese Aesthetic," in *Appreciation of Japan-ese Culture* (Tokyo: Kodansha International, 1981); Ivan Morris, "The Cult of Beauty," in *The World of the Shining Prince: Court Life in Ancient Japan* (New York: Kodansha Amer-ica, 1994); Yuriko Saito, "Aesthetic Egalitarianism" in "Japanese Aesthetics," included in *Encyclopedia of Aesthetics*, ed. Michael Kelly (New York: Oxford University Press, 1998), vol. 2, 545–47.

THE AESTHETICS OF WEATHER

6. Berleant, *Aesthetics of Environment,* 9.

7. For the purpose of my discussion, I give a quick generalization concerning art as an aesthetic object. Particularly among contemporary art, there are exceptions to my description here. Even among traditional art objects, there are a number of controversial and intriguing issues concerning what is and is not a part of a work of art (such as a painter's signature, chips and cracks on the surface of an old painting and sculpture, the title of a painting, sculpture or music, and so on). Or sometimes it may not be possible to ignore what we know to be outside of a work of art, such as if we are "viewing a yellow version of Josef Albers' *Hommage to the square* displayed in a yellow frame on a yellow stuccoed wall." (Paul Ziff, "Anything Viewed," originally published in 1984, included in *Oxford Readers: Aesthetics,* ed. Susan L. Feagin and Patrick Maynard (New York: Oxford University Press, 1997), 27.

8. Again, these are quick generalizations concerning mostly classical music and theater. Many contemporary pieces, such as John Cage's *4′ 33″* and the artistic genre called happening, owe part of their effectiveness and appeal to these conventions because they shock us by breaking them.

9. For example, while the motto of classical and neoclassical art theories in the Western tradition was to "imitate" or "copy" nature, it was never to reproduce empirical nature but rather to present "Nature" in the sense of perfect or idealized nature. In a culture like Japan known for its traditional attitude of affinity to and respect for nature, various arts dealing directly with natural material, such as garden, bonsai, and flower arrangement, are designed to distill and emphasize its essential characteristics, thereby improving its articulation. I explored this aspect of Japanese garden in "Japanese Gardens: The Art of Improving Nature," *Chanoyu Quarterly,* No. 83 (1996):40–61.

10. Paul Ziff, "Reasons in Art Criticism," included in *Philosophy and Education,* ed. Israel Scheffler (Boston: Allyn and Bacon, Inc., 1958), 234, 235.

11. Thomas Leddy reminds us that the sun itself and its light are seldom the direct object of our aesthetic appreciation. "[N]ote that although the sun always shines literally in the sense that it emits rays of light, it is usually not considered beautiful in itself. The beauty of sunshine seems, rather, to depend on indirection: the shimmer of silver linings on clouds, the shine of dawn light on a landscape, the way a sun's ray passes through the clouds, the reflection of a winter sun on a lake. Things sparkle and shine in the sun, for example an island, a lovely pond, a new house or just a beautiful morning." "Sparkle and Shine," *British Journal of Aesthetics* 37 (July 1997):267.

12. Here I am indebted to the notion of "engagement" developed by Arnold Berleant in the following seminal works: *Art and Engagement* (Philadelphia: Temple University Press, 1991); *The Aesthetics of Environment* and *Living in the Landscape: Toward an Aesthetics of Environment* (Lawrence: University Press of Kansas, 1997).

13. Included in *Basho and His Interpreters: Selected Hokku with Commentary,* comp. and tr. Makoto Ueda (Stanford: Stanford University Press, 1991), 151, 177.

14. Included in *Snow Falling from a Bamboo Leaf: The Art of Haiku,* tr. Hiag Akmakjian (Santa Barbara, Calif.: Capra Press, 1979), 76.

15. One discrimination we can make among various ways of experiencing weather is the degree to which our entire being is engaged. For example, viewing the outside from a

window will give us very limited contact with the particular weather condition compared to our outdoor experience.

16. His description of a storm in the High Sierra can be found in "A Wind-storm in the Forests" in *The Mountains of California,* originally published in 1894, included in *The American Landscape: A Critical Anthology of Prose and Poetry,* ed. John Conron (New York: Oxford University Press, 1973), 264–270.

17. Mark Twain, *Life on the Mississippi,* in *Mississippi Writings* (New York: Literary Classics of the United States, 1982), 284–85.

18. Jerome Stolnitz, *Aesthetics and Philosophy of Art Criticism* (Boston: Houghton Mifflin, 1960), 35.

19. Ronald Hepburn, "Aesthetic Appreciation of Nature," in *Aesthetics in the Modern World,* ed. Harold Osborne (London: Thames and Hudson, 1968), 62, emphasis added.

20. Edward Bullough, "'Psychical Distance' as a Factor in Art and an Aesthetic Principle," *The British Journal of Psychology,* vol. 5 (1912–13), 88–89.

21. The modification can be in the form of disillusionment, as pointed out by Cheryl Foster in her "Aesthetic Disillusionment: Environment, Ethics, Art," *Environmental Values* 1 (1992): 205–15. As an example of aesthetic disillusionment, she describes a spectacular sunset that turns out to result from the proliferation of sulphur dioxide emitted from a factory.

22. Sei Shonagon, *The Pillow Book of Sei Shonagon,* tr. Ivan Morris (New York: Columbia University Press, 1967), vol. 1, 1. All the subsequent references from this work are consolidated at the end of this paragraph.

23. All the quoted passages in this paragraph are from Sei Shonagon, ibid. The early morning winter is from 1 (emphasis added); the First Month, 126; March Third, 4; Kamo Festival, 4; Iris Festival, 44; Star Festival, 12; the clear moon, 40; storm in July, 50; Moon Festival, 12–13. This last passage continues: "Sometimes the rain stops early in the morning, but the sky is still overcast, and it looks as if it may start raining again at any moment. This too I find very pleasant." Another description of a morning in the Ninth Month reads as follows:

> I remember a clear morning in the Ninth Month when it had been raining all night. Despite the bright sun, dew was still dripping from the chrysanthemums in the garden. On the bamboo fences and criss-cross hedges I saw tatters of spider webs; and where the threads were broken the raindrops hung on them like strings of white pearls. I was greatly moved and delighted. As it became sunnier, the dew gradually vanished from the clover and the other plants where it had lain so heavily; the branches began to stir, then suddenly sprang up of their own accord (135).

24. Basho, *Basho and his Interpreters,* 225, 320, and 180.

25. Ibid., 275, 303.

26. My translation of section 114 of *Makura no Soshi* (*Pillow Book*), ed. Joji Ishida (Tokyo: Kadokawa Shoten, 1980). The Morris translation has "a very cold winter scene; an unspeakably hot summer scene," along with "Pines. Autumn fields. Mountain villages and paths. Cranes and deer" under the section titled "Things That Gain by Being Painted" (124). But two other Japanese editions, one by Iwanami Shoten, the other by Shogakukan, both have the phrase regarding summer and winter as an independent section, not as a part of things that gain by being painted.

27. This way of appreciating the quintessential nature of an object or a phenomenon is one of the unique features of Japanese aesthetic appreciation, which governs various aesthetic and artistic activities, ranging from Japanese garden and bonsai to cooking, poetry-making to painting.

28. Basho, 378, 240. An excellent discussion of the Japanese view of rain can be found in Barbara Sandrisser's "Fine Weather—the Japanese View of Rain," *Landscape* 26(1982): 42–47.

29. Shinkei's poem is included in *Traditional Japanese Poetry: An Anthology*, tr. Steven D. Carter (Stanford: Stanford University Press, 1991), 290. The other two are my translation from *Shinkokinshu*, compiled by Fujiwara no Teika in 1205. I am using vol. 26 of *Nihon Koten Bungaku Zenshu* (Complete Works of Classical Japanese Literature), ed. Fumito Minenura (Tokyo: Shogakukan, 1974), nos. 663 and 664.

30. Yoshida Kenko, *Essays in Idleness: The Tsurezuregusa of Kenko*, tr. Donald Keene, originally written between 1330 and 1332 (New York: Columbia University Press, 1967), 115.

31. A fifteenth-century tea master Murata Shuko's statement was quoted by Komparu Zenpo and cited by Koshiro Haga in "The *Wabi* Aesthetic," in *Tea in Japan: Essays on the History of Chanoyu*, ed. Paul Varley and Kumakura Isao (Honolulu: University of Hawaii Press, 1989), 197. In his discussion of the aesthetic ideal of the tea ceremony, *wabi*, Haga compiles in this essay a number of descriptions given by the tea masters and others. What is interesting for our purpose is that most of them describe this ideal by the metaphor of landscape or object, such as the moon, hidden or obscured by clouds or mist. To cite just one example, another retired monk, Kamo no Chomei (1153–1216) claims: "When looking at autumn mountains through mist, the view may be indistinct yet have great depth. Although few autumn leaves may be visible through the mist, it is alluring. The limitless vista created in imagination far surpasses anything one can see more clearly," 204.

32. Basho, 102, 137.

33. Immanuel Kant, *Critique of Judgment*, tr. J. H. Bernard (New York: Hafner Press, 1974), section 28, 100.

34. Sei Shonagon, *Pillow Book*, 185–86. Murasaki Shikibu, *The Tale of Genji*, tr. Edward G. Seidensticker (New York: Alfred A. Knopf, 1992), 480–90.

35. Kamo no Chomei, *An Account of My Hut*, tr. Donald Keene, included in *Anthology of Japanese Literature*, ed. Donald Keene (New York: Grove Press, 1960), 197–212.

36. For the purpose of the present discussion, I will not address various complications regarding restoration of art, such as whether it is aesthetically and historically desirable to erase the sign of aging completely from an old work of art.

37. Kevin Melchionne points out that one of the reasons that the art of home-making does not receive aestheticians' attention is because it does not result in objects which stay unchanged for a long time. "Unlike paradigmatic art forms like painting or poetry, interiors do not just sit around after their completion unaltered for the centuries. They are lived in, worked in, and worked on and so they are also transformed, if only by being worn upon daily." "Living in Glass Houses: Domesticity, Interior Decoration, and Environmental Aesthetics," *The Journal of Aesthetics and Art Criticism* 56, no. 2 (Spring 1998):199.

38. Joseph Addison, "Pleasures of the Imagination," 412 (June 23, 1712) included in *Essays in Criticism and Literary Theory*, ed. John Loftis (Northbrook, Ill.: AHM Publishing Corp.,

1975), 142–143. In contrast, Kant seems to represent the general tendency to require permanence of an aesthetic object. For him, constantly changing objects, such as "the sight of the changing shapes of a fire on the hearth or of a rippling brook," do not have beauty, although "they bring with them a charm for the imagination because they entertain it in free play." *Critique of Judgment*, tr. J.H. Bernard (New York: Hafner Press, 1974), section 22, p. 81.

39. Kenko, *Essays in Idleness*, 7.

40. Translated by Asataro Miyamori in *Masterpieces of Japanese Poetry Ancient and Modern* (Westport, Conn.: Greenwood Press, 1970), 395, 446.

41. See 144–45 of "A Record of Nanbo" by Nanbo Sokei (1522–91) in which he documents the instructions left by Master Soeki (Sen no Rikyu), tr. Toshihiko and Toyo Izutsu in *The Theory of Beauty in the Classical Aesthetics of Japan* (The Hague: Martinus Nijhoff, 1981).

42. These and other works are discussed in John Beardsley's *Earthworks and Beyond: Contemporary Art in the Landscape* (New York: Abbeville Press, 1989). My colleague Lucretia Giese called my attention to a new piece titled "Clocktower Project" by Christina Kubisch installed in MASS MoCA in North Adams, Massachusetts, which creates different sounds of the bells depending upon the weather. "Bright sunshine . . . generates bold, sharp strokes" while "on overcast days, the bells speak in more muted, mournful tones." *Wall Street Journal*, 1 October 1998.

43. Andy Goldsworthy, *Hand to Earth: Andy Goldsworthy Sculpture 1976–1990* (New York: Abrams, 1993), 117.

44. Note that I address the topic of everyday aesthetics as a general subject matter in "Everyday Aesthetics," *Philosophy and Literature* 25(2001):87–95.

CHAPTER 10

Sniffing and Savoring
The Aesthetics of Smells and Tastes

Emily Brady

> *Louisiana in September was like an obscene phone call from nature. The air—*
> *moist, sultry, secretive, and far from fresh—felt as if it were being exhaled into*
> *one's face. Sometimes it even sounded like heavy breathing. Honeysuckle,*
> *swamp flowers, magnolia, and the mystery smell of the river scented the atmos-*
> *phere, amplifying the intrusion of organic sleaze.*
> —Tom Robbins, *Jitterbug Perfume*

Introduction

SNIFFING AND SAVORING constitute not only a fundamental route to sensory awareness of our environment, but they also contribute to defining the quality and character of people, places, and events, as illustrated by Tom Robbins in the lines above.
Despite their significance in our lives, however, smells and tastes are a neglected
subject in aesthetics.[1] This stems from the belief that these senses are improper
objects of aesthetic appreciation, a belief that can be traced in part to the philosophical legacy of a distinction between the higher and lower pleasures. A more
general reason for the neglect of these senses arises from the predominance of the
visual in aesthetics and more widely in human experience. In this chapter I want to
put things right and assert the legitimacy and importance of smells and tastes in
aesthetic appreciation. I shall argue first that they can be appreciated as having aesthetic qualities in themselves and they meet the conditions of inclusion in the aesthetic domain set out by traditional aesthetic theories. That domain, normally
reserved for high art and the beauty or sublimity of nature, can be expanded to
include olfactory and gustatory experiences. But I shall argue that our appreciation
of smells and tastes involves valuing them on an instrumental level as well. In our

everyday experience, smells and tastes enable us to understand our environment and find meaning in it, to orient us in it, and connect us to it.

Some Distinctions

I begin with an analysis of smells and tastes. My account here is drawn mainly from the late Frank Sibley's lengthy and detailed analysis presented in a paper on the aesthetics of smells and tastes.[2] Like Sibley, I concentrate mainly on smells. Much of what we commonly call tasting is, more accurately, smelling. Smell is physically defined by receptors in the nose, combined with the olfactory nerve. Taste is physically defined by receptors in the tongue, or taste buds. By these physical criteria, smell is the more important sense, since our sensation of what comes into the mouth is perceived also through olfactory receptors. Furthermore, the nose is typically a more sensitive receptor than the tongue, so all in all, smell is doing most of the work. But the two senses also work together.[3] We can still discern the difference between the two senses, and one way to do this is according to their function. Smell is the sense that involves sniffing or breathing through the nose, while taste is the sense that involves savoring—eating, drinking, and the mouth.

There are different kinds of smells and tastes—the taste of milk, the aroma of coffee—but within kinds, Sibley makes a useful distinction between the particular and the general. Particular smells and tastes are particular instances of them— the taste of this particular cup of coffee, or the smell of a particular person's sweat. The "general" category refers to the general smell or taste associated with something or the generic category of the particular, for example, the taste of Earl Grey tea, rather than this particular cup, the general smell of sweat, as opposed to a particular person's. In many cases it will be hard to distinguish general categories. Against Sibley, one could argue that the general/particular distinction is unfounded. It might be claimed that there are only particulars because there are no common characteristics to create such general categories. Indeed, most of the examples I give here will be of particular instances of smells and tastes. Nevertheless, the distinction is a useful one even if it does not hold categorically. We can usually discriminate between different tastes of water in some sort of way and at the same time discern the taste of water generally. One taste of water is chlorinated, another brackish, yet we still recognize the water-taste they both belong to and can distinguish that water-taste from a milk-taste. The use of general categories does not entail that there is some essential taste to water or to milk but only that we can reasonably identify a generic taste. Even if we wanted to develop an essentialism of smells and tastes, it would be very hard to come up with the appropriate descriptions. Like faces, smells and tastes are easily recognizable, yet the essence of them is very difficult to put into words. These modes of sensory perception are less developed, which is one reason why most people do not have a rich vocabulary for describing them.

A second useful distinction made by Sibley is between single and mixed smells and tastes. Single smells or tastes are simple, where only one smell or taste can be discerned, and where a smell or taste is not distinguishable into separate or different ones. Two examples are the taste of salt or the taste of lemon. Mixed smells and tastes involve compounds, where more than a single smell or taste is discerned. This category is interesting because it locates the complexity of what we experience through the nose and mouth. The soft drink Sprite seems to be a mixture of three tastes—the fresh citrus of lemon and lime with the clean, slightly salty taste of carbonated water. The smell of raspberry yogurt combines the creamy smell of yogurt with the sharpness of raspberry. Although we sometimes find it hard to identify the complex mixture of a smell or taste, I suspect that most are mixed. Certainly it is possible to discriminate the various mixtures there are. Some mammals can discriminate with precision the blend of smells in the scent of a particular person, some humans can distinguish every individual scent in an aroma or fragrance, and even machines can make such distinctions relatively accurately.[4] An admixture of tastes may also create a whole new single taste altogether, which makes the distinction between single and mixed somewhat less sharp.

Defending Smells and Tastes as Objects of Aesthetic Appreciation

With some idea of the subject matter of smells and tastes, I now turn to objections raised against smells and tastes within philosophical aesthetics.[5] Most of these criticisms come from the modernist tradition, typified by Kant's aesthetic theory. My strategy here is to argue that smells and tastes can meet the objections of this tradition, on its own terms, even if the tradition itself too narrowly defines the proper objects of aesthetic appreciation.

One general reason why smells and tastes have been neglected in philosophical aesthetics stems from their association with that which is base. They are associated with the body and with nonhuman animals and relegated to the realm of the crude, so-called lower pleasures. This first prejudice stems from the long philosophical tradition of making a distinction between the lower and higher pleasures, a distinction closely tied to mind-body dualism, which holds that the mind is distinct from and has more value than the body. The lower pleasures associated with the body are eating, smelling, sex, and other bodily functions such as sweating, while the so-called higher pleasures are associated with the mind and the intellect. One early source of this kind of thinking is Plato. In *Phaedo*, for example, the bodily pleasures are considered an obstacle to achieving truth and a desirable afterlife.[6] This idea is continued famously by Mill: "It is better to be a human being dissatisfied than a pig satisfied; better to be Socrates dissatisfied than fool satisfied."[7]

Despite recent emphasis on the body by phenomenologists and some post-modern thinkers, the prejudice continues, no doubt supported by the conventions of everyday life. Many societies in Western culture still dictate that smells and tastes are baser pleasures. For example, smelling socks is considered unseemly and rude—perhaps because our behavior is compared to nonhuman animals. Add to this that we mask natural odors such as sweat with perfumed scents. Another convention that supports the prejudice is our criticism of people who are overinterested in eating and drinking, except when raised to an intellectual art or connoisseurship, which combines smelling and tasting with thorough and refined knowledge.

The prejudice against smells and tastes has also found its way into the art world. Combined with the fact that sight is our dominant sense, smells and tastes have had no role to speak of in the history of art. *Still life* is one genre of visual art in which the other senses are played on, but it is still obviously visual even if some paintings make one's mouth water. It is possible to find olfactory descriptions in literature and many writers regularly use smell and taste descriptions—Proust and Joyce are prime examples.[8] But on the whole the literary imagination tends to be a visual one. A particularly relevant exception is Peter Süskind's *Perfume: The Story of a Murderer,* the story of a perfumer who lacks any personal scent, yet who has an extraordinary sense of smell that leads to his demise.[9] The novel describes a rich olfactory world, using smell to build an image of the central character and the way that his nose constructs the environment around him.

In the other arts, some contemporary works have made progress toward expanding the use of the senses, with installations or sculptures that might include rotting vegetables, blood, or chocolate. In Finland, Helsinki's contemporary art museum has an installation with twenty-nine ceramic pots on a long table, each containing a different scent. Appreciating this art work requires a lot of sniffing and, if you like, checking each scent against a guide with information on each pot.[10]

One way to defend smells and tastes against the lower/higher pleasures objection is to argue that the distinction itself is untenable. This argument would begin by attacking the outdated and challenged belief in mind-body dualism. While I cannot present such an argument here, it is worth pointing out that although recent materialist theories in the philosophy of mind have seriously challenged the mind-body split, their influence on aesthetic theory has been slow.[11] Two other brief points may suffice to make some headway against the entrenched view. The other senses have also been associated with the "distasteful" aspects of the body; sight, sound and touch are all also associated with eating, drinking, sex, and sweating, so why pick on smells and tastes? Furthermore, not all bodily smells and tastes are unpleasant: skin smells like milk or honey, hair smells soft and fresh, kisses are described as sweet.

The claim that smells and tastes belong to the baser pleasures also associates them very closely with consumption and desire. This has led some philosophers to argue that sensations cannot be disinterested.[12] When applied to aesthetic appreciation, disinterestedness stipulates contemplation of an object's aesthetic qualities for their own sake, rather than for some interest they might serve. Eating and drinking in obvious ways are connected to consumption, and we often want more of whatever smell or taste we enjoy. But smells and tastes, as well as other sensations, are not necessarily connected to consumption. The aroma of very ripe stilton cheese can be appreciated without wishing to consume it (or in the moments before we do in fact consume it in order to satisfy hunger). The same is true in the most sophisticated kinds of olfactory and gustatory appreciation, like wine-tasting, in which only a sip of wine is savored.

The opposite is also true. As activities, sniffing and savoring are not always appreciative, that is, we may have sensory responses without making any aesthetic judgments. We may enjoy a walk in the forest for the exercise it brings, only vaguely noticing the fragrant scent of pine trees. Similarly, when meals are consumed quickly to satisfy hunger, or during conversation, complex tastes go unnoticed. On the other hand, sometimes the aesthetic imposes itself: a smell is so strong we cannot fail to notice it, describe it, and judge it as pleasant or unpleasant. The strong scent of cedar slows our gait in the forest, or a rotten salad tomato interrupts the conversation.

Both the appreciative and nonappreciative cases discussed here show that it is possible to appreciate a smell or taste for its own sake, where we value it for its distinctive qualities. Like all sense perceptions, smells and tastes can be pleasant to perception, can be dwelled on in contemplation, have specific and interesting characters, are recognizable and memorable. They offer an object for sustained discriminatory attention.[13]

The association of tastes and smells with the body supports another objection—that tastes and smells lack the mental component considered essential to aesthetic appreciation. Traditional aesthetic theories argue that aesthetic experience involves immediate sense perception but also, importantly, a reflective or contemplative feature associated with thought and imagination. Lacking this, tastes and smells are relegated to the realm of mere sensory experience.[14]

For Kant, tastes and smells belong to the realm of the "agreeable." In his distinction between the beautiful and the agreeable, the beautiful involves disinterested contemplation of an object's form or appearance, while the agreeable involves interest and merely what "the senses like in sensation," and so it is not disinterested and not contemplative.[15] The agreeable also lacks the imaginative engagement of the contemplation of the beautiful.

These claims rest on a limited concept of aesthetic objects. Kant's view assumes that there must be something more than mere sensation; there must be some form or structure in an object in order for it to give rise to an aesthetic judgment.[16] This assumption becomes more explicit when Kant dismisses color alone as a proper object of aesthetic contemplation, as well as single tones of music. If smells and tastes lack structure, like colors, they can never be included in the category of aesthetic objects.

But smells and tastes are more aesthetically interesting than this suggests. Let me first address Kant's claim that smells and tastes have no structure. As shown above, we find single and mixed smells and tastes, particular and generic ones, and we can discriminate the different strands of mixed or complex smells and tastes. The complexity that typifies so many olfactory and gustatory experiences is evidence of their structure, as illustrated by Hugh Johnson's loving description of Château Pétrus:

> The crop is small, the new wine so dark and concentrated that fresh-sawn oak, for all its powerful smell, seems to make no impression on it. At a year old the wine smells of blackcurrant. At two a note of tobacco edges in. But any such exact reference is a misleading simplification. Why Pétrus (or any great wine) commands attention is by its almost architectural sense of structure; of counterpoised weights and matched stresses. How can there be such tannin and yet such tenderness?[17]

Smells too can exhibit structure.[18] Perfume—something many of us use everyday—combines any number of different smells such as spicy, floral or fruity. The terminology of perfumery draws on the compositional descriptions and terms of symphonic music such as 'accords,' 'notes,' and 'tones' to describe the character of a particular scent: "Boronia absolute is a delightful oil rich in violet notes of betaionone. The top note is fresh, the body notes extraordinarily rich and warm."[19] The perfumers in Robbins' novel convey the complexity of perfume scents through metaphorical description:

> Tangerine seems to work okay as the top note. It aerates rather quickly, but it rides the jasmine and doesn't sink completely into it. With a middle note of the vigor of that Bingo Pajama jasmine . . . what we need is a base note with a floor of iron. It can't just sit there, though, it has to rise subtly and unite the tangerine somehow with that bodacious jasmine theme.[20]

Further evidence of the complexity and structure of smells and tastes can be found by examining the act of appreciation itself, the best example being in the principles of olfactory and gustatory connoisseurship. Wine, whisky, and cigar tastings proceed through careful judgmental steps that take in various qualities of the subject. For whisky it is color, nose, flavor, then finish, with additional general notes.[21] Cigar tasting begins with the 'aesthetics' or look and feel of the cigar, followed by: prelight condition, postlight condition, flavor and strength, aftertaste, aroma, and general notes.[22]

In this sort of appreciation discrimination is clearly taking place. But we do not have to turn smells and tastes into a high art in order to find cases where judgments are made. Our everyday life is infused with this kind of appreciation, in appreciating our daily route to work, in choosing the best ingredients for tonight's dinner, and so on. We find one aroma pleasant, another unpleasant, one taste interesting, another uninteresting. That we have preferences like these in our daily lives suggests our ability to discriminate between different smells and tastes. Clearly, the connoisseurs who have spent the most time and thought developing their olfactory and gustatory skills are best equipped to make such judgments, but even when appreciation is less developed, it remains significant and too often overlooked. In any case, that we do make these aesthetic judgments, whether shallow or deep, suggests a complexity to smells and tastes that Kant, and others, miss.

Another reason behind Kant's classification of smells and tastes in the agreeable is his belief that mere sensations are the subject of individual rather than universal liking. This claim is a commonly held belief—that we are more likely to question one's judgment of a work of art than one's preference for strawberries to blueberries.[23] However, if my argument for the legitimate status of smells and tastes as objects of aesthetic appreciation is accepted, it should follow that they may also be the subject of aesthetic judgments that are disputable. I would not argue for strong objectivity in the case of every aesthetic judgment, but at the very least we can justify these judgments. In the case of smells and tastes most of us lack the requisite critical vocabulary that enables justification for such judgments. But once critical abilities are sharpened, it should be possible to formulate justifications, and thus engage in critical discourse. Proof for this can be found in the already existing discourse of wine and food criticism, tea-tasting, perfumery, and other skilled activities that focus on smells and tastes.

The activity of aesthetic appreciation itself also shows that Kant is wrong in his second claim, that the appreciative activity of smells and tastes lacks a mental dimension. In enjoying the taste of a particular kind of ice cream, we may be involved in contemplation; we reflect on the taste, making comparisons, as we try to approximate where the qualities of the taste fit into our experience, and whether the taste itself is pleasant or unpleasant. When we call the taste of vanilla ice cream smooth, silky and mellow, we draw on the concept of smoothness or perhaps make associations to other objects with that aesthetic quality. Imagination comes into play here too, since smells and tastes, just like paintings and poems, evoke images and associations.[24] Smells are notorious for bringing to mind particular times, places, or experiences of the past, so memories may also become part of the reflective activity. The commonplace aroma of coffee may conjure up images of relaxing, sitting comfortably with friends at a favorite cafe.

The more basic feelings of pleasure and displeasure are an obvious part of the aesthetic response to smells and tastes. But emotions, which involve thought, also get a foothold in olfactory and gustatory appreciation. Smells and tastes regularly involve emotional arousal, at least as often and perhaps more so, than aesthetic responses to the visual. To someone who enjoys clean, fresh air, the burning, carbon fumes of exhaust evoke feelings of disgust and dismay at the prevalence of car culture. A hot cup of tea makes some people (even a whole nation) feel relaxed and secure. By contrast, the musky odor of a skunk causes fear in humans (if only fear of being enveloped in the awful smell).

A final objection, suggested already in my discussion of Kant, is the claim that smells and tastes are not easily specifiable as aesthetic objects. Of all the senses, sniffing and savoring offer us the most fleeting experiences. Smells come and go in an instant, tastes leave us soon after food is consumed. Compare this to the fact that art objects are more permanent: paintings sit on the walls of galleries for years, waiting to be contemplated at one's leisure. Even the moving images of films are there to be revisited, and in the age of videos, we can freeze-frame parts of films for careful aesthetic attention.

The points already made concerning the role of reflection, imagination, and emotion should suffice to show that smells and tastes can be the subject of aesthetic appreciation, even if they are not like more traditional objects that sit in galleries. We can identify, individuate, select, and revisit smells and tastes; they can be localized and specified, even if they are not as sustained as other aesthetic objects. Besides, other sensations such as sounds are fleeting too, yet we consider combinations of them to be worthy objects of aesthetic appreciation. The aesthetic-object objection rests on a rather outdated notion of the nature of aesthetic objects. If an aesthetic object cannot be temporary, then on this view it is difficult to see how the natural environment could ever be aesthetically appreciated appropriately. One of the things that makes our experience of environments so rich and dynamic is the very transitory quality of them, such as changes in weather and light, or the effects of growth and decay.

Smells and tastes meet the strict modernist criteria of what counts as an object of aesthetic appreciation. Moving critically beyond modernism, some contemporary aestheticians argue that a key feature of aesthetic appreciation is cognition. Many contemporary art works demand conceptual reflection rather than sensuous or formal appreciation. Can smells and tastes meet this new condition, given the view that they lack content, refer to nothing beyond themselves, and thus are devoid of meaning for interpretation?[25] I have shown that emotional and imaginative associations accompany olfactory and gustatory experiences, but can these kinds of perceptions involve meaning? Carolyn Korsmeyer argues that smells and tastes are primarily valued as aesthetic objects in virtue of the insight and meaning discovered through their appreciation; rather than being merely sensuous objects, smells and tastes are also denotative. Foods in ritualistic settings, for example, a harvest festival, are the clearest cases, but we also find meaning in everyday appreciation:

> Routine uses of foods also may bestow upon them certain expressive properties. Chicken soup is a home remedy for illness in a number of cultures. There may be some medical reason for this. . . . Such palliative features are not likely to be part of the immediate experience of the soup, however, and more relevant for expressive properties such as "soothing" and "comforting" that are exemplified in chicken soup is the very fact that it is a home remedy and means that one is being taken care of.[26]

The value of Korsmeyer's argument is twofold, first because it sets out some good reasons for the cognitive value of smells and tastes, providing another reason to hold that smells and tastes are proper aesthetic objects; and second, it shows that smells and tastes have instrumental value. In the next part of the chapter I show some of the ways in which smells and tastes are valuable everyday resources, not specifically because of their cognitive value, but in virtue of how they place us in our environment.

Smells and Tastes in Everyday Life

The olfactory and gustatory experiences of everyday life constitute two sensuous dimensions of our environment. They help to situate us in it, and at the same time to orient us in various parts of it. J. Douglas Porteous points to this in his comparison of sight and smell:

> Vision clearly distances us from the object. We frame 'views' in pictures and camera lenses; the likelihood of an intellectual response is considerable. By contrast, smells environ. They penetrate the body and permeate the immediate environment, and thus one's response is much more likely to involve strong affect.[27]

Porteous goes on to discuss the significance of smell to understanding place:

> The concept of smellscape suggests that, like visual impressions, smells may be spatially ordered or place-related. It is clear, however, that any conceptualization of smellscape must recognize that the perceived smellscape will be non-continuous, fragmentary in space and episodic in time, and limited by the height of our noses from the ground, where smells tend to linger.[28]

Despite the impermanence of smells, they can environ us. They enable us to discover meaning in the places and situations in which we find ourselves; through a particular kind of aesthetic orientation we both interpret and understand our surroundings. This orientation, an olfactory geography that changes according to place and focus, has various overlapping levels, which I shall discuss in turn.

Familiar and recognizable smells are key to habituating us in an environment, to making us feel at home. This is true even though we so quickly adapt and habituate ourselves to smells that we experience regularly. The smell of a person or a house or the smell of a city are all smells which become so familiar that we hardly notice them anymore. And the fact that we do not notice them just covers up the fact that they remain crucial in our feeling of a sense of place. After being away from a place or a person for awhile, the smells are more noticeable when you return, which signals a feeling of being at home, or in other contexts, a comforting feeling of familiarity. Such familiarity through smell is one feature that grounds a sense of place.

The flip side of familiarity is unfamiliarity. Smells are important here too—they alert us to the strange, to what is dangerous, and make us feel alien to a place.[29] New houses or other strange places have different, new smells. Often there is pleasure in the unfamiliarity, in the freshness of something experienced for the first time. Less pleasurably, smell enables us to discover problems in our surroundings—the sulphuric smell of gas leaking, the suffocating smell of smoke, the smell or taste of rotten food, and the stench of disease or death.[30] In his illuminating history of smell in French society, Alain Corbin cites the eighteenth-century fear of the cesspools of excrement that collected in urban centers. The source of the stench would have been something very familiar, yet in great quantities it became something strange, harmful and fearful:

> Thouret noted that exposure to air and sunlight rendered the faecal matter spread out in the Montfaucon basins innocuous, as was proved by the transmutations in the smells. If old excrement proved dangerous, it was because it had become "alien to ourselves, our food, and our furnishings" by an interplay of "decompositions" and "recompositions". It had lost the odor of the body. It had putrefied.[31]

We are typically attracted to things with pleasant odors and detracted from things with unpleasant odors. Sometimes the response is an immediate one—some smells just are repugnant, such as the smell of almost anything decomposing (autumn leaves being a nostalgic exception). The negative value we assign to the source of the smell follows the immediate response. But we also judge olfactory experiences as negative because of what we associate with them or know about their source. The smell of an animal decomposing is unpleasant and somewhat strange because it is associated with death and our fear of it as something we want to avoid (a fear also played out in terms of a fear of the unknown). The meanings of smells and tastes are thus closely tied to the judgments we make about them, and the environment in which we find them. In this way, smells and tastes play some role in determining our likes and dislikes, or what we value in our environment.

The familiarity and strangeness of smells and tastes contribute to our ability to use these senses to identify and recognize aspects of our environment. Along with our other senses, smell enables us to identify and individuate objects, particular places, and whole environments. I can tell the difference between two similar bath towels—one clean, the other dirty—not by how they look, but by the contrast in their smells. Moving outdoors, one fundamental way the urban is distinguished from the rural is by the different smells associated with each. In the city it is the heavy smell of fog, the earthy smell of rain on pavement, and the noxious fumes of exhaust. In the countryside it is the green smell of new-mown hay, the pungent, sweet smell of manure, and the spicy smell of burning wood. Each identification of a smell or taste provides a description under which we understand things in our environment or the particular environment as a whole.

Turning once again to a literary source, James Joyce creates rich images of urban places like Dublin through sensory descriptions in his various novels. Olfactory and gustatory qualities evoke an intimate feeling of the places visited in the daily lives of the two main characters in Ulysses, Stephen Dedalus and Leopold Bloom. Gustatory qualities are especially significant to Bloom's character and his routines. Bloom's visit to Davy Byrne's restaurant involves detailed, rambling descriptions of the pleasures and displeasures of his experience there:

> Mr Bloom ate his strips of sandwich, fresh clean bread, with relish of disgust pungent mustard, the feety savour of green cheese. Sips of wine soothed his palate. Not logwood that. Tastes fuller this weather with the chill off.[32]

He has a special liking for "the inner organs of beasts and fowls" and "Most of all he liked grilled mutton kidneys which gave to his palate a fine tang of faintly scented urine."[33] Bloom also dwells on his wife's scents and wonders about his own—a way of identifying her and to some extent himself in relation to her.[34]

Smells and tastes also have significance in understanding places that differ culturally. There is some evidence to show cultural differences in olfactory perception itself as well, which is connected to the variety of smells and tastes associated with a particular culture. Paul Rodaway provides a clear example of this, also in an urban setting:

> public spaces in the older part of traditional Arab cities—such as Marrakech, Fes, Kairouan and in particular the souk market areas of Arab cities—have far

richer positive smellscapes than the modern Western city. The streets of cities such as New York and London can often have quite a negative smellscape of traffic fumes, whilst the enclosed shopping malls and department stores are a mixture of zones of relative odourlessness and areas of pungent 'staged' smellscapes, such as the perfume of beauty products counters. The traditional Arab souk, a maze of narrow passageways, small openings and stalls and workshops has a far richer odour of the products sold—from live animals to leather and cloth—and these smells seem to mingle with great abandon.[35]

Given that smells (and tastes) play an important role in everyday experience, olfaction (and to some extent tastes) also contributes to identifying and recognizing people and places in cultures other than our own. An unfortunate and sometimes sinister implication is that this often leads to racial and ethnic stereotyping.

Classes too have been distinguished by olfactory criteria. George Orwell's essay on the unemployment and poverty of Northern England's working class earlier this century, *The Road to Wigan Pier*, evokes strong images of the hardship and squalor of day-to-day living, and working in the coal mines. He reflects on the common belief that "The lower classes smell," and his remarks are telling. Orwell argues that this belief is at the heart of class distinctions, given how fundamental physical feeling is to likes and dislikes. Even if the lower classes do not actually smell, the belief that they do contributes to their oppression, for they are believed to be inherently dirty.[36] This indicates the centrality of smells to daily life not only in the way smells affect our perception and treatment of others, but also in the way that smells reveal the conditions and circumstances of practical living in what we eat, where we work, and how we bathe.

Another striking way our noses facilitate recognition and identification is through olfactory memory. This dimension of memory is especially robust and lasting, and many physiological theories have been put forward to show that our memory is better through the nose than through the eyes. It has been claimed, for example, that olfaction bypasses the conceptual part of the brain, the neocortex, whereas sights and sounds are do not. The result is that odor-related memory is more immediate, and called up more directly than memories connected to sight or sound.[37] Our ability to recognize a smell at some time in the present is dependent upon having had a past experience of the generic category of that smell.

In the present, our everyday recognition of various features of the places we live and work comes through smells. Consider the following smells. In the house: kitchen—warm baking bread, rich red meat, gas oven, grease; bathroom—soap, perfumes, hamper, water. In institutions: library—dust, leather; hospital—sharp disinfectant, sanitized surfaces, illness, urine. In natural environments: sea—salt, fish, sun-scorched sand; mountains—damp, cold stone, dark earth, fresh leaves.

These examples show how olfactory memory operates to recognize and recall smells we associate with types of environments, but it also gives us the extraordinary capacity to call up very specific memories. A single whiff offers a door of recognition into a moment from the past. One of my strongest olfactory memories comes through a particular seaweed soap. The smell is of sand, salt, and rotting seaweed, which takes me back to carefree, childhood summers spent at the beach in North Carolina. The emotional quality of olfactory memories can be quite strong; with childhood memories it is typically sentimental and nostalgic, with other memories it may simply leave one feeling despondent. Olfactory memory also recalls moments or stretches of time, acting as a historical record of smell experiences that provide a more fluid reference point for orientation to our environment. A particular smell is associated with a particular time in our lives or particular smells with times of the day or the year. The morning is the sweet smell of dew on grass; the winter is the smell of snow muffling other smells with its crisp, white scent.

Much of my discussion has focused on the idea of individuals experiencing their environment. So far I have said nothing about human bodies, but the same environing roles of smell and taste apply in this most intimate of environments. Smells and perhaps tastes too help to establish our own identity and to recognize the identity of other people. For all sorts of reasons humans have body odors. They originate in our apocrine glands, which are found on various parts of the body, including the face and armpits. The fat in hair absorbs odors, and what we eat affects body odor (brunettes are said to smell different from redheads, meateaters different from vegetarians).[38] With this range and change of bodily smells, it is not surprising that we can recognize the smell of a particular person, especially someone we know well, and guess something about their habits, based only on scent evidence. For people with no olfactory perception, or "anosmia," the delights of food and the characteristic smell of a loved one are painfully missed.

The experience of smells and tastes in relation to other people as well as to other things in our surroundings may involve a relationship of reciprocity. Another sense, touch offers the clearest case of this since whatever you touch is somehow touching you back. Taste involves touch, too, as we place food or other things in our mouths. When in close proximity to others, we smell their odor and they smell ours. Kant's views on this topic are disappointingly narrow, but consistent perhaps in their prudishness. Smells are the "most expendable" of the senses, and he argues that they repel us from things because most smells are unpleasant. He prefers taste because it promotes "sociability in eating and drinking."[39] Kant may be right about the centrality of taste as a social sense, but he ignores the environing quality of smells. The potential for promoting reciprocity indicates how these senses can establish a special sensory relation between ourselves and our environment.[40]

The individual also experiences herself or himself and has an identity in their environment. The olfactory geography of each person's body constitutes one dimension of bodily knowledge, and it is fundamental to charting the territory of our own bodies. The habituation with our own smells means that we do not overtly notice these smells, but our recognition of them becomes clear when we notice that something has changed. Unfamiliar smells on our bodies may be due to something we have eaten, someone we have been with, or because of illness or disease. Strange or new smells on our bodies confuse ourselves and others who know us.

Personal style is to some extent an olfactory matter. We are accustomed to how we fashion ourselves in visual ways: makeup on our faces, the adornments of jewelry, our choice of clothes, the bodily shape we present or aim for. We are also accustomed to the way we look at ourselves, as much as our consciousness of how others see us. Smell functions in these ways too. A personal style is created with a favorite perfume, and we cover up odors like sweat or garlic breath with scents we and others prefer to smell on our bodies.

Conclusion

I have tried to show why smells and tastes ought to be included in the subject matter of aesthetics. They deserve appreciation in their own right, but they are significant too because they orient us in our environment and contribute to meaning and value we find in it. In environmental aesthetics aesthetic sensitivity depends upon transcending the limits of visual dominance in aesthetic appreciation, and reaching beyond the limits of the walls of an art gallery. This involves exploration using all the senses. If developing aesthetic sensitivity generally is a worthwhile activity, which I think it is, then becoming skilled in olfactory and gustatory perception should be part of this. I would like to conclude by suggesting a few ways in which we might develop these senses in aesthetic appreciation.

First, be aesthetically sensitive: make an effort, break conventions, sniff your food, savor the smell of a friend, and describe what you smell to someone else. Practice identifying smells and combinations of them; as you eat a meal at a restaurant, try guessing the ingredients. Aesthetic sensitivity is a skill, and so like any skill it needs practice and habit to develop. Second, build a smell and taste vocabulary. This vocabulary is quite poor in most of us, but having it can open up a new sensory world by giving us the ability to express what we experience. Porteous suggests some useful ways to do this. Explore and describe smellscapes and tastescapes instead of landscapes. Describe smell events and smell marks. Discuss ways in which you might play the role of a nosewitness instead of an eyewitness. Instead of hearsay, explore the idea of *nosesay*. Practice nose-training and work out descriptions for what you discover. Generally, try to describe every smell or taste event you encounter, avoiding visual terms. Developing an aesthetic sensitivity for smells may have some real benefits: the possibility of more intimate aesthetic experience of our everyday environment and the possibility of finding more meaning in it.

Notes

Earlier versions of this chapter were delivered to the Society for Philosophy and Geography at the American Philosophical Association Eastern Division meeting, December 1997, and the Stapledon Society at the University of Liverpool, February 1999. I thank audiences at these meetings, an anonymous referee, and the editors for their helpful comments.

1. Exceptions to this in philosophical aesthetics include a recent discussion on Aquinas' remarks on smells and tastes. See D. McQueen "Aquinas on the Aesthetic Relevance of Tastes and Smells," *British Journal of Aesthetics,* 33:4, 1993; and N. Campbell, "Aquinas' Reasons for the Aesthetic Irrelevance of Tastes and Smells," *British Journal of Aesthetics* 36, no. 2 (1996). The aesthetic theories of J.O Urmson, Frank Sibley, and Harold Osborne are all more open to the idea that smells and tastes could be objects of aesthetic appreciation.
2. F. N. Sibley, "Tastes, Smells, and Aesthetics," in *Approach to Aesthetics: Collected Papers on Philosophical Aesthetics,* edited by John Benson, Betty Redfern, and Jeremy Roxbee-Cox (Oxford: The Clarendon Press, 2001).
3. 213., Part II, 1. Sibley takes the definition from J.J. Gibson, *The Senses Considered as Perceptual Systems* (Boston: Houghton Mifflin, 1966), chap. eight. Gibson's analysis of smells and tastes as a system is also the basis of Paul Rodaway's discussion of the senses in *Sensuous Geographies: Body, Sense and Place* (London and New York: Routledge, 1994), 61–81. By concentrating on smells in this chapter, I am also guilty of neglecting the special character of taste and thus in some sense this adds to the very problem I wish to overcome. I have more interest in this chapter in smells, but include tastes as well since the two senses are so closely connected. More attention has been paid recently in philosophy to taste in particular, including Marienne L. Quinet, "Food as an Art: The Problem of Function," *British Journal of Aesthetics* 21, no. 2 (Spring 1981): 159–71; Elizabeth Telfer, *Food for Thought: Philosophy and Food* (London: Routledge, 1996); Carolyn Korsmeyer, "Food and the Taste of Meaning" in *Aesthetics of the Human Environment,* ed. Pauline von Bonsdorff and Arto Haapala (Lahti: Institute of Applied Aesthetics, 1999), 90–104 and *Making Sense of Taste: Food and Philosophy* (Ithaca: Cornell University Press, 1999).
4. It seems to be a biological fact that animals walking on all fours, close to the ground, have an especially keen sense of smell (D. Ackerman, *A Natural History of the Senses* (New York: Vintage Books, 1990, p. 30). Perfumers are best known for the ability to distinguish the mix of scents in a fragrance, but machines, gas chromatographs, can do it too. Olfactory and gustatory experts are also found in wine-tasting, whisky-tasting, and cigar smoking, and of course in the culinary arts. In whisky-tasting, for example, the nose of a particular whisky might be a mix of fresh and floral aromas or, by contrast, "peaty with a burnt heather character and hints of ozone" (Talisker whisky, aged ten years; John Lamond and Robin Tucek, *The Malt Whisky File* [Edinburgh: Canongate,

1997], 210). Cigar connoisseurs distinguish the complexity of the flavor and strength of a cigar, its aftertaste and its aroma, among other characteristics, and within each of these a mix of smells or tastes is common (see, for example, the cigar reviews in any issue of *Smoke* magazine.)

5. At the beginning of the chapter I noted a general or underlying reason why smells and tastes are a neglected topic, the predominance of the visual. Eyesight is for most of us the sense we use most, and it is therefore not surprising that it has received the most attention in aesthetics. Emphasis on the visual is not a bad thing in itself, but it provides limited information, since our other senses also have a role in both our awareness and our aesthetic appreciation of our environment. For more on ocularcentrism, see Martin Jay, *Downcast Eyes: The Denigration of Vision in Twentieth-Century French Thought* (Berkeley: University of California Press, 1993) and David Abram *The Spell of the Sensuous* (Vintage Books, 1996).

6. Plato, *Phaedo*, tr. G.M.A. Grube (Indianapolis: Hackett, 1977), 64c–67d, 12ff.

7. J.S. Mill, *Utilitarianism*, in *The Utilitarians* (Garden City: Dolphin Books, 1961), 410.

8. See Marcel Proust, *A Remembrance of Things Past;* James Joyce, *Ulysses, Dubliners,* and *Finnegans Wake.* J.D. Porteous gives several good examples in chapter two of his book, *Landscapes of the Mind: Worlds of Sense and Metaphor* (Toronto: University of Toronto Press, 1990). See also Ackerman, 15–18.

9. Peter Süskind, *Perfume: The Story of a Murderer* (New York: Pocket Books, 1991).

10. The art work is *Babylon* by Christian Skeelin and Morten Scriverin, 1997, in the permanent collection of the Kiasma Museum, Helsinki.

11. The pitfalls of mind-body dualism might be avoided by valuing the work of philosophers such as Merleau-Ponty, who asserts the centrality of the body in human experience, but dissolving dualism does not necessarily dissolve the dualism between the lower and higher senses.

12. See I. Kant, *Critique of Judgment,* tr. W. Pluhar (Indianapolis: Hackett, 1987). Monroe Beardsley also notes this line of argument, although it is not clear that he supports it. See M. Beardsley *Aesthetics: Problems in the Philosophy of Criticism* (New York: Harcourt Brace, 1958), 98–99, 111.

13. David Prall (quoted in Telfer), "The Elements of Aesthetic Surface in General," in *The Problems of Aesthetics,* ed. Eliseo Vivas and Murray Krieger (New York and Toronto: Rinehart, 1958), 187. This point is also supported by Telfer, chap. 3, esp. 41–44; and Korsmeyer.

14. This view has been held by Aquinas, Kant, Hegel, and some recent philosophers such as Roger Scruton. See Aquinas, *Summa Theologiae* (several editions); Kant, *Critique of Judgment;* G.F.W. Hegel, *Aesthetics: Lectures on Fine Art,* trans. T. M. Knox (Oxford: Clarendon Press, 1975), Vol. 1, 35; R. Scruton, *The Aesthetics of Architecture* (London: Methuen, 1979), 113–115, and *Art and Imagination* (London: Methuen, 1974), 156.

15. Kant, §3, Ak. 205–07, 47–48.

16. Kant, §14, Ak. 224–25, 70–71. Beardsley and Scruton make a similar claim. See Beardsley, 98–99; Scruton, 113. McQueen also discusses Aquinas' objections in relation to complexity, see McQueen, 351ff.

17. Hugh Johnson, *Wine Companion,* 3d ed. (London: Mitchell Beazley, 1991), 97.

18. Sibley supports this point, as well as Telfer, in relation to the composition of meals, although she is less enthusiastic (see Telfer, 48–49).

19. E. Morris, *Fragrance: The Story of Perfume from Cleopatra to Chanel* (New York: Scribner's, 1984), 234.

20. Tom Robbins, *Jitterbug Perfume* (London: Bantam Books), 61–62.

21. See also note 4 above.

22. *Smoke,* Summer 1998, 132.

23. See Scruton, *Aesthetics of Architecture.*

24. Both Sibley and McQueen also note the role of associations in olfactory experience. See Sibley, part VI, and McQueen, 353–354.

25. Although Telfer defends food as a minor art form, because food is not representational in the way that art is, it cannot be a *major* art form. See Telfer, 58ff.

26. Korsmeyer, "Food and the Taste of Meaning," 98–99.

27. Porteous, 25.

28. Ibid.

29. For an illuminating discussion of how the strange and familiar operate in our urban sense of place, see Arto Haapala, "Strangeness and Familiarity in the Urban Environment," in *The City as Cultural Metaphor: Studies in Urban Aesthetics,* ed. Arto Haapala (Lahti: Institute of Applied Aesthetics, 1998).

30. Kant notes this as the only redeeming quality of our sense of smell. See Immanuel Kant, *Anthropology from a Pragmatic Point of View,* tr. Mary Gregor, (The Hague: Martinus Nijhoff, 1974), Ak. 159, 37.

31. A. Corbin, *The Foul and the Fragrant: Odor and the French Social Imagination* (Leamington Spa, Hamburg, and New York: Berg, 1986), 28.

32. J. Joyce, *Ulysses,* ed. Hans Walter Gabler (Harmondsworth: Penguin Books, 1986), 142.

33. Ibid., 45.

34. Ibid., 306–07.

35. Rodaway, 80.

36. G. Orwell, *The Road to Wigan Pier* (Harmondsworth: Penguin Books, 1962 [1937]), 112–14.

37. Morris, 37.

38. Ackerman, 22–23.

39. Kant, *Anthropology,* Ak. 159, 37.

40. See Rodaway, 37. I am grateful to Desna MacKenzie for drawing my attention to this relationship.

CHAPTER 11

How Can Food Be Art?

Glenn Kuehn

FOOD IS ART; I am convinced that this is true. Problems arise, of course, when I try to convince others just how food can be art. This project is difficult because food typically has not been considered an art form, and it certainly is not often seen as equal to others genres such as painting, sculpture, and music. In her book, *Food for Thought* (*FT*), Elizabeth Telfer takes on this challenge and contexualizes food as art through evaluation and classification.[1] Telfer uses the notion of reaction for aesthetic evaluation and a modest institutional theory for artistic classification, and concludes that food is art, but only in a "minor" sense because it is inherently temporal, nonrepresentational, and cannot move one emotionally. I have chosen Telfer's work not only because of her overt concern over the new and exciting topic of the artistic potentiality of food, but also because of her overall method of determining how food can be a "work of art."

This chapter is both a response to Telfer's assertions and an attempt to further establish food as a very significant and profound art form far beyond where Telfer leaves it. I believe that her effort and goal of showing food to be art is very significant. However, I also believe that her method of describing the artistic status of food is outdated and does not provide an adequate understanding of the contemporary, everyday context through which we are dealing with the aesthetics of cooking and eating—a philosophy of food. Nor does she offer a context through which food can be seen as part of a profound and significant aesthetic experience. If food is going to be seen as art, it needs a context in which significant experiences of the aesthetic can come out of everyday life.

Part of my concern over Telfer's method is that she relies on a way of viewing the self and its relation to its environment that is based on a metaphor of an ineffable distance between the self and its world.[2] She consistently reaffirms strong mind/body, self/other, subject/object dichotomies through her conclusions, and speaks generally of food as art through historical aesthetic theories that offer neat and clean, though functionally weak in an everyday setting, classifications. Telfer's method of dealing with the art of food neglects the potential aesthetic experiences surrounding food and food-making practices because her classification of food as a "minor art" is unnecessarily limiting for an adequate understanding of what is involved in the aesthetic aspects of life.

My view draws from the work of John Dewey and his notion of transformative aesthetic experience. For Dewey all experiences have the underlying potential to be aesthetic. Similarly, in the context of this chapter, I will claim that as not all food is great art,—not all food is great food—but all food has the potential to be art because its production, presentation, and manner of appreciation (i.e., eating) necessarily involve one in an interactive engagement with the qualitative tensions that underlie experience. Also, unlike the appreciation of things such as painting or sculpture, the appreciation of food brings one to a more direct and organic experience that is potentially aesthetic. I propose that a contextualization of food (and cooking) as art is more productively contextualized in the aesthetic potentiality of experience. This alternate view necessarily appeals to the ideas of process, historical and cultural interaction, transformative experience, and emotion. Dewey held that the major function of art was the illumination of a community of shared experience, and the advantage of this contextualization is that the artistic awareness of food and cooking is understood as a classification-in-progress, that is, this context allows for not only the transiency of food, but also for the intensity of the fads and innovations within contemporary life that involve food; it is an aesthetic awareness that brings with it an extended community.

Food also has a unique characteristic that no other art form has in that it must actually be consumed and destroyed in order to be experienced and enjoyed.[3] Therefore, an adequate assessment of food's artistic status must not only be sympathetic to the notions of temporality and some ambiguity, it must embrace them. Dewey's work offers an interactive depiction of aesthetic experience that is supportive of these characteristics.

This essay is in four parts: an analysis with comments of Telfer's notion of aesthetic reaction; an analysis with comments on Telfer's classificational/evaluational uses of "work of art"; an evaluation of Telfer's conclusion that food is a "minor" art; and my response and attempt to establish food as a profound aesthetic medium worthy of being called "art."

In the end, I hope to show that the question of whether or not food is art, and in what capacity we can classify it as such, is perhaps not the best question we can ask. I believe the more important question is, "Why do we *want* to call it art?" and this question calls for future dialogues on the aesthetic dimensions of everyday life.

Telfer's Overall Project, and
Aesthetics as a Reactive Experience

Telfer makes a systematic attempt to determine the status of food and cooking in the art world. Her claims come forth in the following progression:

1. Aesthetic reactions are not always of works of art.
2. A work of art is man-made.
3. Art forms are types of works of art to which similar arts belong.
4. Works of art and art forms are labeled as such either by classification or evaluation.
5. Some food is art by classification.
6. Food is art by evaluation, but in a weak sense.
7. Food is a minor art, because:
    Food is transient.
    Food is non-representational.
    Food cannot "move" one emotionally.
8. Cooks are performing artists much like musicians.
9. Cooking is possibly a "people's art."

Telfer outlines her view of the food-art scenario.

> With the art of food, we have two problems. We need to strike a balance between the aesthetic claims of the food on a particular occasion and the social claims of that occasion. We also need to find a middle way between two unsatisfactory attitudes to the aesthetic dimension of food: we must not be so heedless as to waste a satisfying kind of aesthetic experience, but not so precious as to expect more of it than it can give.[4]

She begins by pointing to the range of aesthetic reactions in experiences and states that such reactions are not always of art objects per se because the notion of aesthetic reaction is applicable to a wide range of experiences; we can have aesthetic reactions to nonmanmade objects such as landscapes, clouds, and trees. However, she concludes that the general notion of aesthetic reaction that is going to be workable in an artistic context is one that is based on a disinterested feeling of pleasure (*FT,* 41). Telfer uses work of J.O. Urmson (1958, 1962) to focus her conception of aesthetic reactions down to a nonneutral and noninstrumental species of pleasure; that is, one appreciates a thing's look for its own sake and not for the "benefit it brings to me or others" (*FT,* 42).

Telfer further modifies the notion that such reactions be "characterised as non-neutral, non-instrumental, having a certain intensity and often accompanied by judgments for which the judgers claim a kind of objectivity" (*FT,* 43). She offers three claims for this broad definition being useful for an aesthetic investigation of food and food-related activities:

> First, it is generally agreed that there can be aesthetic reactions to tastes and smells. . . .
>
> Second, as with the other examples of aesthetic reaction, we can distinguish liking the taste and smell of food from approving of it instrumentally on the grounds that it is nourishing, fashionable or produced by politically respectable regimes. Likewise we can distinguish the person who "enjoys his food" but does not notice what he eats, from the person whose awareness is more vivid—the latter reaction being the only one which is characteristically aesthetic.
>
> And third, as with the other senses, the non-neutral, vivid and non-instrumental reaction to tastes and smells can be combined with a judgment for which the judger claims objectivity (*FT,* 44).

I find her depiction of aesthetic experiences as based on reaction to be troubling. First, if aesthetic experience is inherently reactive, then there is an implicit separation of self from the environment; we are working with a metaphor of objective distance where one reacts "to" the experience. Telfer never talks about aesthetic experience, only aesthetic *reaction.* She says that aesthetic reactions are applicable to varying experiences, and instead of explaining why they happen, where they come from, or why we should care, she just says that they just "happen." An explanation for how and why the situation is therefore aesthetic is lost because this understanding of art is based on the intensity of sense impressions that have no understandable explanation outside of physical causality.

This approach allows such dichotomies as self/other, mind/body, subject/object, etc., not only to be relevant, but also helpful to the discussion about a philosophy of food.[5] There is no explanation of the connection between the reactee and the reactor—so to speak. And although she makes it clear that aesthetic reactions are not limited to mere sensory pleasures (they must be inclusive of broader notions such as awe and inspiration) she does not tell us where the ability to have these reactions comes from.

The reason I take issue with this choice of words is that an understanding, appreciation, and cultivation of the everyday bits and moments of life seems to necessitate an awareness of the interaction one has with one's environment. If one is simply going around reacting to this or that without an explanation of why these reactions matter or have value, then there is an implied separation between a person and her environment. This disconnectedness seems to work against understanding the great aesthetic potentiality involved in food and cooking that is more accurately presented as an interactive, "theoretical practice," that involves an interacting body-mind working through (not merely "in") a qualitative environment.[6]

Second, since an explanation of the source of aesthetic reactions (something such as the underlying conditions of qualitative experience outlined by Dewey) is lacking in Telfer's work, we are taken into the abyss of a subjectivist, "I like it" theory. Telfer claims that pleasure must be involved in an experience of art, yet without an explanation of why aesthetic reactions can happen, we have no means of saying why anything is art at all apart from the fact that we react to it pleasurably. Further, the judgment of art as being good or bad will be based on the possible degrees of a pleasing, yet unexplainable, reaction. As I understand her claims, in identifying aesthetic reactions, we are distanced, not worried about what it is for or why it is happening, and gratified that it did happen. And while many would say that this is a perfectly fine way of describing artistic experience, I do not think it is an adequate way of evaluating the aesthetic value of food.

In this context it is beneficial to turn to someone such as Dewey, who does offer an explanation of aesthetic experience that is more inclusive. As briefly stated before, for Dewey, the major function of art is not representational or formal or based on reactions to pleasurable sensations—art and aesthetic experience illuminate a community of shared experience. Dewey states,

> To esthetic experience, then, the philosopher must go to understand what experience is. . . . For this reason, while the theory of esthetics put forth by a philosophy is incidentally a test of the capacity of its author to have the experience that is the subject-matter of his analysis, it is also much more than that. It is a test of the capacity of the system he puts forth to grasp the nature of experience itself.[7]

What Dewey offers is a sense of aesthetic experience based on integrated interaction instead of subjective reaction. Metaphorically, reaction requires a separation, a distance between two distinct things. With this distance comes a degree of unknowability of the ineffable way in which one thing reacts to another. Interaction does not necessarily require this grand distinction nor does it necessarily carry the ineffable baggage. Interaction implies a continuous stretch of existence—an integrative connectedness of living through the qualitative possibilities underlying experience.[8] Experience is more than a series of mutually modifying reactions. The interactive aesthetic experience happens in one world, and there is no great ontological (though there is certainly a functional) gap between the experiencer and the experienced.

Aesthetic interaction relies on an awareness of the qualitative tensions that underlie all potential experiences, for, as Dewey held, all experiences are potentially aesthetic. The truly aesthetic experience is a potent and consuming distillation of ordinary experience—an epitome of everyday life. The qualitative tensions within all experiences form the inherent connection of the self with its environment. If we understand the ways in which we experience life then we will see that aesthetics is not merely "reactive," but is in fact imbedded in understanding of interactive experience itself. Dewey states, "I have tried to show in these chapters that the esthetic is no intruder in experience from without, whether by way of idle luxury or transcendent ideality, but that it is the clarified and intensified development of traits that belong to every normally complete experience" (*LW,* 52–53).

For Dewey, we are a part of experience and we undergo experience—life is interactive and environmental and there is no separation of the self from its environment because the self lives through the environment. "For only when an organism shares in the ordered relations of its environment does it secure the stability essential to living. And when the participation comes after a phase of disruption and conflict, it bears within itself the germs of a consummation akin to the esthetic" (*LW,* 20).

Dewey does say that aesthetic experience is one of taking in qualities, "The esthetic or undergoing phase of experience is receptive. It involves surrender" (*LW,* 59). However, it is not a reactive experience of receiving impressions from an unknowable source. Instead, it is an interactive involvement with the qualitative tensions of the environment. "That which distinguishes an experience as esthetic is conversion of resistance and tensions, of excitations that in themselves are temptations to diversion, into a movement toward an inclusive and fulfilling close" (*LW,* 62). These descriptions are not of mysterious reactive feelings, but of an awareness of the inherent qualitative involvement one undergoes when one experiences aesthetically. Art is undergone, and aesthetic experience comes from ordinary experience—art comes out of everyday life. This understanding is not only accommodating to food-related experiences, it is also more widely inclusive of many other experiences into the realm of art.

Telfer claims that art is something to which we react, but she does not offer any reason for the reaction. Things just seem to happen. Dewey offers a more helpful view of experience as an involvement of self and environment out of which aesthetic experience is possible. The aesthetic is undergone through a living interaction and involvement. Aesthetic experience is relational, not reactive. The most tempting, and common, view pertaining to art is the "I like it" theory, where any concrete explanation for why art is important, or even what art is, is cast aside by the view that it is art if "I like it." I see Telfer as being slightly tempted by this view.

Her understanding of works of art as being created for the purpose of eliciting aesthetic reactions is based on pleasure, and this seems to fall prey to a relativistic perspective of viewing art as something you like. For Telfer, the judgment of art as being good or bad will be based on the pleasure of the aesthetic reaction because it is to the reception of an intense sense impression that she appeals for an understanding of aesthetics. For Dewey, the judgment of something being aesthetically "good or bad" is based on the completeness of the interactive experience and the degree to which it transforms the qualitative experience one undergoes. That is, aesthetic value is not based on reaction, but on a coherent transformative interaction, and there not only is little involvement of liking in this judgment, the issue of liking the experience does not even enter into the situation.[9]

Dewey's perspective also avoids the "I like it" problems. While it is easy to say "I don't know what art is, but I know what I like," it is obvious that this statement does not get us anywhere in understanding why we want to call something "art." With Dewey's scenario, we can talk about the types of tension and feeling and emotion and satisfaction we undergo. We can talk about the ways in which our perspectives, feelings, ideas, lifelong outlooks, etc., have been transformed because of the experience. We simply have more ground upon which to stand and more about which we can communicate, and what we are communicating are the qualitative tensions underlying all experiences that can (may or may not) become aesthetic. We are communicating about the reason for experiencing something as art.

Art through Classification and Evaluation

Telfer's greater concern, however, is with the artistic status of food. She claims that "Not all objects that can give rise to aesthetic reactions are works of art. A work of art is by definition a man-made thing, even if the human involvement need consist of no more than putting a natural object in a gallery and giving a title" (*FT,* 44). Her question is: how does food fit into this scenario?

She identifies two ways of dealing with food as art. The phrase "work of art," she claims, can be used in either a classifying or evaluative sense. "To use it in a classifying way is to say something about how the object is regarded, whereas to use it in an evaluative way is to say something about the extent to which it merits the label 'work of art'" (ibid.). Telfer claims that food can be art in both the classifiable and evaluative sense. For Telfer, food turns out to be an object that wobbles in and out of the classificatory and evaluative senses of "work of art" depending on the intention of the cook, recipe maker, and the judgment of the one who eats it.

The classifying use of "work of art" is somewhat vague. Objects are works of art depending on the norms of a particular society at a particular time that says "this is art." Telfer states, ". . . a thing is a work of art for a society if it is treated by that society as primarily an object of aesthetic consideration" (*FT,* 45). The classifying use of "work of art," then, is based on how an object is to be regarded at a particular time and place.[10]

The evaluative use of "work of art" is indicative of the intensity of the reaction to a particular art object. One may know perfectly well that some object is art (i.e., has been classified as such), but the artistic worth is determined by the reaction.

> People who use the phrase 'work of art' in this evaluative way are from one point of view commending the things that they call works of art, but it does not follow that they consider all works of art to be good ones. Thus the person who refuses to call a collection of pipes a work of art might also say of a not very good conventional sculpture, 'That is a work of art, even if it is not very good', meaning that it deserves to be appraised aesthetically, even though it may then be found wanting (*FT*, 45).

Telfer states, "The distinction between the classifying and the evaluative senses of the phrase 'work of art' is relevant to food . . . some dishes clearly constitute works of art in the classifying sense" and "I conclude that there are no limitations . . . which prevent food from giving rise to works of art in the evaluative sense . . ." (*FT*, 45–46, 56). Understandably, the classifying definition of a work of art can apply to some, but not all, food, based on whether or not it was intended for aesthetic consideration. "Run-of-the-mill" food, as she states, is not categorizable as a work of art because it was not intended to be art.[11] Run-of-the-mill food is functional, instrumental, and therefore not art. However, Telfer points out that this method of classification has interesting possible side effects particular to food: whereas instrumental food is not art, food intended to be art may lose its status as food.

> It is obvious that foodstuffs can be made into visual objects which are works of art. The great pastrycook Careme—who was famous for the immensely elaborate models (known as *pieces montees*) which me made out of sugar and other foodstuffs—once said of confectionery that it was the principal branch of architecture (Quintet 1981:164–65). It could be argued that these objects are not food, since they were not intended to be eaten, but food properly so called is likewise often arranged or decorated in creative and attractive ways which constitute a visual work of art (*FT*, 46).

Food as art is confusing because it seems as though it both may or may not be art at the same time. This confusion is one of the reasons I will later claim that the question of whether or not food is "art" begs problematic methods of classification that are not suited for an understanding of the aesthetic potentiality of food.

The artist is her next concern, for it is the chef who (in this context) makes available the tastes and smells of food. Telfer likens the chef to a musician and depicts the artistic role of a chef as one of interpretation and performance. A "particular cook's version of a recipe is an interpretative work of art, like a particular musician's performance of a piece of music" (*FT,* 49). Both the recipe and the "performance" of the recipe, then, can be 'works of art' in the classifying sense; their intention, presumably, is to be regarded as art. Further, both the recipe and the performance can be reacted to aesthetically (one by eating and the other by cooking) and deemed works of art in the evaluative sense.

The artistic status of food is very much like an "interpretative work of art, like a particular musician's performance of a piece of music" (ibid.). Yet, as promising as this scenario seems, Telfer leaves the comparison unresolved. She comes to no great resolution, and instead of explaining which one (the recipe, the chef, or the performance of the recipe) is given priority and why, she seems to conclude that they all are (or can be) art in the same way that we cannot really conclude whether or not the written score, intention of the composer, or the performance itself is "the" art. Thus, the classifying notion of 'work of art' is helpful only in a general sense because it loses its use when we wonder if we should point to the recipe, the food, or the chef (or all three) as the locus of the artistic worth.

Telfer ends up with the claim that, evaluatively, food is art, but not always. "I conclude that there are no limitations in us or in the nature of tastes themselves, which prevent food from giving rise to works of art in the evaluative sense of that phrase, though these will be simpler than in the arts of sight and sound" (*FT,* 56). She claims that the evaluative view of food allows an enhancement of our everyday lives much in the way that clothes can also offer enhancement. Yet the familiarity of eating everyday leads to the marginalization of food as a minor art (*FT,* 56–57).

Food as a "Minor" Art

Telfer's classification of food as a minor art is based on three premises: it is transient, it is not representative of anything beyond the abilities of the cook, and it cannot "move" someone like other arts can. First, the transience of food is a severe limitation of its ability to speak to different generations as something like the works of Shakespeare have; it simply is not around long enough to be contemplated by very many people. Further, in order to be contemplated, it must be destroyed through consumption, and the manner in which one appreciates food precludes its appreciation by any other person. Telfer states,

> We must conclude that works of art in food, whether creative of interpretive, cannot gain the same statue as those of greater permanence. This is one important reason why food must remain a relatively minor art. We might say the same, for the same reason, about any art of the short-lived kind—an art of fireworks,

for example, or of flower arranging. The peculiar poignancy of fireworks and flowers depends on their evanescence, and such art cannot have immortality as well (*FT,* 59).

Second, although food can vaguely symbolize traditions, it does not instill in us anything significant about the world because it is non-representative. It lacks the kinds of meaning that other major art forms have.

> [F]ood does not represent anything else, as most literature and much visual art does. We can see the representational arts—painting and literature—as telling us something about the world and ourselves, and we can see the world and ourselves in the light of ways in which they have been depicted in the representational arts. But we cannot do either of these things with food.[12]

Last, Telfer claims that food is unable to "move us." "Speaking for myself," she states, "I should say that good food can elate us, invigorate us, startle us, excite us, cheer us with a kind of warmth and joy, but cannot shake us fundamentally in that way of which the symptoms are tears or a sensation almost of fear. We are not in awe of good food, and we hesitate to ascribe the word 'beauty' to it, however fine it is" (*FT,* 60). This absence of "earth-shaking" quality further limits food's significance and, along with its lack of permanence and representational shortcomings, classifies it (at best) as a minor art.

First, I am not sure why, except for historical reasons, the transiency of food need render it a minor art any more than music, dancing, or even the reading of a story. It is not explicitly stated, but the distinction between high art and popular art seems to be working in the background for Telfer. Her examples of flower arranging and fireworks would normally be categorized as popular art partly, as she points out, of their transiency. Yet, temporality is something to which some "high" arts must appeal for value (e.g., music, theater).[13] Of course the written score of a particular piece of music is not evanescent, but neither is a recipe. And yet Telfer does not seem to acknowledge that the score, just as the recipe, must be performed to be appreciated; it must be temporally actualized.

Contrary to Telfer, Dewey uses the an appreciation of the transient to cultivate the aesthetic, and, as Thomas Alexander has pointed out, we, as organisms, are always living in an extended period of change and transformation. Dewey did not run from this fact. Instead he used it to depict a profound aesthetic awareness. Alexander states, "Instead, Dewey is indicating that the organizing quality is nothing other than the temporality of the developing event as a whole. It is present throughout the phases either tacitly or explicitly as the guiding sense or context, the horizon of the event."[14] The intensity of someone's artistic experience is indicative of how profoundly it has affected the temporal nature of his/her experience.[15] A rejection of food as being higher up in the art world because it is transient seems to rely on a narrow view of experience and a neglect of the temporal nature of living and appreciation.

In a prior critique of this chapter it was pointed out that Telfer's concern with transiency is simply that food cannot be a Beethoven string quarter. Yet, both experiences can be undergone just once, in only one context, with a specific group of people that can never be exactly reproduced. Both are inherently temporal. Both rely on written guides, skilled performers, and an appropriate context. The question of why I should value a Beethoven string quarter as art more than a great five-course meal is puzzling because I do not see the grand difference between the experience of either one. Why is the conclusion that food is a minor art partially because of its temporal nature not also a cheapening applicable to music, theater, musicals, television, movies, dance, and poetry readings? Appreciating the Mona Lisa something that you have to "do"—looking at it takes time.

Second, I simply cannot disagree more with the claim that food as art lacks meaning because it has no representational ability. At a basic level the ability to put things together in a recipe tells us something about art and technique; there is a fundamental sense and display of harmony in the act of cooking. Further, the manner in which recipes are constructed and prepared represents cultural heritages, traditional culinary techniques, and artistic abilities. Chefs trained in the French tradition continue to learn the methods and techniques of Escoffier. Eating around the world can certainly represent not only the obvious cultural differences of various societies, but also the economic, political, agricultural, religious, familial, and personal differences we have.

To be fair, Telfer does agree with the claim that food can be "other things," and she offers the following examples: a meal can be a religious observance; eating in a particular way can be indicative of one's allegiance to a particular religion or race; the choice of food can be an assertion of your values; a meal can be celebratory; eating together can be an expression of loyalty; preparing meals can be an act of friendship or love; and a meal can be an exercise in civilization and elegance (*FT*, 38–39). However, despite these assurances that food is indicative of many things, it is when food is considered to be art that it suddenly loses all representational ability. For Telfer, food as art tells us nothing about the world or ourselves because, unlike a painting, the artistic appreciation of food is not of anything beyond its taste.

My response to this comes from looking at food as art through Dewey and seeing it as expressive of contextual, not of cognitive (i.e., representational) meaning. For Dewey, cognitive objects occupy the tensive focus of ongoing events—that is why they are cognitive. They are the means whereby we are reconstructing experience. Giving them meaning is the larger context, defined by the more amorphous, qualitative horizon that infuses and provides the tacit supportive structure. Here, the "representational" ability of food is not of cognition, but of context. Our social, political, cultural, spiritual, symbolic, and familial relationships and lives are in part expressed through food because they are contextually constructed around cooking and eating—and cooking and eating with others. Again, art is the illumination of a shared community. Food as art is involved in these contexts through the underlying tensions and resolutions that make up our qualitatively (potentially aesthetic) experienced lives.

It seems that Telfer is attempting to understand an aspect of life as a possible art but coming at it from a formalistic point of view that emphasizes how we cannot look beyond the thing itself to understand its artistic worth.[16] This method precludes an investigation of why we want to say that food is art and where a sense of the aesthetic comes from. To understand the aesthetics and art of cooking and eating, one has to look at culture, time, place, tradition, language, and history. I don't see how one could separate food as art from these contexts and conclude that it isn't representative of anything. Food as art is most definitely representative of and tells us something about the world and ourselves, and, I believe, in a very profound manner.

Third, while Telfer does not explain why food cannot have representational quality, she adds we should not worry because music cannot do it either—yet, music can expresses emotion, and that's something food cannot do.[17] Food can express taste, inventiveness, and discernment. Food can also be expressive of skill and training, of knowledge of ingredients and how they fit together, and even of one's love for another, but this does not offer any profound artistic moments akin to hearing that Beethoven string quartet, or seeing a great painting, etc. Food, as a medium, is not itself (as music is) expressive of anything emotional.

I cannot remember ever tasting something so great that it made me cry (except for an Indian curry that burned my mouth with a searing pain and destroyed my sense of taste for two days). But I have eaten (and continue to eat) foods that have changed me in a productive and cultural way. The sauce on the Hasenpfeffer, that loaf of French bread (such a crust), that first taste of Beluga caviar, the beef jerky from the Pinehurst deli, the martinis at the Mandarin Club, a filet-o-fish from McDonalds with extra tartar sauce, Tony's cheesecake, perfectly cooked scallops, oysters on the half-shell in Boston. These are not merely maudlin memories, they are moments in a food-related context where I was, and sometimes have been again, aesthetically transformed not only by what I thought about that particular food, but how I would from then on experience food. The food was the medium through which I experienced the expression of harmony, arrangement, articulation, skill, and depth of feeling. These were aesthetic experiences; qualitative experiences of art through a food-related (or food-centered) context.

Not surprisingly I have been greatly challenged on this point. The strongest criticism against my position here is that food is, unfortunately, fairly inarticulate, and while one can represent the fact, and maybe degree, of something such as one's love for another in a dinner, one cannot represent the significance of the fact.[18] I will of course grant that eating a meal is qualitatively different than hearing a beautiful and moving piece of music, but the experience of listening to music is qualitatively different from viewing a dance performance, which is different from viewing paintings, which is different from watching a play. The experiences are all qualitatively different because the context is different, and each is perhaps uniquely able to convey certain aesthetic qualities that the others cannot. The aesthetic distinctiveness of experience for Dewey comes through the contextual expression, and a dismissal of food as artistically inadequate because it can't make someone cry depends on an erroneous equivocal application of what art must be when comparing different aesthetic experiences.

This emphasis on contextuality and of the unique expressive capacities of different art forms can also be seen as dependent on the work of Susanne Langer, who said that each art form had a unique and specific "virtual" experience that it alone articulated and made available. If I continue Telfer's comparison of music to food, I can say that I have cried listening to music, but never from eating. But that does not mean food lacks any expressive capacities; it just cannot articulate the emotion that music can.[19]

The experiences surrounding cooking and eating are within the qualitative realm of potentially aesthetic experience. We need food to live, but if merely sustaining life were all that we required we could get by on much more meager, tasteless, and purely functional food. The manner in which food is particularly capable of showing and expressing social, political, cultural, spiritual, symbolic, and familial contexts gives it a unique and significant place in the art world as an art that points to the value of the manor in which we continue to live. Food takes us on an aesthetic journey into different cultures, times, and places—and it does it through something that we need everyday to keep going.

In the end, Telfer's conclusions appear to center around the idea that food could never be on the level of a high art, and is at best something of a popular art. She states that although not all eating experiences are aesthetic, "Aesthetic eating, if I may call it this, is eating with attention and discernment food which repays attention and discernment. And to achieve attention and discernment may well take some practice and some instruction. On the other hand, the art of food is easier to appreciate than arts which require a lot of background information; the art of food is a possible people's art" (*FT,* 57). It is a people's art because it is inherently an everyday activity that, for the most part, is seen as little more than a biological necessity. The accessibility and universality of cooking and eating, along with food's inherent transiency, allow it to be art for everyone, but only in a minor and relatively insignificant way. She clearly employs a working distinction between high and popular (common) art. This distinction will work well in the following discussion as showing why common arts need to be valued more than they are and that the distinction itself is not always coherent or consistent.

An Aesthetic Recovery of Food

A problem with a contemporary method of classifying art is that it must deal increasingly with things that are common. In other words, an historical classification of what was art is a method that is far easier than current assessment of what is now art—or what we currently want to call art. Further, a particular difficulty in situating cooking/food within an artistic context lies in the recent actualization of its presence in the so-called art world. That is, only recently could it be taken seriously that food is an art object; that cooking is an artistic activity; that something can be said about food other than social critique; that aesthetic theory has something to say about food and food-related activities in a way that is similar to other art forms.[20]

I believe that the process of attempting to place food in the art world is better suited to focusing on a description of the aesthetic that appeals to the idea of interactive and qualitative experience as it is undergone by people every day. The advantage of this context over the one offered by Telfer is that we will not be seeking to classify food as art according to traditional art theories and depictions of aesthetic reactions, but instead looking at its role in the current streams of society and figuring out not only why we want to refer to it as art, but why we want to refer to it as art *now*. This overall attempt to classify food as art is couched comfortably in a larger issue of why we want to classify anything as art at all. The benefit of this context is that it allows explanations for food's (and cooking's) artistic and aesthetic ontology without retrospectively trying to place it in a historical art category.

If we really want to worry about whether or not food is art, we need not pine so much because we can situate food in the historical methods of classifying art. For example, food is mimetic in that it is representative of a culture, or a style of cooking, or a tradition; food is pragmatic in that it is instrumental and useful for the preservation of not only life, but also of culture; it is perhaps difficult to think of food as emotive, but given the possibility of expression through food, one may be able to bring in the idea that one can have emotional reactions to food;[21] and, of course, food can be formal in the techniques, traditional preparations and styles in which it is presented. The historical problem is, therefore, not concerning food's general art status, but its status as "fine" art, and here is where Telfer seems to reveal her project: it is not to figure out if food is art, but whether or not food is fine art, and here she dutifully preserves the high art/popular art distinction.

This distinction can be instrumental, but relying on it too heavily can lead to great difficulties. David Novitz refers to this attitude as being inconsistent.

> In our society we pay lip-service to the arts. We speak of their importance and abiding interest, and yet, after all is said, most of us have only the slightest concern for the arts. Paintings and sculptures, poems and plays seem to most people to be in a world removed from ordinary everyday living, and are widely thought to maintain a dignified silence on the really important bread and butter issues that confront us.[22]

Novitz does not buy clear distinctions between high and low arts, and he emphasizes that if we are to make such distinctions, they, like the general determinations of art, are socially constructed. "It would be a good deal easier," he states, "to distinguish the high from the popular arts if all works of art fitted neatly into one category or the other."[23]

What we gain from Novitz's work is the setting up of a context in which not only the classification of art, but also the determination of the art's status is understood as a social construction. The benefit of this is twofold. First, it demonstrates that Telfer's classification theory is subject to changing social attitudes that at some time, perhaps now, could consider without difficulty food as art, and second, it appeals to a contemporary context that can be messy and vague. "How we make or create works of art, what we think of as art, the ways in which we classify the arts, and, of course, what we regard as artistically valuable, are all, I shall argue, a function of the social practices and values which help characterize everyday life."[24]

This scenario is reminiscent of one of Telfer's claims about food as a minor art. Since food is a possible "people's" (common) art, it involves an area of everyday life that can be used to enhance and cultivate the aesthetic in ordinary life. "With food, as with clothes, people have a chance to enhance an area of their everyday lives. So to that extent the aesthetic appreciation of food is not a separate, alien activity, but an aspect of what is done every day" (*FT*, 57). It is puzzling, though, how she can offer this claim and yet not furnish the next step of emphasizing not only the great value of the aesthetic within everyday life, but also that it is the potential qualities that underlie everyday experience that make artistic appreciation possible in the first place. Food is referential and representative of aspects of everyday life, and it has a greater meaning beyond its flavor. The exclusion of something like food from the category "works of art" betrays the aesthetic experiences within our everyday lives.

Yet, for Dewey, it is precisely in so-called ordinary life where one finds the seeds and the heart of the aesthetic attitude. A Deweyan approach emphasizes the importance of transformation resulting from qualitative experience and the awareness of change and growth. Art is undergone—it is experienced as art. And while Dewey does not speak much about food per se, if we look at cooking and eating as potentially aesthetic experiences, food cannot be taken out of an understanding of art simply because it is part of everyday living (and it certainly would not be a "minor" class of art because eating is a biological necessity). In one of the few references to food and eating, Dewey (in a letter to his wife, Alice) states,

> Speaking of civilized places, the nearest dip into civilization I have made was at the Lorings' Thursday evening. There were four or five others in at dinner, Abby doesn't seem to go in for menage, I judge, but Mrs. Loring's dinner was a work of art, just as individualized as everything else. I suppose life in a boarding house makes me unduly aware of this petty side of things, but after all the innate barbarism of America seems to me indicated by the lack of sense for what constitutes a meal; it seems all below consciousness except on the most physical side.[25]

From a Deweyan perspective, food can be seen as qualitatively affective because it has the potential of transforming our experience of living, and it can be art because it offers us an awareness and appreciation of qualitative experience. It is expressive of the ways we interact with others. Interestingly enough, Dewey does include the act of eating together in a brief description of *an experience*—the epitome of a complete and unified aesthetic experience. He states, "An experience has a unity that gives it its name, *that* meal, that storm, that rupture of friendship. The existence of this unity is constituted by a single *quality* that pervades the entire experience in spite of the variation of its constituent parts. This unity is neither emotional, practical, nor intellectual, for these terms name distinctions that reflection can make within it" (*LW,* 44).

Dewey argued that segmenting art off in museums has contributed to a misguided and problematic view of the relation between art and aesthetic experience, and that the desire to classify certain objects as "art" has led to outworn theories that hinder our ability to welcome and appreciate as art the ordinary experiences within everyday life through which we begin to cultivate a sense of the aesthetic. At the beginning of *Art As Experience,* he states, "By one of the ironic perversities that often attend the course of affairs, the existence of the works of art upon which formation of an esthetic theory depends, has become an obstruction to theory about them" (*LW,* 9). Thus it is not through a distanced and objective appreciation that we must seek to understand art. Instead we must illuminate the qualitative potentialities within aesthetic experience to gain an understanding of art. An awareness of these qualities leads to an appreciation of the aesthetic, and this is the source of our desire to label something "art."

The desire to figure out what is and is not art has in many ways led us down a very tedious path. Just as we should use subject/object, self/other, high art/popular art, and other such distinctions primarily in an instrumental or functional manner, the distinction between art objects and aesthetic experience should also not be taken to be more than functional. When we look at the greater concerns of how to live and what we value, the ontological view of the self and its experience that is more productive and healthy is of an integrated, interactive, environmentally connected and aware being. An emphasis on food as involved in aesthetic experiences can lead to labeling it "art," but more importantly it demonstrates how the so-called ordinary aspects of everyday life are as valuable as the refined. An aesthetics of food shows another way in which primal aspects of valuing how we live can be expressed through articulate modes of experience.

The ability of food to change, to transform, is on a level of inherent and (though it is often hard to face) inescapable involvement with one's environment. Food breaks down the traditional dichotomies so easily, elegantly, and obviously, that it seems to have been too easy to overlook its philosophical potential. When you eat you are taking an object, some other "thing" in the world, and adding it to your being. The great distinctions between me and the so-called object world fall away. The complex act of eating is quite beyond mere nourishment and pleasure. It is life-sustaining, and can be life-changing. Food is a part of aesthetic interaction at a very basic and accessible level. And, if you wish to use the word, it is "art."

Notes

1. Telfer, Elizabeth. *Food for Thought: Philosophy and Food* (London: Routledge, 1996). Henceforth *FT* when cited in text.
2. This claim is heavily dependent on understanding meaning as embodied and the use of "metaphor" as outlined by Mark Johnson. Johnson states, "A second, related type of embodied imaginative structure central to my inquiry is metaphor, conceived as a pervasive mode of understanding by which we project patterns from one domain of experience in order to structure another domain of a different kind. So conceived, metaphor is not merely a linguistic mode of expression; rather, it is one of the chief cognitive structures by which we are able to have coherent, ordered experiences that we can reason about and make sense of. Through metaphor, we make use of patterns that obtain in our physical experience to organize our more abstract understanding. Understanding via metaphorical projection from the concrete to the abstract makes use of physical experience in two ways. First, our bodily movements and interactions in various physical domains of experience are structured (as we saw with image schemata), and that structure can be projected by metaphor onto abstract domains. Second, metaphorical understanding is not merely a matter of arbitrary fanciful projection from anything to anything with no constraints. Concrete bodily experience not only constrains the "input" to the metaphorical projections but also the nature of the projections themselves, that is, the kinds of mappings that can occur across domains" (*The Body in the Mind,* xiv–xv).
3. An objection to this claim may be that food could be created such that its decay could be hindered and then placed in a museum. Or, synthetic replicas of dishes (such as in the windows of many restaurants in Japan) could be offered as "food art." I believe that both

of these cases are attempts to make food into something it is not. Food is something that is inherently trapped within the rotting confines of temporality, and to avoid this fact is to treat the art of food as if it were something else.

4. Telfer, 60.

5. I believe part of my reaction at this point is that such dichotomies are simply not helpful to a serious discussion of food and its relation to the self. Food seems to hold an interesting ontological status as the "not yet self," that is, it is an object with the end of being incorporated into the subject. A rigid distinction between me and a tomato that I am about to eat is not all that obvious, therefore, strong ontological divisions between the self and the other simply do not seem to be helpful to a discussion of the philosophy of food.

6. See Lisa Heldke, "Foodmaking as a Thoughtful Practice" in *Cooking, Eating, Thinking: Transformative Philosophies of Food,* ed. Lisa Heldke and Deane Curtin (Bloomington: Indiana University Press, 1992) 203–29.

7. John Dewey. "Art As Experience" in *The Collected Works of John Dewey: The Later Works, 1925–1953,* 10th ed., Jo Ann Boydston (Carbondale: Southern Illinois University Press, 1989), 274. Henceforth cited as *LW* in text.

8. Dewey speaks of this connectedness through ontology and epistemology in one of his few food-related phrases:

    The problem of knowledge *ueberhaupt* exists because it is assumed that there is a knower in general, who is outside of the world to be known, and who is defined in terms antithetical to the traits of the world. With analogous assumptions, we could invent and discuss a problem of digestion in general. All that would be required would be to conceive the stomach and food-material as inhabiting different worlds. Such an assumption would leave on our hands the question of the possibility, extent, nature, and genuineness of any transaction between stomach and food. But because the stomach and food inhabit a continuous stretch of existence, because digestion is but a correlation of diverse activities in one world, the problems of digestion are specific and plural: What are the particular correlations which constitute it? How does it proceed in different situations? What is favorable and what unfavorable to its best performance?—and so on. (John Dewey, "The Need for a Recovery of Philosophy," ibid., 24)

9. A possible objection here is that other profound and transformative experiences, such as rape, beatings, war, should also been seen as aesthetic for Dewey, but he makes the distinction between violence and intensity of action. There is a great experiential difference between trauma and the aesthetic that is based on the ideas of continuity and discontinuity, and reciprocity. Violent experiences are characteristically more sudden, nonreciprocal, and therefore lack the interactive continuity and completeness characteristic of aesthetic experiences. In this way we can avoid having to agree that something such as rape is aesthetic (ibid., 186).

10. Without mentioning the "institutional theory" of art, Telfer does here seem to be making an obvious appeal to this perspective.

11. Though she does not identify what run-of-the-mill food is, I take it to be "typical" board of fare such as cheeseburgers, tv dinners, pot roast, fast food, etc., as distinguished from "haute" cuisine.

12. Ibid. I wonder, though, how anyone could make this claim on a serious level, for food is intrinsically a part of many religious ceremonies, holidays, and familial traditions. To travel to a different country involves an attempt to understand a different culture, which involves different ways of eating and different things to eat. Food can very blatantly tell us something about the world and ourselves because it is an inherent part of culture.

13. And, of course, for Dewey all art is temporal.

14. Alexander, Thomas. *John Dewey's Theory of Art, Experience, and Nature* (Albany: State University of New York Press, 1987), 252.

15. A similar claim can be found in the work of Susanne Langer, who, in her description of the emotive power of music, claimed that music created an experience of "virtual time," where the truly profound musical experience actually altered one's sense of temporality.

16. Here it seems that Telfer is appealing to the work of such people as Clive Bell, Eduard Hanslick, Cleanth Brooks and so on—people who viewed proper art as something completely unrepresentative of the daily aspects and events of living.

17. It must be noted that Telfer's treatment of music as an expression of emotion is cursory at best. She states, "There is a philosophical problem about what it means to say that music expresses emotion, as well as a problem about how music does it, but it is at any rate clear that it does, and that food does not" (Telfer, 59).

18. A counterexample to this claim, though fictionalized, is in the movie "Like Water For Chocolate" where a meal is presented and through the food the other characters become involved in lustful, passionate experiences. The food was the medium through which the depth of love was expressed.

19. This is perhaps very fitting as Langer claimed music made emotions audible by simultaneously creating a realm of "virtual time" where one could directly experience the audible manifestation of emotive qualities. Music, she said, is the tonal analogue of emotive life (Langer, *Feeling and Form* [New York: Charles Scribner's Sons, 1953], 27).

20. Certainly, while comments can be found in the history of philosophy concerning cooking and eating, in was not in an aesthetic or artistic context. It was instead in an ethical context (hedonistic pleasure versus, perhaps, virtue), or in an ontological context (mind versus body), or in a political context (Plato's construction of a just state).

21. A degree of emotional interchange with food can certainly be seen in religious ceremonies and rites as well as with holidays and celebrations.

22. David Novitz, "Ways of Artmaking: The High and the Popular in Art," *British Journal of Aesthetics* 29, no. 3 (Summer, 1989):213.

23. Ibid., 214.

24. Ibid.

25. "John Dewey to Alice Chipman Dewey and children," 1894.07.28,29 (00165), *The Correspondence of John Dewey*, vol. 1, 1871–1918 (Charlottesville, Va.: InteLex Corp., 1999); original, John Dewey Papers 2/6, Special Collections, Morris Library, Southern Illinois University, Carbondale, Ill.

About the Authors

Arnold Berleant is Professor of Philosophy (Emeritus) at Long Island University and Past-President of the International Association of Aesthetics. He has also served as Secretary-General of the International Association of Aesthetics and Secretary-Treasurer of the American Society for Aesthetics. His writings in aesthetics include *The Aesthetic Field, A Phenomenology of Aesthetic Experience* (1970), *Art and Engagement* (1991), *The Aesthetics of Environment* (1992), and *Living in the Landscape: Toward an Aesthetics of Environment* (1997), as well as many essays and reviews. Dr. Berleant has lectured widely nationally and abroad, and his work has been translated into many languages. He has edited *Environment and the Arts* (2002), and two collections of his essays, *Rethinking Aesthetics* and *Aesthetics and Environment* are scheduled for publication in 2005.

Emily Brady is Associate Professor of Philosophy at Brooklyn College–CUNY. Her teaching and research interests range from aesthetics (especially environmental aesthetics) to Kant and the philosophy of mind. Her articles have appeared in various anthologies and in *The Journal of Aesthetics and Art Criticism, Environmental Ethics, Environmental Values, Contemporary Aesthetics,* and *Ethics and the Environment.* She is the author of *Aesthetics of the Natural Environment* (Edinburgh University Press, 2003), and she co-edited *Aesthetic Concepts: Essays After Sibley* (Clarendon Press, 2001).

Allen Carlson is Professor of Philosophy at the University of Alberta, Edmonton, Canada. His teaching and research interests include aesthetics, environmental philosophy, and especially environmental and landscape aesthetics. He has coedited two collections of essays in this latter area and has published articles on the aesthetics of nature, on landscape appreciation, and on environmental assessment and evaluation. His research has appeared in various anthologies and in journals such as *The British Journal of Aesthetics, The Canadian Journal of Philoso-*

phy, Environmental Ethics, The Journal of Aesthetics and Art Criticism, Landscape Journal, and *Landscape Planning.* He has recently published *Aesthetics and the Environment: The Appreciation of Nature, Art and Architecture* (2000).

Arto Haapala is Professor of Aesthetics at the University of Helsinki. He has published some seventy articles on different topics in aesthetics and art theory, that is, problems of interpretation, ontology, and the definition of art. He has edited or coedited thirteen books, *including The End of Art and Beyond—Essays after Danto* (with Jerrold Levinson and Veikko Rantala), *Interpretation and Its Boundaries* (with Ossi Naukkarinen), and *The City as Cultural Metaphor.* He is the author of *What Is a Work of Literature?* and is currently writing a book on existential aesthetics.

Glenn Kuehn is a philosopher, former caterer and a founding member (along with Lisa Heldke and Ray Boisvert) of "Convivium: The Philosophy and Food Roundtable." He has addressed many conferences and colloquia on various topics within the "philosophy of food," and is famous for his cheesecakes and sauces.

Tom Leddy is Professor of Philosophy at San Jose State University. He is a former member of the Board of Trustees of the American Society for Aesthetics and Secretary-Treasurer for the Pacific Division of the ASA. He has published numerous articles in aesthetics including such topics as gardens, architecture, creativity, defining art, metaphor, antiessentialism, interpretation, aesthetic qualities, and organicism.

Andrew Light is Assistant Professor of Environmental Philosophy in the Applied Philosophy Group at New York University and Visiting Associate Professor of Philosophy and Public Affairs at the University of Washington. Light is the author of over sixty articles, and book chapters on environmental ethics, philosophy of technology, and philosophy of film, and has edited or coedited fourteen books, including *Environmental Pragmatism* (1996, with Eric Katz), *Social Ecology after Bookchin* (1998), *Race, Class, and Community Identity* (2000), and *Technology and the Good Life?* (2000). Light is also co-editor of the journal *Philosophy and Geography* (with Jonathan Smith) and the author of *Reel Arguments: Film, Philosophy, and Social Criticism* (2003).

Michael A. Principe is Professor of Philosophy at Middle Tennessee State University. His areas of specialization are Marxism and social philosophy. In addition to publishing in these areas, he has written on aesthetics, ethics, and the history of philosophy.

Yuriko Saito is Professor of Philosophy at the Rhode Island School of Design. Her writings in environmental aesthetics, the aesthetic appreciation of nature, and Japanese aesthetics have appeared in *The Journal of Aesthetics and Art Criticism, The British Journal of Aesthetics, The Journal of Aesthetic Education, Environmental Ethics, Landscape, Chanoyu Quarterly,* and *The Encyclopedia of Aesthetics.*

Jonathan M. Smith is Professor of Geography at Texas A&M University. He is a cultural-historical geographer primarily interested in the history of geographical ideas and geographical thought. He studies the expression of such ideas in cultural landscapes, geographical behavior, geographical scholarship, and other varieties of literature. He has published articles on geographers' use of metaphor, irony, and rhetoric, on the development of geographical concepts such as region, place, and environmental ethics, and on the geographical imagination in 17th-century England and the 19th-century United States. He has also published articles on landscape symbolism, the role of technology in geographical change, and the geographical conditions of contemporary identity. He has coedited six books and is presently coeditor of the journal *Philosophy and Geography* (with Andrew Light).

Pauline von Bonsdorff is Professor of Art Education at the University of Jyväskylä and Docent of Aesthetics at Helsinki University. She has written some forty articles on aesthetics, environmental aesthetics, theory of architecture, art criticism, and phenomenology. She is the author of *The Human Habitat: Aesthetic and Axiological Perspectives* (1998) and has edited and coedited books on environmental aesthetics, everyday aesthetics and feminist aesthetics.

Wolfgang Welsch is Professor of Theoretical Philosophy at Jena University (Germany). He received the Max Planck Research Award in 1992 and has been a fellow at the Stanford Humanities Center. He has written over one hundred articles and published fourteen books (five as editor) on aesthetics, epistemology, anthropology, and cultural philosophy. His books include *Unsere postmoderne Moderne* (1987, 6th ed. 2002), *Ästhetisches Denken* (1990, 6th ed. 2003), *Vernunft* (1995), *Grenzgänge der Ästhetik* (1996), and *Undoing Aesthetics* (1997).

Index

Aalto, Alvar, 49–50; on architecture's central tasks, 77

Adams, Ansel, 101

Addison, Joseph, 169

Adorno, Theodor W., 78; on fraying of arts, 141

advertisements, x

aesthetic object(s), 156; art v. weather as, 159–60; change and, 169; function of, 49; limited concept of, 181–82; sensuous surface of, xiv; smells/tastes as, 184; weather's frameless character as, 157–61

aesthetic properties: dialectical relations to noneveryday of everyday, 17; distinct sets of everyday, 8; everyday, 7–12; in human relations, x

aesthetic qualities, xiii; clean as, 9; everyday, 8–9; neatness as, 8; superlatives as everyday, 16–17, 22n18

aesthetic term(s): applying, 13–14; double, 12–13; nice as, 14–15; nonaesthetic v., 14; tasteful as, 15–16

aesthetics: acceptance in, 26; advancement toward popular of, 141; of art, 19–20; art as instance of, 139–40; body and, 137–38; as contextual, 26–29; continuity/engagement/reciprocity in experience of, 28, 35; discovery in experience of, 27; double terms in, 12–13; of environment, 30; field of, 39; integrated interaction base of experience of, 198; love/art and characteristics of, 33; multiplicity in experience of, 29; natural, 11; nonaesthetic features and judgments of, 13, 21n13; of objects, 24–26; perception in, 26–27; philosophical study of, ix; philosophy of arts transformation of, 138; of place, 50–52; practical in experience of, 163; sensory awareness and, 23–24; sensuousness in experience of, 27, 36n6, 162–63; of smell, 9–10; smells/tastes as neglected subject in, 177, 179, 191n1; of social situations, 30–34; sport as neglected topic of, 149; sport's shift from ethics to, 136–39; of strangeness, x–xi; transience/changeability in experience of, 169; uniqueness in experience of, 27–28, 35; values focused on through, 86. *See also* everyday aesthetics; Japanese aesthetics; social aesthetics

Agamberi, Giorgio, 78

Aldo, Leopold, 97

Alexander, Thomas, 203

Alice in the Cities (1973), 109, 129n25; Alice character in, 119–20; characters in, 116; everyday aesthetics' normative dimensions and, 109–10; first road trip in, 115–16; location in, 115; message of, 126;

Alice in the Cities (1973) (continued)
second road trip in, 120–23; space/identity relation in, 118; spaces shown in, 117; thick space in, 116, 119
American Beauty (2001), 5, 16
Anderson, Richard L., 9
architecture, 25; as art, 29–30; in building/planning context, 73; central tasks of, 77; human beings as part of organic nature suggested by, 83; naturally unplanned elements' effect on, 73–74, 87*n*1. *See also* building(s); landscape; place; space
Arendt, Hannah, 62–63, 76
art(s): aesthetics of, 19–20; architecture as, 29–30; artist's role in, 59; avant garde, 150; through classification/evaluation, 200–202; classifying, 207; common experience of, 159; as context, 66–67; contingency and, 147–48; Danto on uselessness of, 57–58; Danto's neo-Hegelian reading of history of, 56; defining, 140; Dewey on function of, 195; discussion about, 29; as end in itself, 142–44; end of history of, 58–59; environmental, 10; from everyday, 199; everyday aesthetics' relationship with, 18–19; everyday things v. works of, xi; expansion of realm of, 26; experience of, 156; fascination with, 144, 153*n*29; food as, xv, 194, 200–201, 205, 207–208; food as minor, 202–207; fraying of, 141; high/low, 207–208; as instance of aesthetic, 139–40; interpenetrations with life and modern, 140–41, 152*n*13; judgment of, 198–200; landscapes' use in, 101–102; landscapes v. works of, 98; liberation of, 59; love's resemblance to, 32–34; message of, 158–59; morality and, 24; as moving into everyday, 64–65; in museums, 209; nature's relationship with, 158, 173*n*9; performance as work of, 143; personal domain of perceptual experience in, 24;

personal exchange with works of, 33; phenomenal/conceptual transformations of sport's constitution/concept of, 135–36; philosophical disenfranchisement/reenfranchising of, 57, 63; popular, 141; restoration, 169; restrictions applied to objects of, 158; rules created in, 144; as safe, 65; situational, 30; smell/taste in, 180; social thought related to theory of, 24; as speech, 62; sport art v., 149–50; sport as, 135, 141–50, 153*n*25, 154*n*32; sport viewed as art by changes to concept of, 139–41, 151*n*11; sports as lacking traits of, 148; symbolic status of, 142; technology's relationship with, 123; thin spaces and, 112; types of work implied in, 142–43; weather as art object as different from, 159–60; weather v. objects of, 157
Art As Experience (Dewey), 209
artifacts: as art, 136; everyday aesthetics and, 112, 128*n*4; space dominated by, 111–12, 127*n*8
attachment: as emotional relation to place, 49; familiarity and, 51–52

Bad as I Wanna Be (Rodman), 136
Balázs, Béla, on films, 114
Baruchello, Gianfranco, xi, 56; art's liberation and, 59; Danto v., 67–68; environment for, 61; everyday aesthetics of, 60, 63; as politically engaged, 62
Bates, Marston, 97
Baumgarten, Alexander Gottlieb, 23, 137
Beardsley, Monroe, 17–18
beauty: of everyday environments, xi; of everyday things, xi; Kant's use of, 7; as love, 34; love parallels with, x; love's relationship with, 32; maximum of, 94; natural, 11; as social character in humans, 31; transient, xiv; understood in nature, 23
Beicken, Peter, 115–16
Bell, Clive, 94–96

Benjamin, Walter, 123

Berleant, Arnold, 156–57; on environmental aesthetics, 4–5

Beuys, Joseph, 11–12, 140

Borgmann, Albert, xii; device paradigm of, 111–12, 116, 126; devices/things distinction of, 110–11, 127*n*3; ontology of technology of, 111; on technological reform, 109; technology approach of Feenberg v., 112–14, 128*m*7

building(s): as cultivation/dwelling, 74–78; as culture/nature relationship's articulation, 81; existential dimension of, 83–86; Heidegger on, 77, 88*m*2; materials used in, 84–86; nature as element of, 75–76; as planned, 74–75; process/object of, 74–75; symbolism and issues of, 84; understanding of, 81–82; unplanned elements of, 71–75, 87*m*

built space: everyday aesthetics of, 114–15; identity and, 118; thick, 118; thin space of suburban, 117

Bullough, Edward, 8, 163

Burden, Chris, 65

Burke, Edmund, 168

Burroughs, John, 97

Cage, John, 148

Carlson, Allen, 5, 60

Carrighar, Sally, 97

Carroll, Lewis, 119

Carroll, Noël, 39

Cartier-Bresson, Henri, 51

Casey, Edward S., 41, 54*m*5

chefs, 201–202

Christie, Linford, 137

clean, aesthetic quality of, 9

climate: built environment's dependence on, 73

Close Encounters of the Third Kind (1977), 102–104

Corbin, Alan, 186

Critique of Everyday Life (Lefebvre), 112, 121

culture(s): building as articulation of nature's relationship with, 81; as cultivation, 76–77, 87*n*7; everyday aesthetics in different, 157; films as critical of, 124–25; Heidegger's critique of, 78; nature as distinct from, 75–76, 87*n*6; nature's separation from, 79–80; sense/spirit of place and, 42–43; smells/tastes associated with, 187–88

Danto, Arthur, xi; on art's uselessness, 57–58; Baruchello v., 67–68; everyday aesthetics in work of, 56–57, 65; on liberation of, 59; neo-Hegelian reading of art history by, 56; on reenfranchising art, 57

Davies, Douglas, 84

device paradigm, 111–12; everyday aesthetics examined by, 113, 116; space and, 116

Devils Tower, 98–99, 101

Dewey, John, 40; aesthetic experience explanation of, 198–99; on art, xv; cognitive objects for, 204–205; on food, 206; on function of art, 195; ordinary life for, 208–209; transformative aesthetic experience notion of, 195; transient used to cultivate aesthetic of food according to, 203–204

Duchamp, Marcel, 57, 59–60, 148

Dufrenne, Mikel, 86

Eisley, Loren, 97

Emerson, Ralph Waldo, 84

emotion: attachment as relation to place through, 49; food and, 205–206; music as expressing, 205; taste/smell and, 184, 189

environmental aesthetics: Berleant on, 4–5; everyday aesthetics' relationship with, 4; landscape appreciation in, 92–93. *See also* building(s); landscape(s)

environments: aesthetics of, 30; aesthetics of everyday, xi–xii; for Baruchello, 61;

environments: (continued)
    beauty of, xi; continuity experienced in,
    83–84; flattened experience of, 80–81;
    habitation qualities and, 82; human
    beings' relation with, 79–80; losing touch
    with, 80; naturally unplanned elements of
    built, 73–74; place as interpretation by
    existence of, 47; self as connected to, 199;
    self relationship with, 194–95. 210n2;
    shaping of, 18; smells habituating one to,
    186; society's values embodied in, 84;
    strangeness experience in new, 43; tempo-
    ral depth/tacit knowing and, 81–83
ethics, sports and, 136
etiquette, 32
everyday aesthetics: agreeable concept and, 6;
    art's relationship with, 18–19; Baruchello's,
    60, 63; of built space, 114–15; in Danto's
    work, 56–57, 65; defining, 3; device para-
    digm for examining, 113, 116; environmen-
    tal aesthetics relationship with, 4; field of,
    ix–x, 19, 20; inquiry into, 109; issues in, 3;
    Kantian attempt to define, 6–7; kitsch
    and, 15; neglect of, 51; normative dimen-
    sions of, 109; as ordinarily/extraordinarily
    experienced, 18; place in, 40–41; proper-
    ties of, 7–12; qualities of, 8–9, 16–17,
    22n8; scientific knowledge and, 5; sensu-
    ous/imaginative dimensions of experience
    of, 7–8, 27, 36n6; spaces/artifacts and, 112,
    128n4; strangeness and, 52; as subjective,
    19; subject/object relationship in, x, xii,
    xv; traditional field of aesthetics and, 3–4;
    in Wenders' work, 109. See also environ-
    mental aesthetics; place; smells; tastes

familiarity: attachment and, 51–52; nature of,
    45; place and, 43–46; smells and, 186–87;
    strangeness' distinction from, 43
Farber, Marvin, 24
Feenberg, Andrew, xii; subversion thesis of,
    113; on technological reform, 109; tech-

nology approach of Borgmann v., 112–14,
    128n7
films: culture and, 124–25; historical authen-
    ticity in, 114, 129n22; as medium, 114; per-
    spective in, 119; philosophical debates'
    contributions from, 109–10; social role of,
    124; technological practice of medium of,
    121; as technology, 123–25
Foi society, 32
food: aesthetic recovery of, 207–10; apprecia-
    tion of, 195; as art, xv, 194, 200–201, 205,
    207–208; art world status of, 196; artistic
    status of, 200, 202; artists making,
    201–202; classifying, 207–208; as con-
    sumed/destroyed to experience, 195,
    210n3; contexts expressed by, 206;
    dichotomies in discussion about, 197;
    emotion and, 205–206; inherent transfor-
    mation of, 210; meaning as art of, 204; as
    minor art, 202–208; as nonrepresentative,
    203; potential for art of, 195; religion and,
    204; representational ability of, 204–205;
    as transient, 202–203. See also smells;
    tastes
Food for Thought (Telfer), 194
Ford, John, 115
form, in landscape appreciation, 94–96

Gehlen, Arnold, 149
Girardelli, Marc, 138
Goldsworthy, Andy, 171
Goodman, Nelson, 8

haiku, 164–68
Harries, Karsten, 78, 84
health, sport and, 138–39
Hegel, G. W. F., 39, 58, 136
Heidegger, Martin, 40, 45, 47–51, 53n12; cri-
    tique of culture of, 78; dwelling notion
    of, 77, 88n12
Hepburn, R. W., 83, 93–94, 97, 162–63
Hitchcock, Alfred, 102

Horkheimer, Max, 78
Hoskins, W. G., 98
How to Imagine (Baruchello), 56–57, 65–66

identity: built space and, 118; relations and, 47–48; thin spaces effect on, 126
interpretation: place and, 46–47; process of, 47
Isenberg, Arnold, 13

Jackson, J. B., 98
Japanese aesthetics: art/everyday aesthetics relationship seen in, 18
Jessup, Bertram, 157
Johnson, Hugh, 182
Joyce, James, 180, 187

Kant, Immanuel, xiv, 39, 168; aesthetic experience types distinguished by, 6; aesthetic theory of, 179; on agreeable, 19; beauty as used by, 7; on purposiveness without purpose, 26; on tastes/smells, 181–83, 189; on universality, 23
Keinholz, Edward, 65
Kenko, Yoshida, 167, 169
kitsch, 15, 155n38
Klee, Paul, 149
knowledge: aesthetic appreciation of landscapes as dependent on articulate, xii; landscapes and common, 96; tacit component in, 82, 90n41. *See also* scientific knowledge
Kolker, Robert Philip, 115–16
Korsmeyer, Carolyn, 184–85
Kurtch, Joseph, 97

landscape(s): aesthetic appreciation of, xii, 94–97; appreciating, 92; articulate knowledge dependence of aesthetic appreciation of, xii; art's use of, 101–102; artworks v., 98; common knowledge in appreciation of, 96; contemporary use of, 99–100; curriculum for teaching appreciation of, 93, 105; effect of, 43; form/content in aesthetic appreciation of, 94–96; historical use of, 97–99; histories of production of, 102; mythical/symbolic/artistic use's relevance to aesthetic appreciation of, 102–103; myth's use of, 100–101; pluralism, 104–105; postmodern view of appreciation of, 93–94, 103; science and aesthetic appreciation of, 96–97; symbolic uses of, 101; visualization in modernity, 79; as work in progress, xii. *See also* environmental aesthetics
language, limits of, 77
Lefebvre, Henri, 112, 121
Lopez, Barry, 97
love: art's resemblances to, 32–34; as beauty, 34; beauty parallels with, x; beauty's relationship with, 32; forms of, 32
Lyotard, Jean-Francois, 80

The Making of the English Landscape (Hoskins), 98
memory: olfactory, 188; smell as evoking, 10, 188–89
Mill, John Stuart, 179–80
mind, materialistic philosophies of, xiv
morality, art and, 24
Morris, William, 78
Mount Rushmore, 98–99
Muir, John, 97, 161
museums, 209
music, 205
Myllylä, Mika, 139, 143–44
myths, landscape use in, 100–101

nature: architecture's suggestion of organic, 83; art's relationship with, 158, 173n9; building as articulation of culture's relationship with, 81; building's element of, 75–76; concept of, 75, 87n4; culture as distinct from, 75–76, 87n6; culture's

nature: (continued)
  separation from, 79–80; impermanence
  in, 170; in natural sciences, 75; reduction
  to material of, 75
Naukkarinen, Ossi, 39–40
neatness, 8
nice, as aesthetic term, 14–15
North by Northwest (1959), 102–103
Novitz, David, 39–40; on high/low arts,
  207–208

Olson, Sigurd, 97
On the Aesthetic Education of Man (Schiller),
  24
Orwell, George, 188
O'Sullivan, Sonya, 145
Ottey, Merlene, 137

Papanek, Victor, 157
perception: in aesthetic appreciation, 26–27;
  aesthetic emphasis on, 35; senses in, 27
performance: as artwork, 143; in sport,
  142–45, 153*n*24
perfume, 182; personal style and, 190
Perfume: The Story of a Murderer (Süskind),
  180
Picasso, Pablo, 62–63
The Pillow Book (Shonagon), 164–65, 168
place: aesthetics of, 50–52; attachment as
  emotional relation to, 49; concepts of,
  40–43, 53*n*13; as defined by reference to
  human body, 41, 54*n*15; everyday and,
  48–50; familiarity and, 40; interpretation
  and, 46–47; lifeworld and, 47; person
  relation to, 47–48; sense/spirit of, 41–43,
  54*n*17; significance of, 45–46; smell's significance to understanding, 185–86; space
  appearing as, 83–86; strangeness/familiar-
  ity and, 43–46; thick spaces giving sense
  of, 112, 127*n*9; thickness of, 123
pleasure: smells/tastes as lower, 179–81; Telfer
  on, 198

pluralism, xi, 58–59, 67; landscape, 104–105
Polanyi, Michael, 82
Porteous, J. Douglas, 185–86
Prall, David W., 10–11

Quammen, David, 97

Rader, Melvin, 157
Rauschenberg, Robert, 11–12
reciprocity: in aesthetic experience, 28, 35; in
  democratic experience, 35
religion, 204
rightness, 8–9
Robbins, Tom, 177, 182
Rodaway, Paul, 187–88
Rodman, Dennis, 136
Rorty, Richard, 40
Rossi, Aldo, 74

Sandrisser, Barbara, 18
Santayana, George, 92–96, 98, 104–105; on
  sport, 142
Schiller, Friedrich, 24, 36; on Aesthetic State,
  34–35; on social character's source, 31–32
Schlink, Bernhard, 48
Schopenhauerian artists, everyday aesthetic
  experience transformed into extraordinary by, 17
scientific knowledge: everyday aesthetics and,
  5; landscapes and, 96–97; natural objects
  experienced in terms of, 5; nature and, 75
The Sense of Beauty (Santayana), 92
sensory experience: aesthetics, awareness and,
  23–24; factors shaping, 26–27; love/art as
  dwelling in perceptual domains of, 34;
  sensuousness, aesthetics and, 27, 36*n*6,
  162–63
Shonagon, Sei, 164–66
Shusterman, Richard, 39, 141
Sibley, F.N., 13–14; on tastes/smells, 178–79
smells: aesthetic appreciation of, xiv–xv,
  182–83; aesthetic domain's inclusion of,

177–78; aesthetic orientation by, 186; aesthetic reactions to, 184, 197; aesthetics of, 9–10; classes distinguished by, 188; consumption and, 181; cultures' particular, 187–88; as denotative, 185; emotions and, 184–85, 189; in everyday life, 185–90; familiarity/unfamiliarity from, 186–87; as lower pleasure, 179–81; memories evoked by, 10, 188–89; as neglected subject in aesthetics, 177, 179, 191*n*1; particular/general, 178; personal style and, 190; as physically defined, 178; place and, 185–86; sight v., 185; single/mixed, 179; structure of, 182; as sustained discriminatory attention object, 181; taste working with, 178, 191*n*3; vocabulary, 190–91

social aesthetics, 24, 29; aesthetics of objects leading to, 25–26; defining, 30–31; human relations approach of, 36; love's forms as occasions of, 32; politics of, 34–36, 38*n*5; theater and, 30

societies: aesthetically integrated, 32. *See also* culture(s)

space(s): appearing as place, 83–86; device paradigm applied to everyday aesthetics of, 116; dominant artifacts of, 111–12, 127*n*8; encountered in everyday life, 109; evaluating social, 111; everyday aesthetics and, 112, 128*n*14; public, 120–21; significance of, 120; of sports, 142; thick, 111–14, 116, 119, 122, 126; thin, 111–14, 126. *See also* built space

speech: action linked to, 63; art as, 62

Spielberg, Steven, 102

sport(s): aesthetic perfection as intrinsic to, 137; aesthetic shift of, 136; as art, xiii, 135, 141–50, 153*n*25, 154*n*32; art traits lacking in, 148; artistic character of, 144–45; art's character as end in itself and, 142–44; clothing, 136–37; contingency celebrated in, 147–48; creativity in, 144; as elitist, 148–49; erotic element in, 138, 151*n*6;

ethics to aesthetics shift of, 136–39; fascination with, 144, 153*n*29; health and, 138–39, 151*n*7, 151*n*8; as neglected topic of aesthetics, 149; as paradigm example of aestheticization, 135; performance in, 142–45, 153*n*24; as popular art, 149; relationship to body in, 137–38; rules followed in, 144; semantics of, 145–46; space of, 142; status of contemporary, 135; symbolic status of, 142; winning in, 143–44, 153*n*25

Stolnitz, Jerome, 162; on disinterestedneess, 157

strangeness: aesthetics of, x–xi; everyday aesthetics and, 52; familiarity's distinction from, 43; place and, 43–46

superlatives, as everyday aesthetic qualities, 16–17

Süskind, Peter, 180

Symposium (Plato), 34

tastes: aesthetic appreciation of, xiv–xv, 182–83; aesthetic domain's inclusion of, 177–78; aesthetic reactions to, 197; aesthetic response to, 184; consumption and, 181; cultures' particular, 187–88; as denotative, 185; emotions and, 184–85; in everyday life, 185–90; as lower pleasure, 179–81; as neglected subject in aesthetics, 177, 179, 191*n*1; particular/general, 178; as physically defined, 178; single/mixed, 179; structure of, 182; as sustained discriminatory attention object, 181; touch involved in, 189; vocabulary, 190–91. *See also* smells

technology, 40; art's relationship with, 123; Borgmann's ontology of, 111; devices/things distinction and, 110–11, 127*n*3; film as, 123–25; human identities/relationships affected by, 109, 112; philosophies of, xii–xiii; political intents built into, 113; public involvement causing subversions of, 113; social relations' forms created by types of, 110

Telfer, Elizabeth, xv; on chefs, 201–202; on food as art, 194, 200–201, 205; on food as minor art, 207–208; food as popular art for, 206; on food/cooking status in art world, 196; on food's representational ability, 204; on judging art, 199–200; on pleasure, 198; self/environment relationship metaphor of, 194–95. 210*n2*

theater, social aesthetics and, 30

topography, 73

Twain, Mark, 162

unplanned: building's elements of, 71–75, 87*n. See also* building(s)

Urmson, J. O., 196

values, 48; aesthetics' focus on, 86; of society embodied in environments, 84

Waldenfels, Bernhard, 79

Warhol, Andy, 57

weather: aesthetic appreciation of, xiii–xiv, 160; as aesthetic object, 157–61; aesthetic value of, 158; aesthetics experience and negative effects of, 164; appreciation of negative conditions of, 167–68; as art object as different from art, 159–60; art objects v., 157; built environment's dependence on, 73; change in, 169; in context of nature, xiii–xiv; daily living effects of, 163–64; everyday concerns and, 161–68; experience of, 158, 161, 173*n15*; feelings aroused by, xiv; impermanence of, 168–71; positive aesthetic value of types of, 171; practical consequences of, xiv; seasons and, 164–66; as uncontrollable, 171–72; well-being affected by, 161–62

Weil, Simone, 33

Wenders, Wim, xii; characters of, 116; on commercial television's effects, 125; everyday aesthetics in work of, 109; films of, 124–25; focal things for, 114, 129*n23*; new social relations' creation seen in work of, 114; technologies' transformative potential seen in work of, 114

Weston, Edward, 101

Zen Buddhist Monks, everyday aesthetic experience transformed into extraordinary by, 17

Zwinger, Ann, 97